Progress in Child Health

VOLUME THREE

EDITED BY

J A Macfarlane MB BChir FRCP

Consultant Paediatrician with special interest in Child Health;
Clinical Lecturer in Paediatrics, University of Oxford

CHURCHILL LIVINGSTONE
EDINBURGH LONDON MELBOURNE AND NEW YORK 1987

CHURCHILL LIVINGSTONE
Medical Division of Longman Group UK Limited

Distributed in the United States of America by
Churchill Livingstone Inc., 1560 Broadway, New York,
N.Y. 10036, and by associated companies, branches and
representatives throughout the world.

First published 1987

ISBN 0 443 03404 4
ISSN 0265-2013

British Library Cataloguing in Publication Data
Progress in child health.
   Vol. 3
   1. Children——Care and hygiene
   I. MacFarlane, J. A.
   613'.0432   RJ101

Printed at The Bath Press, Avon

G

Progress in Child Health

PROGRESS IN CHILD HEALTH

Preface

This, the third volume in the *Progress in Child Health series,* covers, as do previous volumes, a wide variety of subjects. Some people have suggested that each volume should be limited to one or two specific topics; I, however, would rather each reflected the diversification of the field, which increasingly concerns communication between many different professionals and specialties. This has resulted in a need to understand many different subjects — even those outside the ones we are most directly involved with.

This volume therefore covers both specific aspects of child health, such as screening for congenital dislocation of the hip, screening for hearing problems and management of siblings of children who died from suddent infant death, as well as other broader issues, such as child health surveillance in general practice and the use of paediatric nurse practitioners. Further afield, but still essential to child health, there are chapters on family centres, the Home-Start Programme and other subjects.

Overall, however, the aim continues to be the same: that is, to present up to date summaries of different areas of child health in easily digestible form so that the reader can easily gain access to fields of which he or she, although probably not directly involved, certainly needs to have a knowledge. This is whether it is for clinical practice, managerial or administrative needs or to take the Diploma of Child Health examination.

It will, I think, benefit Child Health if this volume comes anywhere near to achieving this aim.

Oxford, 1987   J. A. Macfarlane

Contributors

Dora Black MB FRCPsych DPM
Consultant Child Psychiatrist, Royal Free Hospital; Honorary Consultant, Hospital for Sick Children, London

Graham Curtis Jenkins MA MB BChir DRCOG MRCGP
General Practitioner, Ashford, Middlesex

Peter M. Dunn MA MD FRCP FRCOG DCH
Reader in Perinatal Medicine and Child Health, University of Bristol; Honorary Consultant in Neonatal Paediatrics, Southmead and Bristol Maternity Hospitals

Bridget Edwards BM BCh MRCP DCH
Consultant Paediatrician, Community Child Health, Brent Health Authority

Edward Goldson MD
Staff Paediatrician, Department of Paediatric Medicine, The Children's Hospital, Denver, USA

James Gray BA
Research Assistant, Department of Educational Studies, Oxford University

Margaret Harrison MA
Home-start Consultant, Home-start Consultancy, Leicester

Linda Hart BEd
Training Consultant, Home-start Consultancy, Leicester

Martin Herbert MA PhD FBPsS
Professor of Clinical Psychology and Head of Psychology Department, University of Leicester

Roy Howarth BA
Head Teacher, Northern House School, Oxford

David Isaacs MD MRCP FRACP
Clinical Lecturer, Infectious Diseases Unit, Department of Paediatrics, John Radcliffe Hospital, Oxford

Arthur Rory Nicol FRCP FRCPsych MPhil
Professor of Child and Adolescent Psychiatry, University of Leicester

John Richer MA PhD DipPsych
Principal Clinical Psychologist, John Radcliffe Hospital, Oxford

Michael J. Rigby BA FSS
Regional Service Planning Officer, Mersey Regional Health Authority; Vice Chairman, Child Health Computing Committee

Teresa Smith MA
Lecturer in Applied Social Studies, University of Oxford

Madeleine St Denis RNC MS
Paediatric Nurse Practitioner, Harvard Community Health Plan, Boston, Massachusetts, USA

Sarah Stewart-Brown MA BM Bch MRCP
Senior Registrar in Community Medicine, South Western Regional Health Authority; Research Associate, Department of Child Health, University of Bristol

Alison J. Waite BN SRN SCM HV
Project Co-ordinator, Infant Home Surveillance Research Project, London School of Hygiene and Tropical Medicine

Tony Waterston MB ChB MRCP DCH DRCOG
Consultant Community Paediatrician, Newcastle-upon-Tyne

Nicholas Wells BA
Associate Director, Office of Health Economics, London

A. F. Williams BSc MRCP
Lecturer in Child Health, University of Bristol

Contents

Screening for congenital dislocation of the hip

'I am the owner of my shoulders, the tenant of my hips'.

Chazal

INTRODUCTION

Definition

Congenital dislocation of the hip (CDH) may be defined as a deformation of the hip joint, present at birth, in which the head of the femur is, or may be, partly or completely displaced from the acetabulum. The term embraces secondary hip joint dysplasia whether or not hip instability or dislocation persists. In this definition the word deformation is used to distinguish those congenital anomalies which are alterations in the shape or structure of a previously normally formed part of the body (fetopathies) from those that are malformations or structural defects due to primary errors in morphogenesis (Dunn, 1969, 1976a).

Aetiology

By far the most important group of deformations is that of the congenital postural deformities, involving the musculo-skeletal system and believed to be caused by mechanical factors operating in utero whether intrinsic or extrinsic in origin. Any part of the body may be involved. They include deformities of the skull, face and jaw; congenital sternomastoid torticollis; congenital postural scoliosis; CDH; bowing of the legs; genu recurvatum and a variety of talipes. At least 2% of all babies exhibit one or more congenital postural deformities at birth. Fortunately, the great majority spontaneously resolve following delivery while the remainder will usually respond to early mechanical correction.

The congenital postural deformities not only occur in association with each other (a third of affected infants having two or more deformations) but also share common aetiologically related pregnancy characteristics, which include primiparity, uterine malformation, oligohydramnios, maternal hypertension, fetal malpresentation (especially breech), fetal growth retardation and

1

Table 1.1   Estimated increased incidence of CDH at birth in relation to certain perinatal factors

Family history of CDH (parents/sibs)	× 5+ (?)
First pregnancies	× 2
Maternal hypertension	× 2
Oligohydramnios present	× 10 (?)
Breech presentation	× 10
Fetal growth retardation/distress	× 2+ (?)
Prolonged gestation (42 weeks +)	× 2
Female sex of infant	× 4
Presence of talipes	× 8

Note: An overall incidence of 1.5% is assumed. Many of the above factors occur in association with each other. No multivariate analysis has been used in making these approximate estimates. It would not therefore be appropriate to calculate cumulative increases in incidence when more than one perinatal factor is involved.
This table does not take into account CDH associated with severe malformation.

prolonged pregnancy. The way in which these factors may inter-react with deformation has been described elsewhere (Dunn, 1969, 1976b).

CDH shares the above characteristics (Table 1.1) and has, in addition, a predeliction for girls, the condition being at least four times more common in girls than in boys. It is thought that this is due to hormone induced laxity of the ligaments of the hip joint, especially in the perinatal period. Increased joint laxity may also help to explain the familial occurrence of CDH. CDH is twice as common on the left side as the right, once again due to intrauterine postural factors (Dunn, 1976c).

Natural history and incidence

CDH is the commonest and, after congenital postural scoliosis, potentially the most crippling of all the congenital deformations. While the condition is rare among negroes, and extremely common among some races such as the Lapps, the incidence at birth among Caucasian peoples would seem to be about 1%–2%. This figure does not include cases occurring secondarily to malformations such as spina bifida or Potter's syndrome. In perhaps 90% of cases the hip is dislocatable rather than dislocated at birth, and even without treatment the majority of these unstable hips will rapidly become stable, certainly by the time walking commences. However, 10% of the initially unstable hips will become shallow and dysplastic and prone to osteoarthritis in adult life. Another 10% of hips that are dislocatable, with most of the 10% that were fully dislocated at birth, will present later as classic CDH, usually at the age of about 18 months (Fig. 1.1). Such children walk with a limp, or waddle, which is unsightly as well as physically handicapping.

In spite of treatment most late diagnosed hips eventually become painful when osteoarthritis develops in adult life. The incidence of this classic late presentation is roughly 1–2 per 1000 live births. Unfortunately, there is no known way of distinguishing at birth between the dislocatable hips that will become normal and those that will progress to dysplasia or dislocation.

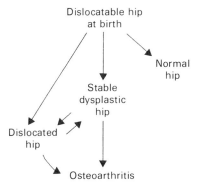

Fig. 1.1 The unstable hip at birth: possible outcomes

Diagnosis

Classic presentation

When the dislocation is unilateral there may be asymmetry of the thighs (and buttocks), both in the set of the thigh into the trunk and in the skin creases and buttock folds. The affected leg may be shorter and abduction of the thigh limited. The hip may be noted to 'snap', either spontaneously or on abduction during examination. Pushing and pulling on the flexed adducted thigh may elicit the sign of 'telescoping'. With bilateral CDH, the separation of the thighs may create a perineal gap. Once walking has commenced, the child may be noted to fall to one side, to limp or, in bilateral cases, to waddle. There is a lumbar lordosis with bilateral CDH. While the majority of children with CDH commence walking at the normal age, the incidence of not walking at 18 months is five to six times more common than in the population as a whole (unpublished data). After the age of 2 years it becomes possible to persuade the child to balance on one leg; then Trendelenberg's test may be found to be positive if, when the patient stands on an affected leg, the gluteal fold on the opposite side falls. Normally it should rise as the body is balanced over the weight-bearing hip.

Neonatal presentation

The classic signs of dislocation are rarely present at birth. Limitation of abduction and/or shortening of the affected leg occurs in 3%–5% of cases. CDH has to be revealed by manipulation of the hip, preferably using a slight modification of the Ortolani-Barlow manoeuvre (Ortolani, 1948; Barlow 1962).

The Ortolani-Barlow manoeuvre The examiner's hands should be warm and the examination gentle. If possible the baby should be relaxed. The infant lies on his/her back with legs towards the examiner and with hips adducted and *fully flexed*. The examiner grasps the upper thighs with the middle finger of each hand over the greater trochanters, with the flexed legs in the palms of each hand, and with the thumb on the inner side of the thigh opposite the lesser trochanter (Fig. 1.2). An attempt is now made to move each femoral head in turn gently forwards into or backwards out of the acetabulum. In the first part of the manoeuvre the middle finger of each hand is pressed on the greater trochanter in an attempt to relocate a posteriorly dislocated head of the femur forwards into the acetabulum. If the head is felt to move (usually not more than 0.5 cm), with or without a palpable and/or audible 'clunk', then dislocation is present. The second part of the manoeuvre test is for dislocatability. With the thumb on the inner side of the thigh, backward pressure is applied to the head of the femur. If the latter is felt to move backwards over the labrum onto the posterior aspect of the joint capsule (again a movement of not more than 0.5 cm and often accompanied by a 'clunk') the hip is said to be dislocatable. It may prove preferable to examine one hip at a time with the free hand steadying the pelvis between thumb on the symphysis pubis and fingers over the sacrum. Note that ligamentous clicks *without* movement of the head of the femur in or out of the acetabulum may be elicited in 5%–10% of all hips and should be disregarded (Dunn et al, 1985).

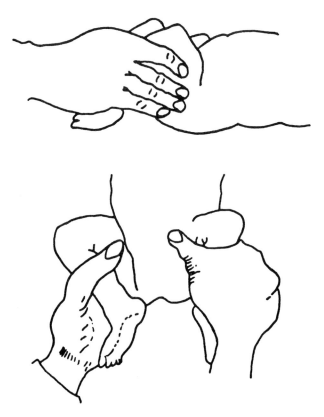

Fig. 1.2 Neonatal examination of the hip for CDH

Management

The earlier the diagnosis is made the simpler and safer is treatment. With occasional exceptions, the dislocatable or dislocated hips may be cured by six to 12 weeks in a light abduction splint. No pressure should be applied in order to achieve abduction. Follow up with X-ray at six and 12 months ensures that the outcome is satisfactory. Avascular necrosis should be exceptionally rare. There is minimal interference with the infant's development or with family life (Dunn et al, 1985).

At diagnosis in later infancy, limited abduction and upward displacement with shortening of the leg are often present. Usually there is a need for an arthrogram, a period in traction, an adductor tenotomy and several months' treatment in a hip spica. There is a much greater risk of avascular necrosis. Provided this last complication does not occur the long-term outcome is usually fairly satisfactory.

If the diagnosis is delayed until after walking has commenced, treatment becomes more complex and prolonged. Most cases require surgery, which may include open reduction, acetabuloplasty and derotation osteotomy of the femur, in addition to arthrograms, adductor tenotomies and periods in traction or in a hip spica. Several general anaesthetics and hospital admissions may be required. Hospital admission leads to separation from parents and psychological trauma at a very vulnerable age. Many pelvic X-rays are required, and treatment often lasts two to three years. Although the short term outcome may be satisfactory, the majority of these children will eventually develop further problems, particularly problems due to osteoarthritis in middle adult life.

Cost benefit considerations

The cost of early versus late treatment in financial terms is hard to judge accurately. Recent medico-legal judgements have awarded £60 to £70 000 to the plaintiff in missed CDH negligence cases, and the cost to the health service of late diagnosis (at 18 months) is unlikely to be less than an equivalent sum. On the other hand, neonatal management probably costs only 1% of this amount.

Arguments for and against a screening programme

Not everyone will agree with all I have written in the introduction, though it is based on an extensive study of the literature and from a personal interest in the problem for over 25 years, during which time 883 infants with CDH have been diagnosed and treated at birth and another 345 cases with 'late' diagnosis have been studied and documented. A lengthy introduction was felt to be necessary in that the need for neonatal screening for CDH has been challenged in recent years. In addition, the safety and effectiveness of diagnostic manipulation of the hip joint, as well as of early treatment in abduction, has been questioned. This has been discussed elsewhere (Dunn et al, 1985).

To justify the introduction of a screening programme it is necessary that the condition to be identified should be relatively common and serious, that it should be distinguishable from the normal by a test that is relatively specific, reliable, acceptable and cheap, and that a satisfactory method of treatment is available. All these criteria would appear to be very adequately satisfied in respect of neonatal screening for CDH (Table 1.2).

Table 1.2 Neonatal screening for CDH

Is the problem important (serious and common)?	Yes
Is an accepted treatment available?	Yes
Is the natural history understood?	Yes
Is there a latent or early stage?	Yes
Is a suitable test available?	Yes
Is the test safe and acceptable?	Yes
Is there an agreed policy of when to test?	Yes
Are facilities available for diagnosis and treatment?	Yes
Is case finding a continuing policy?	Yes
Is there a cost-benefit advantage?	Yes

One argument against neonatal screening requires further discussion. This is that, because four out of every five dislocatable hips become stable spontaneously and develop normally, the introduction of screening leads to a great deal of unnecessary and potentially iatrogenic treatment as well as parental anxiety. (It is even alleged that such hips are not abnormal in the first place, which is rather like saying that a primary tuberculous complex that resolves spontaneously cannot be real tuberculous infection!) The same argument is used to suggest that screening should be delayed for a week or even a month after birth in the hope that natural resolution of the condition will take place in the meantime (Fig. 1.3). This approach fails to appreciate that serious structural damage may progressively occur within weeks of birth and that there is good evidence for believing that some dislocatable hips that have become stable subsequently become either dysplastic or dislocated. It should be added that parental anxiety may be minimised by a sympathetic explanation coupled with a confident and optimistic prognosis (Stratton, 1983).

A second criticism is that neonatal screening has on occasion apparently failed to reduce the incidence of late CDH and that, furthermore, early treatment may cause avascular necrosis of the head of the femur (Catford et al, 1982). In reply it can be said that many screening programmes *have* been shown to be both effective and safe (Von Rosen, 1962; Barlow, 1962; Mitchell, 1972; MacKenzie, 1972; Fredensborg, 1976; Cyvin, 1977; Lehmann, 1981; Paterson, 1982; Palmén, 1984; Dunn, 1982; Dunn et al, 1985). It surely behoves those whose programmes have been unsuccessful to consider why they have failed and to make the necessary modifications to their methodology and organisation (Fig. 1.4). The price to be paid for missing the diagnosis in the neonatal period is unacceptably high (Table 1.3).

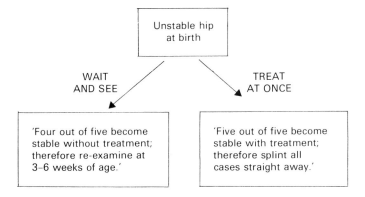

Fig. 1.3 Management alternatives

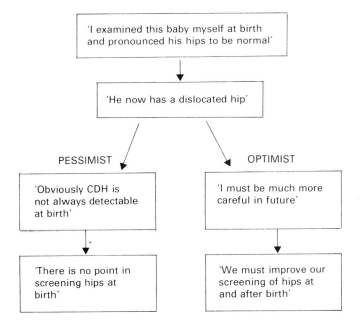

Fig. 1.4 Reflections following 'missed' CDH

Table 1.3   Effects of missing CDH diagnosis at birth

1. Diagnosis usually delayed till $1\frac{1}{2}$–2 years
2. Long and complicated treatment including multiple hospitalisations, leg traction, plaster of Paris splinting, operations on hip joint, rotation osteotomy
3. Emotional trauma
4. Risk of avascular necrosis of the head of the femur
5. Poor long term results — the aching hip, osteoarthritis
6. Much greater expense

SCREENING PROGRAMME

Neonatal screening

The way in which hips should be examined has already been discussed. The question remains: who is the best person to undertake the screening? The simple answer is that it may be any member of the medical team who is both conscientious and competent at examining hips. In some programmes all infants are examined by the same person whether an orthopaedic surgeon or someone specifically allocated to this duty, such as a general practitioner or midwife. The advantage of such a scheme is that the examiner becomes very proficient; the disadvantage is that the programme becomes very dependent on one or two individuals while the remaining members of the team are deprived of experience in diagnosing a common and important condition. There is also the matter of logistics. Almost all babies in the UK are now born in hospital, but about half will have returned home within two to three days. It may not prove easy for one individual (or even two) to examine every infant on the first day of life, or even before discharge home.

The alternative arrangement is to screen the hips as part of the normal complete neonatal examination which is, or should be, undertaken on the first day of life and again prior to discharge from hospital. Such examinations take only a few minutes of the doctor's time, and, once the infant is undressed, examination of the hips usually takes only a few moments more. No extra expense is involved, and the paediatric (or obstetric) residents who undertake most of these neonatal examinations soon gain competence and confidence in the Ortolani-Barlow manoeuvre. The main disadvantage is that the junior staff are constantly changing and there is always the danger that new members of the team will overlook cases of CDH while they are gaining experience. Several strategies may be used to minimise this risk.

First, new members of the team need to be made aware of the importance of the diagnosis and trained and supervised until they become competent in the examination. Excellent models are available for demonstrating the 'feel' of a dislocating hip*.

Second, residents should be encouraged to report all doubtful hips to a senior member of the staff so that they may be re-checked, whenever possible in the presence of the initial examiner. This checking should be done at once and certainly whenever possible on the same day. Ideally the hips should be examined first by the resident and then by the expert so that the resident has the opportunity of drawing attention to any change in the state of the hip that may have taken place in the interval since the earlier examination.

Third, all infants at high risk of CDH, as for instance those with a family

---

*'Baby Hippy': a model for demonstrating and teaching examination of the newborn hip, whether dislocated or dislocatable. Made by Medical Plastics Laboratory Inc, Export Department, Medica International, 205 West Wacker Drive (Suite 621), Chicago, Illinois 60606, USA.

history, those presenting by the breech and those with other deformities, should be double checked by the most experienced examiner available.

Fourth, it is important that, when a case is missed and diagnosed later, the doctor involved in the initial examination be informed so that he can check his technique.

The second neonatal examination prior to discharge from hospital is important as it provides another chance of picking up an abnormal hip. Experience in Bristol has revealed that one in seven of all neonatal diagnoses may be made at this time (Dunn et al, 1985).

No mention has been made of the use of radiological or ultrasound examination in screening for CDH. This is because, though these methods may be of value in confirming or further investigating the diagnosis in the neonatal period (Bertol et al, 1982; Clarke et al, 1985; Berman et al, 1986), they are time consuming, expensive and probably less reliable than clinical examination. They therefore have little or no place in neonatal screening.

Postneonatal screening

Even the most successful neonatal screening programmes have their missed cases and surveillance therefore needs to be continued throughout the first two years of life and indeed until the child is walking with a normal stable gait. Inspection and manipulation of the hips for the classic signs of dislocation should form part of every medical examination during this period. The regular developmental assessments that most infants have at 6–12 weeks, 6–8 months, 12–15 months and 18–24 months should in particular include careful screening for CDH. Suspicion of CDH, at least from 3 months onwards, should lead to radiological examination. A single A-P film with the legs adducted and parallel is all that is required in the first instance. Some authorities consider that in very high risk groups, as for instance when there is a strong family history of CDH, screening at 3 months should include radiological examination; others feel that X-ray should be reserved for diagnosis after clinical examination has led to suspicion.

Organisation

A multi-disciplinary programme lasting two or more years requires quite a complex organisation. Probably the best way of setting up and supervising such an organisation is through the creation in each district or area of a special committee whose membership includes representatives of obstetrics, midwifery, paediatrics, orthopaedics, radiology, health visiting, general practice and community medicine. This committee is best coordinated and chaired by the person most interested in the problem, usually either a paediatrician or an orthopaedic surgeon. The responsibilities of the committee should include the planning of the programme, including the times of regular examinations at birth and thereafter of all infants in the population, the training of the staff who will be responsible for examination, the delineation of clear guidelines for the referral of suspected or confirmed cases, the maintenance of a register of confirmed cases, the feedback of information on late diagnosed cases to those who missed the opportunity of making the diagnosis earlier, the on-going audit of the whole endeavour, including the results of treatment and late outcome, and research on the subject.

Referral

When CDH is diagnosed with confidence after the neonatal period, referral should be to an orthopaedic surgeon. In the early weeks of life, though, when the diagnosis may still be in doubt, it may be preferable in the first instance to refer the infant back to the paediatrician responsible for care in the neonatal period. Such a policy may cause less anxiety to the parents, especially if a follow up appointment has already been arranged for other reasons. The diagnosis can then be clarified and further referral made to the orthopaedic clinic when appropriate. Another advantage of this approach is that it may help to spare already busy orthopaedic clinics from a further increase in workload.

Reasons for failure

The results of some reported studies in recent years have been disappointing, with the incidence of classic late presentation apparently remaining as high as it was before screening was introduced (Walker, 1971; Wilkinson, 1972; Williamson, 1972; Bjerkreim, 1974). Such observations of course assume that we know what the incidence of postneonatal CDH would be without early diagnosis and treatment. In fact we have few reliable data on this subject and such as we have relate only to children with dislocation and ignore the probably equally large number of children with stable but dysplastic hips following the partial resolution of CDH after delivery. Indirect evidence suggests that without early diagnosis and treatment the incidence of classic CDH is unlikely to be less than two per 1000. If, as seems likely, an equal number of children have hip dysplasia without dislocation, the incidence of all late hip pathology due to CDH might be expected to be at least four per 1000.

CDH may be missed at birth or later either because the hips are not examined or because they are examined by an unskilled person; or they may be examined by someone with experience who slips up, as all of us do from time to time. Alternatively, if examination is delayed for a day or more after birth, the hip may have become temporarily stable, only to dislocate again later in infancy. Very occasionally too, infants are born with shallow, dysplastic, stable hip joints which may become unstable or remain dysplastic in later infancy or childhood (Table 1.4).

Another problem is that responsibility for care and the diagnosis of CDH is often divided between several disciplines. Too often there is a lack of communication, including the feedback of information regarding later

Table 1.4 Reasons for missed early diagnosis of CDH

1. Hips not examined
2. Hips examined by unskilled person
3. Hips examined by skilled person but diagnosis missed
4. Hips stable on examination but dysplastic
    a) from birth
    b) becoming so after birth

diagnosis, to those who had responsibility for earlier examinations. The need for proper training of the staff who undertake most routine checks has been stressed, including the need to distinguish between 'clicks' and 'clunks'.

Successful screening

There are many reports in the world literature on the success of neonatal and infant screening programmes in reducing the incidence of late diagnosis. None have been better documented than those from Sweden which have recently been reviewed by Hanssen et al (1983). Thus in Malmö it has been estimated that 90% of all cases of CDH were diagnosed and successfully treated at birth (Fredensborg, 1975), while in Göteborg the figure was 85%. For the whole of Sweden 50% of cases were diagnosed on the maternity wards and 80% during the first six months of life.

The results of a 10 year screening programme in Bristol have recently been reported (Dunn et al, 1985). From among 23 002 infants born during 1970–9 in the University department, 445 cases of CDH were identified. Altogether 99% were successfully treated with between six and 15 weeks' abduction splinting. The remaining 1% required adductory tenotomy and further splinting. None required open operation. None developed avascular necrosis. Radiological assessment of the 90% seen at 1–5 years was excellent. Very careful searches revealed only 10 cases of postneonatally diagnosed CDH among the University infants. These late cases for the most part required long and complicated surgical treatment and had much less favourable outcomes. The University results were statistically significantly better than those for other groups of infants born in Bristol during the same period (that had also been screened for CDH). While at first sight it would appear that 98% of all cases in the University cohort were diagnosed at birth, this estimate fails to take account of cases that were missed but resolved spontaneously. Probably 90% would be a more accurate figure.

CONCLUSIONS

1. Classic CDH is a common and potentially crippling deformity with repercussions throughout childhood and adult life.
2. The great majority of cases may be clinically diagnosed at birth and safely treated within a few weeks or months.

3. The earlier that treatment is instituted the shorter the period needed and the more favourable the outcome.
4. The cost of early diagnosis is only a small fraction of that of later treatment.
5. All infants should be screened at birth. Continuing regular surveillance is necessary until the child is walking with a stable gait at 2 years of age.
6. The multi-disciplinary approach needed requires the creation of a representative committee to supervise the organisation and audit of screening the whole population (under 2 years) in an area.

Acknowledgement

I am grateful to the Van Neste Foundation and the Department of Health and Social Security for their support.

REFERENCES

Barlow T G 1962 Early diagnosis and treatment of congenital dislocation of the hip. Journal of Bone and Joint Surgery 44B: 292–301
Berman L, Catterall A, Meire H 1986 Ultrasound of the hip: a review of the applications of a new technique. British Journal of Radiology 59: 13–17
Bertol P, Macnicol M F, Mitchell G P 1982 Radiographic features of neonatal congenital dislocation of the hip. Journal of Bone and Joint Surgery 64B: 176–9
Bjerkreim I 1974 Congenital dislocation of the hip in Norway, Acta Orthopaedica Scandinavica 157 (Supplement)
Catford J C, Bennet G C, Wilkinson J A 1982 Congenital hip dislocation: an increasing and still uncontrolled disability? British Medical Journal 285: 1527–1530.
Clarke N M P, Harcke H T, McHugh P, Lee M S, Borns P F, MacEwan G D 1985 Real-time ultrasound in the diagnosis of congenital dislocation and dysplasia of the hip. Journal of Bone and Joint Surgery 67B: 406–412
Cyvin K C 1977 Congenital dislocation of the hip. Acta Paediatrica Scandinavica 263 (Supplement)
Dunn P M 1969 The influence of the intrauterine environment in the causation of congenital postural deformities, with special reference to congenital dislocation of the hip. MD Thesis, Cambridge University
Dunn P M 1976a Congenital postural deformities. British Medical Bulletin 32: 71–76
Dunn P M 1976b The anatomy and pathology of congenital dislocation of the hip. Clinical Orthopædics and Related Research 119: 23–7
Dunn P M 1976c Perinatal observations on the aetiology of congenital dislocation of the hip. Clinical Orthopaedics and Related Research 119: 11–22
Dunn P M 1982 Congenital dislocation of the hip. British Medical Journal 285: 1737
Dunn P M, Evans R E, Thearle M J, Griffiths H E D, Witherow P J 1985 Congenital dislocation of the hip: early and late diagnosis and management compared. Archives of Disease in Childhood 60: 407–414
Fredensborg N 1975 Congenital dislocation of the hip (Thesis) Lund, Sweden, University of Lund
Fredensborg N 1976 The results of early treatment of typical congenital dislocation of the hip in Malmo. Journal of Bone and Joint Surgery 58B: 272–278
Hanssen G, Nachemson A, Palmén K 1983 Screening of children with congenital dislocation of the hip joint on the maternity wards in Sweden. Journal of Paediatric Orthopaedics 3: 271–279
Lehmann E C H 1981 Neonatal screening in Vancouver for congenital dislocation of the hip. Canadian Medical Association Journal 124: 1003–1008
MacKenzie I G 1972 Congenital dislocation of the hip. The development of a regional service. Journal of Bone and Joint Surgery 54B: 18–39

Mitchell G P 1972 Problems in the early diagnosis and management of congenital dislocation of the hip. Journal of Bone and Joint Surgery 54B: 4–12

Ortolani M 1948 La Lussazione Congenita Dell'Anca. Nuovi Criteri Diagnostici E Profilatico. Correttivi. Bologna, Editore Capelli

Paterson D 1982 The early diagnosis and screening of congenital dislocation of the hip. In: Tachdjian M O (ed) Congenital Dislocation of the Hip, Churchill Livingstone, New York, p. 145–157

Palmén K 1984 Prevention of congenital dislocation of the hip. Acta Orthopaedica Scandinavica 55: 208 (Supplement)

Stratton D 1983 Your baby's hips. A parent's guide to congenital instability or dislocation of the hip. Cow & Gate Ltd, Trowbridge, UK, 1–9

Von Rosen 1962 Diagnosis and treatment of congenital dislocation of the hip in the newborn. Journal of Bone and Joint Surgery 44B: 284–291

Walker G 1971 Problems in the early recognition of congenital dislocation of the hip. British Medical Journal 3: 147–148

Wilkinson J A 1982 A post natal survey for congenital displacement of the hip. Journal of Bone and Joint Surgery 54B: 40–49

Williamson J 1972 Difficulties of early diagnosis and treatment of congenital dislocation of the hip in Northern Ireland. Journal of Bone and Joint Surgery 54B: 13–17

Visual defects in school children: screening policy and educational implications

INTRODUCTION

Screening for visual defects in school children has become a time honoured practice in the School Health Service. As with many other well established clinical practices, studies attempting to appraise and quantify its merits and deficiences are hard to find.

Individual voices have been heard (Youngson, 1977) to question the value of these programmes as they are currently practised, and some recent research on the 1958 and 1970 birth cohort studies suggests that a reappraisal should be undertaken. This chapter endeavours to present some of these research findings and to encourage further questions and debate.

People who have been screening children in school for many years believing in its importance to the children's health and well being, will not welcome the implication that some of this effort has been to no avail. On the other hand, critical debate can benefit any service: though this may require that clinical practice changes, the outcome should be a service where everyone participating understands its costs and benefits.

CURRENT SCREENING PRACTICE

Anecdotal reports suggest that programmes of vision screening in school children vary widely from one health district to another. Information was therefore collected on the children of the 1970 birth cohort, about the screening tests which they had undergone in school, and this evidence allows us to make a more precise statement about current practice.

The 1970 birth cohort is a representative sample of over 13 000 children resident in England, Wales or Scotland who were selected by their date of birth and were studied at intervals during their childhood. Together with the two previous birth cohort studies (those of 1946 and 1958), it was described in Volume I of *Progress in Child Health* (Golding, 1984). For further relevant information on the 1970 study, the reader is referred to other publications (Stewart-Brown, 1986; Stewart-Brown & Butler, 1985; Stewart-Brown et al, 1985).

When the 1970 cohort was surveyed at 10 years of age, clinical medical officers were asked to consult each child's school medical record (forms 10M and 10BM) and to provide information about the screening tests that had been carried out on the child at school.

Distant vision screening

Table 2.1 shows the ages at which the 13 871 children in the survey had had their first distant and near vision screening tests. Most children (66.9%) had had their distant vision screened by the time they were 6 years old. Only 1.7% of the children had never had their distant vision tested. For 9.4% of the children this question was either unanswered or answered 'not known', because the 10M and 10BM forms were not available at the time of the medical examination.

Table 2.1   Age at first vision screening test for 13 871 children

Age	Distant vision (%)	Near vision (%)
≤ 5 years	66.9	13.8
6 or 7 years	16.2	7.2
≥ 8 years	5.9	8.9
Not tested	1.7	26.8
Not known if tested	9.4	43.4

Data from the 1970 birth cohort at age 10 years

Near vision screening

The picture for near vision screening was very different. Altogether 26.8% of the children had definitely never had their near vision screened and only 29.9% definitely had been tested. For 43.4% of the children the question was unanswered. School medical records were available for over three quarters of this group, and the most likely explanation for the size of this 'unknown' group is that nothing had been written about near vision screening in the school records. Although it is possible that these children were screened and no record was kept, it seems more probable that they had never had their near vision tested.

My interpretation of this table is that nearly all children have their distant visual acuity tested in primary school but only a small proportion also have their near vision screened.

Other vision screening tests carried out in school

Of the cohort children, 52.8% had had their colour vision screened at least once by the time they reached 10 years of age and 11% had been screened for squint at least once since school entry.

Frequency of screening and geographical differences

Table 2.2 shows the frequencies with which the children in the 1970 cohort had undergone visual acuity testing, and Table 2.3 shows that screening patterns differed somewhat in different parts of the United Kingdom.

Altogether 10.7% of children appeared to have had their distant vision screened nearly every year. Roughly a third had had a single screening test, and another third had had two. In Wales 3% of children had never had their distant vision screened, but this was true of less than 1% in England and Scotland. In Scotland less than 20% of children had definitely had their near vision screened. Information on the frequency with which children had been tested for colour vision and squint was not collected in this survey.

It is clear from Tables 2.1, 2.2 and 2.3 that there is no generally accepted pattern for visual acuity screening and that different children receive a widely differing service. Although there appears to be agreement, in England and Scotland at least, that all children should have their distant visual acuity tested at some time in primary school, it appears that some health authorities believe that this should be done frequently and others that it should be done only once. Opinion is much more divided about near vision screening, and it would appear

Table 2.2   Frequency of vision screening at school before 10 years for 13 871 children

No. of times	Distant vision (%)	Near vision (%)
1	28.9	19.3
2	30.3	7.1
3	19.0	2.2
≥4	10.7	1.2
Not tested	1.7	26.8
Not known if tested	9.4	43.4

Data from the 1970 birth cohort at age 10 years

Table 2.3   Geographical variation in vision screening

Country (No. of children*)	Distant vision			Near vision		
	Screened (%)	Not screened (%)	Not known (%)	Screened (%)	Not screened (%)	Not known (%)
England (11 657)	89.9	0.7	9.4	31.7	23.0	45.3
Wales (805)	83.0	3.0	14.0	34.8	28.6	36.7
Scotland (1375)	93.2	0.7	6.1	18.8	42.4	38.8

*34 children were included whose current house address was overseas
Data from the 1970 birth cohort at age 10 years

that most authorities feel that near vision screening is not worth while in addition to distant vision screening.

THE PURPOSE OF VISION SCREENING

Screening is carried out either to detect a disease process at a stage where it can be successfully aborted or treated (primary or secondary screening) or to detect a potentially handicapping condition in which the handicap can be ameliorated by some form of treatment (tertiary screening).

Vision screening in children is performed for different reasons at different ages. In infancy babies are screened to detect partial sight or blindness. Some of these children have conditions such as congenital cataracts which can be treated; in others the aim is to detect blindness, because knowledge of the condition by parents and professionals is thought to minimise the associated handicap. In the pre-school period children are screened to detect squints, which are unsightly and may lead to unilateral loss of sight. Treatment for squint may both cure the squint and prevent the development of amblyopia.

By school age partially sighted children will have been identified and by 6 or 7 years of age squints will have become resistant to treatment. Thus, although an initial school entry check for the presence of squint may be useful, school vision screening programmes are primarily of value only for detecting the less severe degrees of visual impairment caused by refractive errors — that is, myopia, hypermetropia, anisometropia and astigmatism — and for detecting colour vision defects. Hypermetropia and astigmatism very rarely develop anew between the ages of 5 and 16, but myopia commonly does; it is, therefore, to detect new cases of myopia that vision screening is carried out repeatedly during the school years.

COSTS AND BENEFITS OF VISION SCREENING

All screening activities have their costs; and as whole populations need to be screened to detect the few individuals who would benefit from identification, the costs of screening programmes can be very high. This may be difficult to believe because individual screening tests are rarely expensive and the potential benefit, for example to a child who has a severe and treatable visual defect that is identified and corrected as a result of a vision screening programme, is immense. However, guidelines have been laid down that describe screening tests for which the benefits to society are likely to outweigh the costs, and it is worth examining these criteria in some detail with respect to school vision screening. The criteria are as follows:
1. The condition is common.
2. It constitutes an important public health problem.
3. Treatment for the condition is available and not too costly.
4. The screening test is both reliable and cheap.

HOW COMMON ARE VISUAL DEFECTS IN CHILDREN?

Prevalence at 10 years

The children of the 1970 birth cohort were medically examined by clinical medical officers and school nurses at 10 years of age; they were requested to test distant visual acuity in each eye using a Snellen chart or an equivalent alternative if more appropriate for the child. They were given instructions which included standing the child in a good light 20 feet from the chart, occluding first one eye and then the other, but they were not given special training for the survey. Near vision was tested using a Sheridan Gardiner near vision chart, which was provided for the survey together with instructions on how to use it ('Place the child in a good light and hold the chart at a comfortable distance not more than 10 inches from the eye being tested; occlude first one eye, then the other'). Results of visual acuity testing for this sample of children are shown in Table 2.4.

Table 2.4 shows that over 20% of children had less than perfect visual acuity but that most of these had only very minor or unilateral defects. Only 1.8% had a distant visual acuity of 6/24 or worse in both eyes. 3.5% of children had perfect vision on distant acuity testing but had some defect of near vision; most of this group had only minor defects.

The acuity data collected on the cohort children are likely to contain inaccuracies for several reasons. Unless the distance between the child and the chart is measured correctly it is possible both to overestimate and to underestimate acuity. If the eye not being tested is not occluded properly unilateral visual loss will be underestimated. If care is not taken to ensure good lighting and concentration by the children visual loss may be overestimated. However, as the people who carried out acuity testing on these children were the people responsible for routine screening the picture provided by these data is likely accurately to represent screening test results as currently practised in schools.

Table 2.5 shows the geographical variation in prevalence of defects in the three different countries: England, Wales and Scotland. The overall prevalence of defects was much the same from country to country, but there were significantly more children with isolated distant vision defects in Wales and significantly more with isolated near vision defects and other types of defects in Scotland. This would suggest that myopia may be more common among Welsh children and hypermetropia more common among Scots. It is worth noting in passing that the country in which children were least likely to have had their near vision screened was the one in which such defects were most common.

Changes in prevalence over time

The children of the 1958 birth cohort study also had their visual acuity examined, and in that study acuity testing was carried out at several different ages. Using data published in one of the papers from that study (Peckham and

Table 2.4 Prevalence of visual defects in 12 853 children of 1970 birth cohort at 10 years of age

Description of defect	Acuity in better eye / Distant Near	Bilateral defects*					Acuity in affected eye	Unilateral defects				
		6/9 9 (%)	6/12 6/18 12 18 (%)	6/24 6/36 24 36 (%)	6/60 <6/60 60 <60 (%)	Total bilateral defect		6/9 9 (%)	6/12 6/18 12 18 (%)	6/24 6/36 24 36 (%)	6/60 <6/60 60 <60 (%)	Total unilateral
Distant Vision defect only		3.7	1.3	0.7	0.2	5.9		3.6	0.8	0.1	0.0	4.5
Near vision defect only		1.4	0.1	0.0	0.0	1.5		2.0	0.1	0.0	0.0	2.1
Both near and distant vision defects†		2.9	1.3	0.7	0.2	5.1		0.8	0.8	0.8	0.4	2.8
Total		8.0	2.7	1.4	0.4	12.5		6.4	1.7	0.9	0.4	9.4

*Classified by severity of defect in better eye. † Classified by severity of distant vision defect
< = worse than

Table 2.5   Geographical variation in visual defects

	England (n = 10 720)	Scotland (n = 1338)	Wales (n = 763)
Percentage of children with:			
Perfect vision (6/6 6/6 6, 6)	78.2	76.7	77.2
Distant vision defects only (acuity ≤ 6/9)	10.7	8.5	12.3
Near vision defects only (acuity ≤ 9)	3.4	4.9	2.8
Other defects	7.8	9.9	7.7

Data from the 1970 birth cohort at age 10 years

Adams, 1975) it is possible to compare the prevalence of defects in the two cohorts.

The children in the two cohorts were studied in very similar ways, and the methodological flaws of acuity testing in the 1970 study were also present in the 1958 cohort. Paradoxically, unless we have reason to believe that the reliability of acuity testing in schools changed significantly over the period in question this means that we can have more confidence in differences between the two samples than in the absolute values generated in either alone.

Table 2.6 contrasts the prevalence of distant visual defects in the 1958 cohort at age 11 with that in the 1970 cohort at age 10. Children who had near vision defects but perfect distant vision have been excluded from the table.

Table 2.6   Secular changes in distant visual acuity

	1958 cohort	1970 cohort
Date of testing	1969	1980
Age at testing (years)	11	10
No. of children	12 772	12 985
Visual acuity (%):		
6/6 6/6	77.6	81.4
6/6 6/9 6/9 6/9	10.0	9.0
6/6 6/12 6/6 6/18 6/9 6/12 6/9 6/18	3.8	3.6
6/6 ≤6/24 6/9 <6/24	2.0	1.6
6/12 ≤6/12 6/18 ≤6/18	3.3	2.7
≤6/24 ≤6/24	3.3	1.7

There were very significantly fewer children in the 1970 birth cohort with distant vision defects. This difference was present at all levels of visual acuity loss but was most marked among children with the most severe loss ($\leqslant 6/24$ bilaterally). In this group the prevalence of defects in the 1970 birth cohort was almost half that in the earlier study ($p < 0.0001$).

The problem with comparing these two samples and attributing differences to secular changes is that between 10 and 11 years of age children enter puberty. As the development of myopia has been observed clinically to accompany puberty we would expect there to be more children with defects of distant visual acuity at 11 than at 10. A study (Tibbenham et al, 1978) was carried out on the 1958 birth cohort data, to look at differences in visual defects among the children when they were tested at 7 and 11 years.

There was a 2% increase in defect prevalence over the four year period. We would therefore be hard pressed to ascribe the 4% difference in defect prevalence between the two cohorts to the one year age difference. The prevalence of visual impairment would appear to have fallen over the decade 1970–1980 to a very significant degree.

Evidence that this may have happened can also be gleaned from another study (Ismail & Hall, 1981), which looked at the visual acuity of all school entrants in two outer London boroughs. The results from this study can be compared with those of the 1958 cohort children at 7 years of age. Table 2.7 shows that the prevalence of all defects among the 7 year olds in 1958 was 20.9% and of defects more severe than 6/9, 8.2%. Among 5 year olds in 1980 the corresponding figures were 10.4% and 3.4%. The prevalence of defects would appear to have more than halved during this time. Clearly, in comparing those two studies possible geographical variation needs to be taken into account in addition to the possibility of a secular improvement in screening technique. The impression left by these four studies, however, is that visual defects in children are much less common now than they were a decade ago.

Table 2.7

	1958 Cohort*	School entrants in 2 outer London Boroughs**
Age (years)	7	5
Date of testing	1965	1980
No.	14 197	4239
Vision		
6/6 6/6	79.1	89.6
6/6 6/9	12.7	7.0
6/9 6/9		
$\leqslant 6/12$ either eye	8.2	3.4

* Alberman et al, 1971a
** Ismail & Hall, 1981

The development of defects during the school years

The children in the 1958 cohort had their vision tested at 7, 11 and 16 years, and one study (Tibbenham et al, 1978) had used these data to examine the development of defects during childhood. Studies of this type are necessary to assess the need for repeated screening of children and to identify the optimum frequency of testing.

About 15% of the 5680 children assessed as having normal vision at 7 years of age had some defect when they were tested at 11; 1.8% of them had bilateral vision of 6/24 or worse, and 1.7%, 6/12 or 6/18 vision. Of the 5678 children with normal vision at 11, 12.5% had a defect at 16 years, 1.2% had a bilateral defect of 6/24 or worse and 2.0% a defect of 6/12 or 6/18.

Data are also presented which show that a significant proportion of children recorded as having a defect at 7 years of age had perfect acuity at 11, and a proportion of those with defects at 11 had perfect acuity at 16. These findings could be explained on the basis of measurement error, but it is also biologically plausible that refractive errors develop and then disappear during different phases of growth in the eyeball. There are many different anatomical structures in the eye which grow during childhood, and different growth in the different parts could lead to refractive errors which would be corrected as 'catch-up' growth occurs in another structure. It is in many ways remarkable that growth is normally so well coordinated and that most children maintain perfect acuity throughout their school years.

There are some problems about using the 1958 cohort data to assess the value of current screening programmes. First, we have shown that defects are less common now than they were when the children in this cohort were in school and it is likely that the rate of development of new defects has also changed. Secondly, what we really want to know is the annual rate of development of new defects. We could arrive at a figure for this by assuming a steady rate of development; if we do this we can calculate that defects appeared between 7 and 11 at a rate of 0.8% per annum. There are certain flaws in this method, and these could make the assessment misleading if measurement error was large. Therefore, although it is reasonable to predict that in the 1980s around 0.5% of children will develop new defects of 6/12 or worse in each primary school year, further studies are urgently needed.

Implications of prevalence data

Is 6/9 vision abnormal?

Imperfect visual acuity is very common in school children, but most of these children have only a very minor visual loss. Although opinion on the significance of 6/9 vision is clearly divided, some clinicians would hold that anything less than 6/6 visual acuity is bound to interfere with a child's development and should be treated. This belief warrants further consideration. The Snellen chart has a somewhat arbitrary cut-off point at 6/6, and many children can actually read 6/5 or even 6/4. Why then should we not regard 6/6 vision as an impairment? Alternatively, perhaps we should regard 6/9 as part of a normal range for 10 year old children. If this level is regarded as 'abnormal' or 'pathological', visual acuity stands out from other clinical areas as something of an anomaly.

In other areas of clinical practice a statistically defined normal range is accepted. This normal range usually encompasses individuals where measurement lies within ±2 standard deviations; 95% of individuals should fall within this range. Although the concept of a normal range may not be applicable to visual acuity where the relevant measurement varies from condition to condition, it is very likely that there is an underlying normal range of refractive indices. On the scale of measurement defined by acuity charts, 20% of the 1970 birth cohort children had acuities which fell outside the normal range as currently defined (i.e. 6/6 or better). Acuity of 6/12 in this sample corresponded much more closely to the definition of abnormality used in other clinical areas because 5% of the sample had acuities of this value or less.

So we should perhaps bear in mind in this discussion on screening that 'abnormality' could begin at 6/12 acuity and that 6/9 vision could be 'normal' for a 10 year old. In relating this to screening practice it is necessary to make the transition from acuity to refractive indices. Vision of 6/9 due to myopia may be normal whereas 6/9 vision due to hypermetropia is not.

Workload generated by current screening programmes

If we assume that the prevalence we found in the 1970 cohort study at 10 years of age represents the average prevalence of vision defects at all ages 5–15, and if we look at the worst possible situation where all school children are screened every year and all those with acuity of 6/9 or worse are referred for a further opinion, we can calculate that in an average size health district of 250 000 (school population 40 000) 8000 children would need a second opinion every year (160 children per week). This is unlikely to represent the true picture because children identified and treated appropriately in one year should not be referred again in the next unless their vision had deteriorated significantly; but allowing for this it is possible to calculate that around 5% of children would be referred every time the school population was screened (Stewart-Brown & Brewer, 1986). This represents 40 children per week in an average size health district screening every year.

Other implications

The other fact to emerge from Table 2.4 is that districts that do not use near vision screening will fail to detect visual defects in the 3.5% of children with isolated near vision defects. The most likely cause of defects in this group of children is hypermetropia. Severe hypermetropia causes distant as well as near visual acuity loss, and children with mild hypermetropia can record normal acuities both distant and near because their power of accommodation is sufficient to overcome the refractive error. This small group therefore had a degree of hypermetropia which could be overcome for distant vision but not for near. Because powers of accommodation in children are variable it is impossible to predict the degree of refractive error from acuity tests, but whatever their precise refractive error it is likely that these children had to exercise their maximum accommodation to achieve their recorded near visual acuity. Whether this would have been associated with any disability in these children has not been rigorously studied, but there are some indications from a study discussed later in this chapter that they may do so (Stewart-Brown et al, 1985).

DO ALL VISUAL DEFECTS MATTER? (PUBLIC HEALTH IMPORTANCE)

Visual defects are held to interfere with children's schoolwork; they are said to prevent some children achieving their optimum performance on the sports field; they are thought to cause symptoms such as headaches and fatigue, and some clinicians believe that they may have subtle influences on a child's social and psychological development. Once again, the information collected on the three birth cohorts has provided an opportunity to examine some of these beliefs in further depth.

Educational attainment of children with visual defects

Children with visual defects are not a homogeneous group. If the different refractive errors do cause problems in the classroom, it is unlikely that they cause the same problems. Children who have unilateral loss of sight from, for example, amblyopia could be predicted to suffer from a different set of difficulties from those with bilateral loss of vision. To investigate the possible educational consequences of vision defects in the 1970 cohort study we divided children into a series of 10 categories according to the pattern of their visual acuity loss. The categories are shown in Table 2.8. This classification was chosen for several reasons: first, because it allowed children with minor visual defects (6/9) and children with defects in one eye only to be identified; secondly, because using this system it was possible to attach a probable diagnosis to some of the groups; and, thirdly, because it permitted us to investigate the group of children with defects which would not have been identified in screening programmes in which only distant vision screening was performed.

Although this classification has been very useful in our studies, there are several reasons why the 1970 cohort data set is not ideal for investigating the educational consequences of visual defects. The first reason is the degree of error likely to be present in the visual acuity measurements. Ideally this sort of study requires precise optometric and ophthalmological measurement on a large representative sample of children. Secondly, in all the different categories

Table 2.8 Categories of visual defect

Category	Description of defect	Visual acuity			Predominant diagnostic category
		Distant	Near		
0	No defect	6/6	6/6	6 6	Perfect vision
1	Bilateral minimal distant defect†	6/9	≤6/9	6 6	Myopia of increasing severity
2	Bilateral mild distant defect†	≤5/12≥6/18	≤6/12	6 6	
3	Bilateral marked distant defect†	≤6/24	≤6/24	6 6	
4	Unilateral distant defect	≤6/9	6/6	6 6	Unilateral myopia
5	Bilateral near defect†	6/6	6/6	≤9 ≤9	Mild and moderate hypermetropia
6	Unilateral near defect	6/6	6/6	≤9 6	Unilateral hypermetropia
7	Unilateral mild mixed defect*	<6/9≥6/18	6/6	≤9 6	Amblyopia of increasing severity
8	Unilateral marked mixed defect*	≤6/24	≥6/9	≤9 ≥9	
9	Bilateral mild mixed defect*†	≤6/9≥6/18	≤6/9	≤9 ≤6	No predominant diagnostic category
10	Bilateral marked mixed defect*†	≤6/24	≤6/24	≤9 ≤6	

< = worse than; > = better than; ≤ = worse than or equal to; ≥ = better than or equal to
*Mixed defects are those in which both near and far visual acuity is affected
†Where visual acuity differs between the two eyes, defects have been classified to the level of acuity in the better eye

some children have been treated with spectacles and some have not. We do not know why those who had spectacles had been given them, at what age they were prescribed or whether the children actually wore them. Among children with more serious defects, virtually all had spectacles and educational scores for these groups allow us only to make a comment on how well children with visual impairments perform after treatment. The few truly partially sighted children in the cohort were unable to complete the standard educational tests administered to the cohort as a whole and so they are not in this sample at all. The data set therefore has most to contribute to an investigation of the effects of minor visual defects. Among the latter, most of the children did not have spectacles and unless they had some other impairment all of them would have been able to perform the educational tests.

The ideal data set for investigating this problem, including detailed optometric and ophthalmic examination together with a series of educational tests on a very large representative sample of children, does not exist and would be exceedingly expensive to collect. It is right therefore to make the best possible use of the 1970 cohort data, but results should be interpreted with the methodological difficulties in mind.

In Table 2.9 the mean scores for three different educational tests are presented for children with perfect vision and children in each of the 10 visual defect categories. The scores presented have been adjusted for social class and sex; both of these are to some extent associated with visual defects and both have an influence on educational scores. All scores were standardised to a mean of 100 and a standard deviation of 15. Their derivation is described more fully elsewhere (Haslum et al, 1983).

Table 2.9   Educational performance of children with and without visual defect

Visual defect category†	No. of children	Standardised BAS score adjusted for sex and social class	Reading score adjusted for intelligence, sex and social class	Mathematics score adjusted for intelligence, sex and social class
0	7520	100.9	101.1	101.3
1	330	100.2	100.4	101.6
2	124	105.4****	101.4	101.8
3	78	106.5****	103.8*	102.0
4	428	100.3	101.1	101.2
5	138	98.8	98.8**	100.2
6	185	99.4	100.5	101.8
7	167	99.4	100.6	100.4
8	107	98.3*	100.1	99.9
9	391	98.4***	100.0	100.2
10	77	100.2	100.8	100.2

†See table 2.8
BAS = British Ability Scales
Significance of difference between adjusted mean score of this category and that for children with no defect (category 0) p values: *<0.05; **0.01; ***0.001; ****0.0001
Data from the Child Health and Education Study at 10 years of age

The first column in the table shows the mean scores on the four core tests of the British Ability Scales (BAS). These are a battery of tests designed to measure intelligence (Elliott et al, 1978). Six out of the 10 groups of children had mean intelligence scores within the normal range; two groups had above average intelligence scores; and the scores of two groups fell below the mean. The groups with above average intelligence scores were those where the predominant diagnostic category was likely to be myopia. Myopes in the 1946 and 1958 cohorts (Peckham et al, 1977; Douglas et al, 1967) were also shown to have above average intelligence scores; the evidence that myopes are on average more intelligent than their peers is now very impressive.

The two groups of children who had below average intelligence scores were those in which there were likely to have been a high proportion of children with amblyopia. Children with squints have been shown in a previous study to have reduced intelligence scores (Alberman et al, 1971b), and so this was also an expected finding.

The second column in Table 2.9 shows the reading scores for children in the different groups. These scores were derived from a shortened version of the Edinburgh Reading Test (Godfrey Thompson Unit, 1978). They have been adjusted to take account not only of social class and sex but also of the child's intelligence. This statistical manoeuvre makes it possible to determine whether children in a particular group were reading better or worse than expected for their intelligence. There is a strong positive correlation between intelligence scores and reading scores, and it is children who are not performing as well as would be expected on the basis of their intelligence who are of particular interest.

Children in group 3, those with myopia of 6/24 or worse, had reading scores which were above average, even once their superior intelligence had been taken into account. Almost all of the children in this group had, of course, been prescribed spectacles. Children with 6/9, 6/12 or 6/18 acuity (groups 1 and 2), many of whom did not have spectacles, were reading at a level expected for their intelligence. Only one group of children was reading less well than expected. These were the children with bilateral near vision defects, all of whom were likely to have had mild to moderate hypermetropia.

The third column in Table 2.9 shows the adjusted mathematics scores for these groups of children. They were derived from a mathematics test designed specifically for this survey (Haslum et al, 1983). None of the groups' mean scores was significantly different from one another.

From these data we can conclude that there *are* differences in educational attainment which are associated with different types of visual defect but that overall more children have defects associated with above average achievement than defects associated with below average achievement.

The question which needs to be addressed, however, is 'do the visual defects cause the variation in educational test scores?' Does myopia cause children to score better on intelligence tests and amblyopia prevent children doing so well? The question has more than just academic significance because if the association is causal, spectacles might have an effect on educational attainment; if the association is not causal, that is the two things just happen to go together like blond hair and blue eyes, spectacles are unlikely to affect the educational scores.

If we argue a causal association for myopia, that is, if we say that myopia causes children to do better at school than their peers, should we then be treating the condition? The argument takes on a somewhat different form for amblyopia; if amblyopia causes children to fail intelligence tests, it would clearly be a good idea to treat it. The problem with amblyopia is that by the time children reach school, treatment is rarely effective.

A priori, it seems more likely that refractive errors have an effect on 'learning' than that they affect 'intelligence', and therefore it is probably more appropriate to concentrate on reading and mathematics scores. It is possible that myopes read better than their peers because they are less good at outdoor activities and are more inclined towards reading for pleasure. There is also a plausible biological hypothesis to explain a causal association between mild to moderate hypermetropia and reading difficulty (Stewart-Brown et al, 1985). The latter group (group 5) is interesting because it is not one which is normally recognised to exist clinically. This may be because few health districts screen children with near visual acuity charts and the group is therefore never identified. Since this group is the only one where there is some real suggestion that educational achievement might have been affected by visual defects it would seem to warrant further investigation.

Physical education attainment

The cohort provides data not only on educational achievement in children with visual defects but also on physical coordination and ability on the sports field, so it is possible also to comment on the likely consequences of visual defects in this area of development.

In one of the many assessments that were made on the cohort the child's mother was asked to rate on a 0–100 analogue scale the child's ability to perform certain activities like throwing and catching balls, ability at sport, riding a bicycle, swimming etc. Responses were subjected to principle component analysis, and a sports score was derived from factor loadings. The mean score for children in each of the visual defect categories is shown in Table 2.10.

With the exception of two categories, the scores of all children with defects were significantly below those of children without defects. The differences are small but nevertheless consistent.

Another assessment was made by the clinical medical officers who examined the children for the study. They carried out a battery of tests including catching balls, sorting match sticks, walking backwards along a line and standing on one leg. Results from each test were dichotomised into pass and fail categories (Haslum et al, 1985). A child was deemed to have failed the test if his score was

Table 2.10 Sports scores of children with and without visual defects

Visual defect category†	No. of children	Sports score adjusted for sex and social class	p*
0	8792	0.03	–
1	399	–0.06	0.05
2	151	–0.18	0.01
3	95	–0.30	0.001
4	520	–0.11	0.001
5	159	–0.08	NS
6	228	–0.15	0.01
7	191	–0.08	NS
8	130	–0.13	0.05
9	479	–0.12	0.001
10	95	–0.56	0.0001

†See table 2.8
*Significance of difference between adjusted mean score of this group and that for children with no defect (group 0)
Data from the Child Health and Education Study at age 10 years

in the bottom 10%. Table 2.11 shows the proportion of children failing each test for each visual defect category.

Although the series of analyses on the relationship of physical coordination and visual defects is still in its early stages and more work needs to be done, both assessments seem to tell the same story. Children with visual defects perform activities requiring physical coordination on average less well than their peers. It should be noted that the differences in mean sports scores are very small and are statistically significant only because of the very large number of children in the study. Nevertheless, their consistency is remarkable, and, as might be expected, children with the most severe defects (groups 3 and 10) have the lowest scores.

Table 2.11 Proportion (%) of children in each visual defect category failing physical coordination tests

Visual defect category*	Ball catch test	Sort matches test	Standing on one leg test	Walking backwards test
0	12.9	9.8	8.4	8.5
1	15.2	13.6	14.6	10.5
2	15.7	10.5	10.6	10.7
3	16.8	10.4	8.1	11.4
4	13.5	9.5	12.3	8.4
5	16.8	10.5	13.3	7.5
6	18.7	8.0	8.7	7.7
7	17.2	13.2	14.6	12.7
8	21.5	13.8	20.6	13.7
9	19.7	13.4	16.8	12.2
10	19.8	17.1	23.1	20.7
Significance of differences	p<0.0001	p<0.001	p<0.0001	p<0.0001

*See table 2.8
Data from the Child Health and Education Study

In the same way as it is questionable whether the association between myopia and intelligence is causal, we need to consider whether visual defects cause children to be clumsy or whether defects and clumsiness are associated for some other reason. Two out of the four motor coordination tests, the standing on one leg test and the walking backwards test, do not require precise visual discrimination and it is difficult to see how 6/9 or 6/12 visual acuity could actually cause children to fail these tests. It is also difficult to imagine how the same biological theory could be used to explain test failure by children with myopia, hypermetropia and amblyopia, all of which cause very different visual difficulties. Finally, it may be worth bearing in mind that squint can be a manifestation of motor incoordination when it is caused by muscle imbalance rather than by accommodation, convergence difficulties.

The argument about causation is as relevant to physical coordination as it is to reading scores: if children with visual defects are less coordinated than their peers because they cannot see well (and only if this is so) it may be worth while to detect and treat these defects in an attempt to improve performance.

Visual defects and headaches

In addition to causing children to fail at school, it is the conviction of many doctors, nurses, parents and opticians that visual defects cause headaches. Mothers of the 1970 cohort children were asked to record how frequently their children experienced headaches and so it has been possible to test this conviction.

The proportion of children who were reported to experience headaches more often than once a month was statistically no different among those who had defects (11.9%) and those who did not (10.8%) (Table 2.12). Among children who had defects, 13.4% of those with spectacles had headaches compared with 11.4% of those without (Table 2.12). Although these data do not allow us to comment on individual cases, they would not support the hypotheses either that visual defects cause headaches very commonly or that spectacles can prevent headaches. Indeed, the only group of children who had a higher than average prevalence of headaches was that of children who had perfect vision but who had been prescribed spectacles (this interesting group of children is discussed more fully elsewhere (Stewart-Brown, 1986).

Table 2.12 Proportion of children with headaches

	Children with spectacles (%)	Children without spectacles (%)	Total	Statistical significance
Visual defect present	13.4	11.4	11.9	NS
No defect	18.2	10.6	10.8	$p < 0.001$

Although this finding might suggest that instead of preventing headaches in children who do not need them spectacles could actually cause headaches, there is an alternative explanation. If parents believe that visual defects cause headaches, they will be more inclined to take children who suffer from headaches for an eye test than children who do not. If opticians believe that visual defects cause headaches they may be more inclined to treat very minor refractive errors in these children. So a child with a very minor refractive error is more likely to be given a pair of spectacles if he also complains of headaches. Whether the very minor refractive errors which are present without detectable visual acuity loss could possibly cause headaches must, however, remain debatable, and evidence from the cohort presented here does not seem to support the hypothesis.

TREATMENT FOR VISUAL DEFECTS

Refractive errors, which constitute the great majority of conditions causing 10 year olds to have less than perfect visual acuity, are correctable. It is always possible to fit a lens that can bring the acuity to 6/6, and the temptation to do so is very strong. The cost of an individual pair of spectacles is not great; it is around £15.00 a pair at present. This is likely to increase the temptation to prescribe if in doubt, but whether it is always desirable is another question. Between 10% and 12% of 1970 cohort children had been prescribed spectacles by the time they reached 10 years of age; the number who had had more than one pair during childhood is unknown, and multiple prescriptions could considerably increase the spectacle prescription rate. Thus, although the cost of an individual pair of spectacles is not high, the total spectacle bill of a single health district may be surprisingly high (Stewart-Brown, 1986).

It is clear from studies on both the 1958 (Peckham et al, 1979) and 1970 cohorts (Stewart-Brown, 1986) that opinion is divided about treatment for children with minor acuity loss. Thirty per cent of children with bilateral 6/9 distant acuity had been prescribed spectacles as had 20% of those with 6/9 in one eye. Three per cent of children with apparently perfect acuity were said to have been prescribed spectacles. Because perfect acuity and 6/9 acuity were so very much more common than were the more severe defects, almost half of all spectacle prescriptions in the 1970 cohort had been made to children with this level of defect (Table 2.13).

Evidence that some spectacle prescriptions may be unnecessary has been presented from both 1958 and 1970 cohorts in a different series of analyses. Over a third of both the 1958 cohort 16 year olds (Peckham et al, 1979) and the 1970 cohort 10 year olds (Stewart-Brown, 1986) were unable to produce their spectacles when asked to do so at their school medicals. This was particularly common among children with 6/9 visual acuity. Whatever the academic arguments, this must be strong evidence that many children do not regard 6/9 acuity as an impairment or regard treatment as beneficial.

Undoubtedly, there are costs other than financial ones which can arise from

Table 2.13 Distribution of spectacle prescriptions among children with different levels of visual acuity loss

Visual acuity		%(No) of all spectacle
Distant	Near	prescriptions
6/6 6/6	6 6	20.4 (307)
6/9 ≤6/9	6 6	10.0 (151)
6/6 ≤6/9	6 6	8.9 (134)
6/6 6/6	9 <6	4.3 (65)
All other defects		56.4 (849)
Total		100.0 (1506)

Data from the 1970 birth cohort age 10 years

treatment with spectacles. Possible social and psychological consequences of spectacles have not been researched in detail, but it may be that the children who do not wear their spectacles are only stating that the latter costs outweigh for them any minor visual benefits.

Some evidence was presented earlier in this chapter that a few visual defects were associated with small but significant reductions in educational performance. In addition, almost all children with visual defects performed less well at tasks involving physical coordination than their peers, and it must remain an open question whether visual defects actually cause these problems.

Table 2.14 Spectacle prescription and educational achievement

Visual defect category*	Spectacles	No. of children	Reading score† adjusted for intelligence, sex and social class	Mathematics† score adjusted for intelligence, sex and social class
0	Yes	150	100.6	100.3
	No	7350	101.2	101.3
1	Yes	93	99.5	100.5
	No	236	100.0	99.7
2	Yes	80	104.6	105.1
	No	42	108.0	106.4
4	Yes	88	101.0	100.5
	No	340	100.6	100.8
5	Yes	22	98.7	98.1
	No	115	97.3	98.6
6	Yes	23	98.1	98.1
	No	162	99.6	99.9
7	Yes	77	100.4	97.8
	No	90	98.6	100.4
8	Yes	56	97.1	97.0
	No	51	97.5	97.4
9	Yes	239	98.1	97.9
	No	151	97.4	97.6

*See Table 2.8

†There was no statistical significance in the differences between scores for reading or mathematics of children with and without spectacles in any visual defect category.

Data from the Child Health and Education Study at age 10 years

Table 2.15 Spectacle prescription and sports scores for children with different visual defects

Visual defect category*	Spectacles	No of children	Sports score† adjusted for intelligence, sex and social class
0	Yes	172	−0.08
	No	8614	−0.03
1	Yes	119	−0.14
	No	279	−0.04
2	Yes	98	−0.12
	No	53	−0.31
4	Yes	103	−0.04
	No	417	−0.14
5	Yes	27	−0.35
	No	131	−0.06
6	Yes	24	−0.31
	No	205	−0.14
7	Yes	86	−0.05
	No	105	−0.10
8	Yes	65	−0.12
	No	65	−0.10
9	Yes	290	−0.10
	No	188	−0.13

*See Table 2.8
Data from the Child Health and Education Study at age 10 years
†There was no statistical significance in the differences between sports scores of children with and without spectacles in any visual defect category

In considering the likelihood of this it is worth asking whether children with defects which had been treated performed better than those without. In Tables 2.14 and 2.15 the scores of children with visual defects are shown separately for those with and those without spectacles. The two groups of children who had the most severe defects (categories 3 and 10) are excluded from the table because the small number of children without spectacles in these groups made useful comparisons impossible.

Children with spectacles were not perceived as better at sport than their peers, suggesting that the visual defects were not causing the poor sports performance.

Children with mild hypermetropia (category 5) who had been given spectacles were not reading significantly better than those without. The latter finding needs to be interpreted with a little caution because only a small proportion of children in the group had been given spectacles and the lack of statistical significance may be due to the small sample size. More research on this group of children is needed. If the group has difficulty learning to read because of refractive error it is likely to be worth while identifying these children in screening programmes. At present, few schools include tests for hypermetropia in their vision screening programmes, but the addition of this test to the distant vision screening on a single occasion, perhaps at school entry, would add little to the costs of these programmes and might enhance the benefits greatly.

COST OF SCHOOL VISION SCREENING PROGRAMMES

I am unaware of any published costings of school vision screening programmes, but it is possible to assess the order of magnitude of this cost simply by identifying the activities involved.

Primary screening

The costs can be divided into those for primary screening, those for secondary screening, the costs of unnecessary treatment and opportunity costs. For vision screening the principle activity involves school nurse time. Initial reactions to quantifying the amount of time spent by school nurses in screening children's vision is that it is likely to be insignificant. In many schools this procedure is carried out as part of a routine health check and the extra time involved to test vision is theoretically small. However, the situation could be different in practice. Few schools now boast a designated medical room, and even fewer a room which is 20 feet long. Many nurses therefore need to take children to a corridor or playground to test vision, which may take a significant amount of time. In addition, if the benefit of the other components of the routine medical check is questionable and their continuation is justified on the grounds that the children are being seen for vision testing anyway, the entire cost of the routine medical check could perhaps be laid at the door of vision screening.

Secondary screening

The school screening programme identifies children who need to be examined in specialist clinics, and this secondary screening should be included in calculating the programme's total cost. The costs of specialist examinations are not only those of the specialist but also the administration of the clinic, the nurse's time and the cost of the parent's time in taking the child to the clinic. As discussed earlier, screening programmes which operate at a 6/9 referral level and take place annually incur this secondary screening cost on around one in 20 of all school children. This is likely to be one of the most significant costs of the entire programme and it is one that is frequently ignored.

Costs of unnecessary treatment

Analysis of spectacle prescribing in the 1970 birth cohort showed that the more often a child had been screened the more likely he was to be wearing spectacles regardless of whether or not he had a visual defect (Table 2.16; Stewart-Brown & Brewer, 1986). It is likely, therefore, that school vision screening programmes are responsible for a proportion of unnecessary spectacle

Table 2.16 Observed and expected numbers of spectacle prescriptions in each distant vision screening category

	No. of screening tests					
	0	1	2	3 or more	Not known	X_3^2
% children with spectacles:	7.5	9.7	10.7	15.1	11.0	
Number observed	17	398	447	623	125	$p<0.001$
Number expected*	22.8	439.4	463.4	537.4	94.6	

*The expected number of spectacle prescriptions was calculated from data showing the visual defect rate in each of the screening groups and the spectacle prescription rate for children with defects and those without. This statistical manoeuvre allows us to take into account and adjust for the fact that there was a slight excess of visual defects among children who had been screened three or more times

prescriptions (Stewart-Brown, 1986), and the programme should therefore also bear the cost of these.

Opportunity costs

If the school nurse were not spending her time screening children for visual defects she could be doing something else. In costing screening programmes we need to consider the cost of those activities foregone. How valuable would it be to allow school nurses more opportunity to undertake preventive health education? The question is not easy to answer but should not be ignored because of this.

RELIABILITY OF SCREENING

Anecdotal evidence about school vision screening suggests that reliability may be low. The topic is one which could be fruitfully researched. High false positive and false negative rates could add to the cost of screening programmes. These are aspects of the total cost which are amenable to correction. In-service training for school nurses is likely to improve reliability where this is low, and it would therefore be very useful to know the current level of reliability.

CONCLUSION

The overall costs of school vision screening programmes may be much greater than would appear from an initial superficial view. Primary screening costs need to be multiplied by the total school child population, secondary screening costs by the proportion of children referred for investigation, and to both these costs must be added unnecessary treatment costs and opportunity costs.

The cost benefit ratio depends not just on the costs but also on the benefits. If the programme benefits only a small number of children and if the benefits to a proportion of these are no more than modest, then the cost benefit ratio of the programme could be very high.

Severe visual impairments undoubtedly cause disability, and children with such impairments unequivocably benefit from detection and treatment. If school vision screening programmes and clinical practice in prescribing spectacles were directed towards identifying and treating these children few would argue that they were unjustified. However, because children with severe impairments are almost always identified before school entry, these children constitute only a tiny proportion of all children picked up in school screening programmes. They also constitute a small minority of children who are treated with spectacles. It is these problems which cause the vision screening programme to assume such a doubtful cost benefit ratio.

The argument has been advanced that the refractive errors causing 6/9 visual acuity are part of a normal range for 10 year old children — that is, that these defects do not constitute an impairment at all. Even if we were to accept that they do constitute an impairment it is hard to detect any evidence from current research that they are associated with disability. It must therefore remain doubtful that these defects constitute an important public health problem worthy of a screening programme.

The evidence that 6/12 acuity is associated with disability in a 10 year old is not at all clear, and more critical research is urgently needed to identify exactly which visual defects matter to children.

Epidemiological studies, such as those which this chapter has drawn on, rarely provide definitive answers. They can raise serious questions about the value of health care activities and point to anomalies in practice. To decide unequivocably which visual defects are worth treating, and therefore which are worth screening for, requires randomised controlled trials. Such trials would not be difficult to perform if ophthalmologists, opticians and community health staff were committed to identifying a cost effective service.

In the meantime, the evidence presented in this chapter may be sufficiently convincing to persuade some of those managing school vision screening programmes to re-think their current practice. It must be very doubtful that the benefits of an annual distant vision screening programme from which all children with 6/9 vision are referred could outweigh the costs. A move towards a lower frequency of testing and a more stringent referral level are likely to be in almost everybody's interests.

REFERENCES

Alberman E, Butler N R, Sheridan M 1971a Visual acuity of a national sample (1958 cohort) at 7 years. Developmental Medicine and Child Neurology 13: 9–14
Alberman E, Butler N R, Gardiner P A 1971b Children with squints — a handicapped group. The Practitioner 206: 501–506
Blum H, Peters H, Bettman J 1959 Vision Screening for Elementary Schools. The Orinda Study, Berkley University, California Press
Douglas J W B, Ross J M, Simpson H R 1967 The ability and attainment of short sighted pupils. Journal of Royal Statistical Society 130: 479–493
Elliott C, Murray, Pearson L 1978 British ability scales. National Foundation for Educational Research, Windsor

Godfrey Thompson Unit 1978 Edinburgh reading test. Hodder and Stoughton, Sevenoaks, Kent

Golding J 1984 Britain's national cohort studies. Macfarlane J A (ed) Progress in Child Health, Vol. 1. Churchill Livingstone, Edinburgh

Haslum M N. Morris A, Butler N R 1983 A cohort study oif special educational needs of 10 year olds in the United Kingdom. In: Duane D, Leong C C (eds) Understanding Learning Disabilities. Plenum Press, New York

Haslum M N, Brewer R I, Howlett B C 1985 Assessing clumsiness in children in child health and education study. Third report to the Department of Health and Social Security on the 10 year follow up. Vol 1. Clumsy Children. Available from Dr M Haslum, Child Health Research Unit, Department of Child Health, University of Bristol

Hirsch Monroe J 1964 Predictability of refraction at age 14 on the basis of testing at age 6. Report from the Ojai Longitudinal Study. American Journal of Optometry, Archives American Academy of Optometry 41(10): 567–573

Ismail H, Hall P 1981 Visual acuity of school entrants. Child: Care, Health and Development 7: 127–134

Morris E, Peckham R 1936 An investigation of the visual efficiencies of 10,000 school children. American Journal of Optometry 48: 376–382

Peckham C, Adams B 1975 Vision screening in a national sample of 11 year old children. Child: Care, Health and Development 1: 903–106

Peckham C S, Gardiner P A, Goldstein H 1977 Acquired myopia in 11 year old children. British Medical Journal 1: 542–544

Peckham C S, Gardiner P A, Tibbenham A 1979 Vision screening of adolescents and their use of glasses. British Medical Journal i: 1111–1113

Stewart-Brown S 1985 Spectacle prescribing in 10 year old children. British Journal of Ophthalmology 69: 874–880

Stewart-Brown S, Brewer R 1986 The significance of minor defects of visual acuity in school children. Implication for screening and treatment. Transactions of the Ophthalmological Society of the United Kingdom (In press)

Stewart-Brown S, Butler N R 1985 Visual acuity in 10 year old children. Journal of Epidemiology and Community Health 39: 107–112

Stewart-Brown S, Butler N R, Haslum M N 1985 Educational attainment in children with treated and untreated visual defects. Developmental Medicine and Child Neurology 27: 504–513

Tibbenham A, Peckham C S, Gardiner P A 1978 Vision screening in children tested at 7, 11 and 16 years. British Medical Journal i: 1312–1314

Youngson R M 1977 Screening for visual defects. British Medical Journal ii: 1221–1222

Why do children get colds?

"The family is a unit composed not only of children, but of men, women the occasional animal, and the common cold.

Odgen Nash, *Family Reunion*

A formidable folklore has grown up over the common cold, promoted by grandparents and ill-advised dogma from Nobel prize winners. When the various myths surrounding colds have been subjected to scientific scrutiny the evidence has been that catching chills, getting cold feet, exposure to draughts and so on have no effect on susceptibility to colds. Despite ignorance about them, colds and other minor respiratory illnesses cause more visits to general practitioners than any other complaint and more days of childhood illness and are among the major causes of absenteeism from school and work. Children are particularly susceptible to colds and this chapter is an attempt to explain their susceptibility and to deal briefly with management.

DEFINITION OF THE COMMON COLD

Donald Court (1973) defines the common cold as 'the presence of excessive clear or mucopurulent nasal discharge, frequently associated with cough, mild erythema of the pharynx, and fever'. Sneezing and nasal stuffiness are often associated. In adult colds the sufferer has little or no fever, but 'febrile colds' are common in children.

The chief differential diagnosis of the common cold is an 'upper respiratory tract infection', or URTI, characterised by nasal discharge, red pharynx, pink shiny tympanic membranes and cervical lymphadenopathy with or without fever. The viruses isolated from children with colds or URTIs are virtually identical (Isaacs et al, 1982), and the distinction, therefore, is to some extent an academic one. Nevertheless, for epidemiological purposes the presence or absence of cervical lymphadenopathy is the most useful distinguishing feature.

Allergic rhinitis may be confused with recurrent colds, but this condition seems to be rare in pre-school children. An atopic family history, raised serum IgE level and the presence of nasal eosinophilia on a smear of nasal secretions suggest a diagnosis of allergic rhinitis.

IMPORTANCE OF THE COMMON COLD

There are a number of reasons to be interested in a condition that at first glance would seem almost completely benign. The first is that the same viruses which cause a mild cold in most children can also cause severe disease.

Infections with the respiratory syncytial virus (RSV) cause colds or mild upper respiratory tract infections in school age children. The same virus, however, causes bronchiolitis in some infants, and this condition still carries an appreciable morbidity and mortality. Because RSV tends to re-infect children, albeit with decreasing severity with age, there is a risk of school age children being reinfected at school and infecting their infant siblings.

The same viruses that cause common colds in most children will cause wheezing in asthmatic children (Isaacs et al, 1982). The reason for this is unclear, although it may be due to multiplication of virus in the lower respiratory tract (Horn et al, 1979).

Finally, the important recognition that colds and URTIs are caused by viruses and are frequently associated with fever and that antibiotics do not prevent complications, which are anyway very rare, permits a logical approach to management. Overprescribing of antibiotics is associated with the development of resistant organisms (Soyka et al, 1975).

AETIOLOGICAL AGENTS

An understanding of the number and type of organisms that can cause colds helps to explain why children are susceptible to so many colds and URTIs. Rhinoviruses are the commonest cause of colds in adults and children. There are over 100 different serotypes of rhinovirus, and these are mostly antigenically distinct, so that recovery from infection with one rhinovirus does not confer immunity against other serotypes. Rhinovirus infections occur throughout the year, although the peak incidence is between April and October, accounting for many summer colds.

As already mentioned, respiratory syncytial virus can cause colds, and, although there is only one serotype, incomplete immunity is conferred by infection, and reinfections are common. The parainfluenza viruses, which may cause croup and pneumonia, also cause colds, as do the influenza viruses. The enteroviruses, echoviruses and coxsackieviruses, can cause the common cold and URTIs, particularly in the late summer and early autumn (August, September and October).

Coronaviruses were first isolated, from the nasal secretions of a boy with a cold, by Tyrrell and Bynoe (1966) at the Common Cold Research Unit in Salisbury. Because of the difficulty of growing these viruses in tissue culture, elucidation of their role in causing colds has taken a long time. Serological studies have suggested that children are more susceptible than adults to coronavirus infections: over a three year period in Tecumseh, Michigan, the highest infection rate, 22%, occurred in the youngest age group studied, aged 5 to 9 years, and during a community outbreak 29% of children under 5 years of age seroconverted (Monto & Lim 1974). Using an enzyme-linked immuno-sorbent assay (ELISA) to detect coronavirus antigen in nasopharyngeal secretions, Isaacs et al (1983) found 30% of specimens from children with respiratory infections to be positive. Coronavirus infections peak in the winter and early summer in the United Kingdom.

There are almost certainly other viruses which cause colds. Larson et al (1980) attempted to isolate viruses from nasal washings from 38 adults with naturally acquired colds. Twenty-five specimens yielded known viruses; the remaining 13 secretions were inoculated into volunteers and caused colds in five cases, but with no known virus identified despite exhaustive efforts.

The rhinoviruses and coronaviruses have been associated with wheezing and occasionally pneumonia, RSV can cause bronchiolitis, pneumonia or wheeze, and parainfluenza and influenza viruses can cause croup and pneumonia. Thus, the same agents which often cause mild colds are capable of causing more severe disease.

PATHOPHYSIOLOGY

The pathophysiology of the common cold has been studied extensively only in adults. Virus replicates in the respiratory epithelium causing an increase in nasal secretions with a high protein content. Symptoms begin after two to three days and coincide with maximum virus shedding. Submucosal oedema is followed by shedding of ciliated epithelial cells. Maximum epithelial damage is at five days and regeneration occurs over the next 10 days (Hilding, 1930). The initially clear nasal discharge becomes mucopurulent after two to three days owing to the presence of desquamated epithelial cells and polymorphs. This is not due to superimposed bacterial infection as is sometimes presumed; the bacterial flora of the nose does not alter when the nasal discharge becomes mucopurulent (Bradburne et al, 1967; Tyrrell, 1965) and treatment with antibiotics does not alter the outcome (Todd et al, 1984)

MODE OF TRANSMISSION

Although it may seem obvious that colds are transmitted by respiratory droplet, it is in fact extremely difficult to transmit colds under volunteer conditions. In attempting to transmit rhinovirus colds between adults, Dick and co-workers persuaded nine donors to kiss 12 recipients for between one and one and a half minutes and only one recipient developed a cold (Dick & Chesney, 1981). When fingers contaminated with infected nasal secretions were placed in the recipient's nose and rubbed in his eyes 73% of recipients became infected (Gwaltney et al, 1978), and there was an 85% transmission rate when men were crowded together in a small hut on the Arctic Peninsula (Holmes et al, 1976).

Coughing and talking do not lead to shedding of virus, whereas sneezing, nose blowing and rubbing one's nose transmit a large amount of virus into the atmosphere and on the sufferer's hands. Most children probably get infected by close contact with droplets of contaminated nasal secretions or contaminate their own hands with infected secretions from a sibling or friend.

EPIDEMIOLOGICAL CONSIDERATIONS

There is great variability in the incidence of childhood respiratory infections reported in different studies (Table 3.1). To an extent this reflects environmental factors such as socioeconomic status, family size and urban or rural environment. However, the intensity of observation is also important; in the Newcastle study, where a low incidence was recorded, families phoned to report colds, and in the Seattle virus watch study the observed incidence of infections rose markedly when families were visited at home instead of being telephoned.

Table 3.1 Mean number of respiratory infections per child per year observed in different studies

Study	Place	Age (years)				
		0–1	1–2	2–3	3–4	4–5
North Carolina (Loda et al, 1972)	Day care	9.6	8.6	8.1	7.2	7.6
Cleveland (Dingle et al, 1964)	Home	6.9	8.3	8.5	8.6	8.1
Seattle virus watch (Fox et al, 1966)	Home (visited)	4.4	4.9	4.8	4.8	4.8
Seattle virus watch (Fox et al, 1966)	Home (telephoned)	3.2	2.2	2.7	2.7	2.7
Newcastle 1000-Family (Miller et al, 1960)	Home	1.0	0.9	1.1	1.0	0.8

The studies in Table 3.1 do not separate colds from other upper respiratory infections, but where the incidence of colds has been specifically looked at, children suffer three to eight colds on average per year (Brimblecombe et al, 1958; Dingle et al, 1964; Loda et al, 1972).

The incidence of respiratory infections is dependent on both exposure and susceptibility. Thus, many studies have reported the peak incidence being at age 2 to 3 years. In the North Carolina day care study, however, when children were placed in day care from as young as 6 weeks of age and there was a high exposure to infections, the peak incidence was observed in infants under 1 year of age (Loda et al, 1972). The tendency to send children to play groups, nursery schools and day care centres at a younger age, although this may be important for educational and family reasons, results in increased exposure and thus increased frequency of infections.

By comparing the number of infections a subject experiences with the estimated number of times he is exposed to a new organism it is possible to calculate the subject's susceptibility. In a rural area where exposure is limited, infants were found to be more than twice as susceptible to infections as school children or adults (Lidwell & Somerville, 1951).

Most colds are introduced into the family by school age children. Dingle et al (1964) found that pre-school children under 5 years of age had, on average, six to seven respiratory infections a year if they had no siblings at school, up to nine infections a year if they had a sibling at school, and up to 12 infections a year if they themselves were already at school. Similar results showing that school children introduce respiratory infections into the family have been obtained in Britain in urban (Brimblecombe et al, 1958) and rural communities (Lidwell & Somerville, 1951). In a study of pre-school children with recurrent respiratory infections, the only epidemiological risk factor for infections identified was the attendance of one or more children in the family at school (Isaacs, 1984). It is usually the toddler who infects his bronchitic grandfather, causing an exacerbation of his chronic bronchitis, and not vice versa as is sometimes feared.

Boys tend to have more colds than girls (Brimblecombe et al, 1958; Dingle et al, 1964), although, like the even greater susceptibility of boys to asthma, this tendency is unexplained.

Over 200 years ago Benjamin Franklin said that colds were caught from other people rather than from exposure to cold weather. Nevertheless, perhaps because of the increased frequency of colds in the winter months, it is widely believed that colds may be caught by exposure to cold weather. In experimental conditions, however, chilling (cooling sufficient to cause shivering for an hour or immersion in cold water with a fall in rectal temperature), wet feet and draughts do not increase volunteers' susceptibility to colds (Douglas et al, 1968; Jackson, 1964).

Parental smoking results in an increased incidence of bronchitis and pneumonia in the first year of life, but not of colds or upper respiratory tract infections, suggesting the major effect of passive smoking is on the lower airways (Colley et al, 1974). Breast feeding protects against respiratory infections and otitis media (Chandra, 1979).

THE CATARRHAL CHILD

John Fry (1961) has described the child with a perpetual mucopurulent nasal discharge as the catarrhal child. In fact, these children seem to be having recurrent infections with respiratory viruses, and nasal discharge persists for two to three weeks after each infection (Isaacs, 1984). If the children have six to eight colds annually, often occurring successively in winter, the impression is of continual catarrh.

RESISTANCE TO INFECTION

It is by looking at the factors conferring resistance to colds that one can start to understand why children are more susceptible to colds than adults.

Serum antibody

High levels of virus-specific serum antibodies are protective against colds with that virus. Repeated infections lead to specific serum antibody, and by adult life, for example, antibody can be detected to about half of the serotypes of rhinoviruses. Experimentally the level of serum antibody is critical; high levels protect against all except very large inocula of virus, whereas low levels of antibody may scarcely protect at all.

Secretory antibody

Serum antibody is not the sole, or probably the major, factor in resistance to colds. Perkins et al (1969) found that administration of an intranasal rhinovirus vaccine to volunteers resulted in the production of nasal and serum antibody and protection against experimental infection, whereas two intramuscular doses of the same vaccine produced only serum antibody and no protection. The important secretory antibody is IgA, which appears in nasal secretions within 24 to 48 hours of infection with a respiratory virus and, if specific for the virus, may abort the infection or limit the spread of the virus.

Children have lower levels of serum and secretory IgA than adults, but like adults respond to respiratory viral infection by producing a sharp rise in nasal IgA (Cohen et al, 1970). It may be the ability to produce this rise in nasal IgA that is important in resistance to infection. Yodfat and Silvian (1977) found that children on a kibbutz who produced high levels of nasal IgA in response to respiratory virus infections had a far lower incidence of infection. Isaacs et al (1984), however, found that the level of salivary IgA when healthy correlated best with resistance to respiratory infection, rather than the ability to produce a rise in nasal or salivary IgA.

Emotional factors

Boyce et al (1977) have shown a correlation between major family life events, such as parental divorce or the death of a grandparent, and the severity, but not the frequency, of respiratory illnesses in children. Emotional factors may well affect susceptibility to colds either directly or indirectly, but evidence of this is difficult to obtain and so far lacking.

Breast feeding

As already stated, Chandra (1979), among others, has shown that breast feeding protects against respiratory infections in the first year of life. The mechanism is probably via passage of secretory IgA in the breast milk.

RECOVERY FROM COLDS

Recovery from colds seems to depend partly on local production of secretory IgA specific against the virus and also on local production of interferon. Virus titre falls as local inferferon levels rise. However, in volunteer studies interferon administered after the onset of infection did not abort colds, whereas if given before inoculation of virus, it protected almost completely against infection (Scott et al, 1982).

TREATMENT

Although treatment of colds does not fall within the brief of the title, there are some points too important to be ignored.

In 1970 Linus Pauling, double Nobel prize winner (for Chemistry and for Peace), published *Vitamin C and the Common Cold*, a monograph advocating high dose vitamin C for both prophylaxis and treatment of the common cold. Vitamin C has subsequently been shown to have no effect on prophylaxis or treatment of colds in children in studies on Navajo Indians (Coulehan et al, 1976), boarding school children (Coulehan et al, 1974) and identical twins (Miller et al, 1977). Furthermore, the hazards of high dose vitamin C have been stressed by Barness (1975).

Antihistamines are often given to children with colds but have no effect on symptoms and may even thicken secretions (West et al, 1975). They may cause drowsiness, not necessarily a bad thing as far as the parents are concerned, but when combined with decongestants significant side effects have been reported (Todd et al, 1984).

Aspirin, another traditional remedy for colds, has actually been shown to increase viral shedding in adult volunteers (Stanley et al, 1975). Furthermore, the possible link between aspirin and Reye's syndrome, although still not proven, has been strengthened by a recent pilot study in the USA (Kolata, 1985), and until the controversy is resolved it would seem wise to recommend paracetamol as the preferred antipyretic for children with febrile respiratory infections.

Antibiotics have no effect on colds or upper respiratory tract infections (Taylor et al, 1977) and do not prevent complications (Davis & Wedgwood, 1965). In a large controlled trial Todd et al (1984) showed that antibiotics had no effect on purulent nasopharyngitis.

The last word on treatment should perhaps be from Sir William Osler, who stated, 'There is just one way to treat a cold and that is with contempt'.

SUMMARY

Children get more colds than adults because there is a huge number of common cold viruses, and resistance develops with exposure. Breast feeding protects against colds. Pre-school children are particularly susceptible to colds, probably because of an immature secretory immune response. Colds are introduced into the family by school children, and placing children in day care increases their frequency of injection. Fever should be treated with paracetamol, but no other treatment is indicated.

Acknowledgement

I should like to acknowledge my indebtedness to Dr D A J Tyrrell and Dr H B Valman for their advice and encouragement at all times.

REFERENCES

Barness L A 1975 Safety considerations with high ascorbic acid dosage. Annals of the New York Academy of Science 258: 523–528

Boyce W T, Jensen E W, Cassel J C, Collier A M, Smith A H, Ramey C T 1977 Influence of life events and family routines on childhood respiratory tract illness. Pediatrics 60: 609–615

Bradburne A F, Bynoe M L, Tyrrell D A J 1967 Effects of a 'new' human respiratory virus in volunteers. British Medical Journal iii: 767–769

Brimblecombe F S W, Cruickshank R, Masters P L, Reid D D, Steward G T 1958 Family studies of respiratory infections. British Medical Journal i: 119–128

Chandra R K 1979 Prospective studies of the effect of breast-feeding on incidence of infection and allergy. Acta Paediatrica Scandinavia 68: 691–694

Cohen A B, Goldberg S, London R I 1970 Immunoglobulins in nasal secretions of infants. Clinical and Experimental Immunology 6: 753–760

Colley J R T, Holland W W, Corkhill R T 1974 Influence of passive smoking and parental phlegm on pneumonia and bronchitis in early childhood. Lancet ii: 1031–1034

Coulehan J L, Reisinger K S, Rogers K D, et al 1974 Vitamin C prophylaxis in a boarding school. New England Journal of Medicine 290: 6–10

Coulehan J L, Eberhard S, Kapner L, et al 1976 Vitamin C and acute illness in Navajo school-children. New England Journal of Medicine 295: 973–7

Court S D M 1973 The definition of acute respiratory illness in children. Postgraduate Medical Journal 49: 771–776

Davis S D, Wedgwood R J 1965 Antibiotic prophylaxis in acute viral respiratory diseases. American Journal of Disease in Childhood 109: 544–553

Dick E C, Chesney P J 1981 Rhinoviruses. In: Feigin R D, Cherry J D (eds) Textbook of Pediatric Infectious Diseases. Saunders, Philadelphia, p. 1167–1186

Dingle J H, Badger G F, Jordan W S 1964 Illness in the home. Press of Western Reserve University, Cleveland, Ohio

Douglas R G, Lindgren K M, Couch R B 1968 Exposure to cold environment and rhinovirus common cold. Failure to demonstrate effect. New England Journal of Medicine 279: 742–747

Fox J P, Elveback L R, Spigland I, Frothingham T E, Stevens D A, Huger A 1966 The virus watch program: a continuing surveillance of viral infections in metropolitan New York families. I. Overall plan, methods of collecting and handling information and a summary report of specimens collected and illnesses observed. American Journal of Epidemiology 88: 389–412

Fry J 1961 The catarrhal child. Butterworth, London

Gwaltney J M, Moskalski P B, Hendley J O 1978 Hand to hand transmission of rhinovirus colds. Annals of Internal Medicine 88: 463–467

Hilding A 1930 The common cold. Archives of Otolaryngology 12: 113–150

Holmes M J, Reed S E, Stott R J, et al 1976 Studies of experimental rhinovirus type 2 infections in polar isolation and in England. Journal of Hygiene (Cambridge) 76: 379–393

Horn M E C, Reed S E, Taylor P 1979 Role of viruses and bacteria in acute wheezy bronchitis in childhood: a study of sputum. Archives of Disease in Childhood 54: 587–592

Isaacs D 1984 The epidemiology and immunology of the syndrome of recurrent respiratory infections in the pre-school child. MD thesis, Cambridge University

Isaacs D, Clarke J R, Tyrrell D A J, Valman H B 1982 Selective involvement of the lower
    respiratory tract by respiratory viruses in children with recurrent respiratory tract
    infections. British Medical Journal 284: 1746–1748
Isaacs D, Flowers D, Clarke J R, Valman H B, McNaughton M R 1983 Epidemiology of
    coronavirus respiratory infections. Archives of Disease in Childhood 58: 500–503
Isaacs D, Webster A D B, Valman H B 1984 Immunoglobulin levels and function in
    pre-school children with recurrent respiratory infections. Clinical and Experimental
    Immunology 58: 335–340
Jackson G G 1964 Understanding of viral respiratory illnesses provided by experiments in
    volunteers. Bacteriological Reviews 28: 423–430
Kolata G 1985 Study of Reye's-aspirin link causes concern. Science 227: 391–392
Larson H E, Reed S E, Tyrrell D A J 1980 Isolation of rhinoviruses and coronaviruses from
    38 colds in adults. Journal of Medical Virology 5: 221–229
Lidwell O M, Somerville T 1951 Observations on the incidence and distribution of the
    common cold in a rural community during 1948 and 1949. Journal of Hygiene (London)
    49: 365–381
Loda F A, Glezen W P, Clyde W A 1972 Respiratory diseases in group day care. Pediatrics
    49: 428–437
Miller J Z, Nance W E, Norton J A, et al 1977 Therapeutic effect of vitamin C — a co-twin
    control study. Journal of the American Medical Association 237: 238–241
Monto A S, Lim S K 1974 The Tecumseh study of respiratory illsness. VI. Frequency of
    and relationship between outbreaks of coronavirus infection. Journal of Infectious Diseases
    129: 271–276
Pauling L C 1970 Vitamin C and the common cold. W H Freeman, San Francisco
Perkins J C, Tucker D N, Knopf H L S, et al 1969 Comparison of protective effects of
    neutralizing antibody in serum and nasal excretions in experimental rhinovirus type 12
    illness. American Journal of Epidemiology 90: 519–526
Scott G M, Philpotts R J, Wallace J, Gauci C L, Greiner J, Tyrrell D A J 1982 Prevention
    of rhinovirus colds by human interferon alpha-2 from Escherichia coli. Lancet ii: 186–188
Soyka L F, Robinson D S, Lachant N, Monaco J 1975 The misuse of antibiotics for
    treatment of upper respiratory tract infections in children. Pediatrics 55: 552–556
Stanley E D, Jackson G G, Panusarn C, et al 1975 Increased virus shedding with aspirin
    treatment of rhinovirus infection. Journal of the American Medical Association
    231: 1248–1251
Taylor B, Abbott G D, McKerr M, Fergusson D M 1977 Amoxycillin and co-trimoxazole in
    presumed viral respiratory infections of childhood: placebo-controlled trial. British Medical
    Journal ii: 552–554
Todd J K, Todd N, Damato J, Todd W A 1984 Bacteriology and treatment of purulent
    nasopharyngitis: a double-blind placebo-controlled evaluation. Pediatric Infectious Diseases
    3: 226–232
Tyrrell D A J 1965 Common colds and related diseases. Edward Arnold, London
Tyrrell D A J, Bynoe M L 1966 Cultivation of viruses from a high proportion of patients
    with colds. Lancet i: 76–77
West S, Brandon B, Stolley P, et al 1975 A review of antihistamines and the common cold.
    Pediatrics 56: 100–107
Yodfat Y, Silvian I 1977 A prospective study of acute respiratory tract infections among
    children in a kibbutz: the role of secretory IgA and serum immunoglobulins. Journal of
    Infectious Diseases 136: 26–30

Recent advances in infant feeding

Approximately one in two mothers in the United Kingdom seek infant feeding advice from a professional source; in 1980, 48% chose the health visitor, 30% a midwife or nurse and 12% a doctor (Martin & Monk, 1982). Opinions about infant feeding can vary greatly and are often strongly held so that mothers can receive conflicting advice. A sound understanding of the physiological basis of infant feeding and the nutritional requirements of the infant is clearly a prerequisite to the agreed formulation of advice and assistance with practical problems; how much has been learnt in recent years?

BREAST FEEDING

Between 1975 and 1980 the proportion of mothers initiating breast feeding in England, Wales and Scotland increased from 51% to 67% (Martin & Monk, 1982). This change no doubt reflects an increased public awareness of the contribution of breast feeding to infant health. However, there is still considerable room for improvement in these figures, which conceal a marked social class and geographical distortion: in London and the south east of England in 1980, 76% of mothers initiated breast feeding, but in Scotland only 50% did so. Altogether 81% of mothers from social class I attempted breast feeding compared with only 57% from social class V. Furthermore, of the mothers who began by breast feeding, one third had stopped by the time the infant was 6 weeks of age. Even at this early stage the mother's belief that she produced 'insufficient milk' was the commonest reason for abandoning breast feeding. Houston and Howie (1981) claimed that regular professional support could increase the duration of breast feeding and pointed out that many problems (including mothers' perceptions of 'milk insufficiency') 'were simply variations within the normal range and could have been solved by appropriate reassurance at the correct time'. One common fault among both mothers and professional attendants is failure to appreciate the normal variability in both feeding patterns and the dynamics of milk transfer between mother and infant

(Howie et al, 1981a). This can lead to the imposition of inappropriate feeding schedules with reduction in sucking time and milk production. How can the transfer of milk between mother and baby be measured, and what messages of practical value can be gleaned from studies of this aspect of breast feeding?

Breast milk transfer during a feed

Test-weighing is the conventional means of assessing the volume of milk which the infant has taken, but its accuracy and precision are limited by the performance of the scales chosen. *Routine* clinical test-weighing on conventional mechanical scales may under- or over-record the milk intake at a single feed by as much as 100%, and the average amount taken over a number of feeds is likely to be an underestimate of the true intake (Whitfield et al, 1982). However, the introduction of electronic scales has extended the potential applications of test-weighing; suitable balances may now be obtained in portable, battery operated form (Drewett et al, 1984). These instruments calculate an average weight, thereby overcoming errors due to the movement of the baby, and display the measurement in digital form to reduce errors associated with reading. The weight of milk taken at a single feed can be recorded to within ±4 g on 95% of occasions (Williams A F, Greasley V, Baum J D, unpublished findings).

The precision of these instruments is adequate to examine the dynamics of individual feeds so that questions such as 'How long should a breast feed last?' can be asked. In one study (Lucas et al, 1979) a population of newborn babies was randomly divided into groups, each member of the group being weighed at the start of the feed and at a single later point in the feed, which was predetermined for the group in question. The average weight of milk taken by infants in each group was then calculated so as to produce a profile of the rate of milk intake for the population. It appeared that 50% of the average final feed volume was consumed by the two minute stage in the feed and 80–90% by four minutes. It is important to understand that findings from such a population study indicate trends only and should not form the basis of guidance for individual mother–infant pairs. Further work has examined the rate at which *individual* babies obtain milk by test-weighing at intermediate points in the feed and reattaching the infant to the breast (Woolridge et al, 1982a; Howie et al, 1981a). These studies have shown remarkable variation in the rate at which babies obtain milk, although, interestingly, for a given mother–baby pair the rate of intake at each breast shows a high degree of concordance (Woolridge et al, 1982a). The question remains as to which is the predominant influence on the rate of milk transfer — the baby's sucking efficiency or the rate at which the mother releases her milk? This problem was ingeniously approached using a 'cross-nursing' design in which two mothers exchanged babies between the feeds studied (Woolridge et al, 1982a). This case study suggested that both the mother and baby influenced events, but further work of this nature is needed before generalisations can be made.

Sucking at the breast

The behaviour of babies sucking at bottle teats has been extensively studied and shown to exhibit organisation into bursts interspersed with pauses. When infants suck at a blind teat they characteristically show rapid rates of sucking in short bursts with frequent pauses in between ('non-nutritive sucking'). In contrast, infants obtaining milk from a teat show slower rates of sucking with fewer interruptions ('nutritive sucking') (Wolff, 1968).

An analysis of the sucking behaviour of infants on the breast showed that this dichotomy of patterns seen in bottle feeding infants did not appear during breast feeding: infants showed a continuum between these two extremes. Furthermore, by intermittently weighing babies during the feed, it was possible to show a relationship between sucking pattern and the rate of milk transfer (Bowen-Jones et al, 1982). When babies sucked slowly and evenly on the breast, milk flow was high, but when sucking was rapid and pauses frequent, milk flow was low or absent. The practical potential of this finding was pointed out by the authors — such observations of sucking behaviour may assist in the clinical assessment of breast feeding problems, being an indirect measure of milk availability.

The validity of these findings has found further support through the development of a miniaturised ultrasound breast milk flowmeter, which may be housed in a thin latex nipple shield. This allows simultaneous recording of milk flow and sucking so that the flow of milk at each suck may be measured. Clinical studies (Woolridge et al, 1982b) have indicated that sucking tends to be uninterrupted at the start of the feed whereas, towards the end, sucking is intermittent and the volume of milk obtained with each suck smaller (Fig 4.1).

This finding in turn raises the question *why* do babies finish feeding? Does the supply of milk become limiting, or can the breast fed baby become satiated, and, if so, what cues may be responsible?

Satiation during breast feeding

In a study in which the order of presentation of the breasts was randomised it was found that newborn babies take significantly less milk from the second breast than from the first (Drewett & Woolridge, 1981). Since randomisation ensured that, overall, milk would have been equally available from either breast it may be inferred that the newborn baby displays satiation of appetite during the feed.

About 10 years ago Hall (1975) hypothesised that the rising milk fat content observed during a breast feed constituted a cue for the cessation of feeding. This suggestion was based on her observation that a baby fed ad libitum on one breast would suddenly refuse to take milk which was available to expression but 'would feed vigorously again when put on the other breast'. However, little objective evidence can be adduced in support of this hypothesis. When babies were bottle fed in randomised sequences with human milk of high or low fat

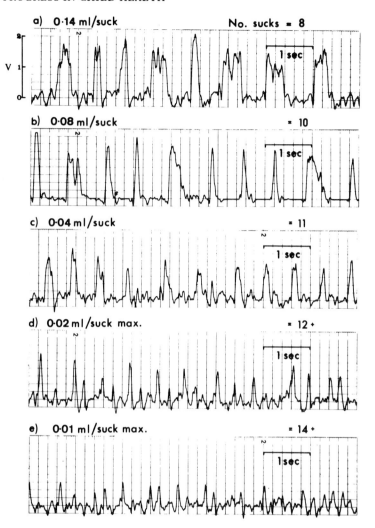

Fig. 4.1 Trace showing changes in sucking during a breast feed measured using a miniaturised flowmeter (Woolridge et al, 1982b). The volume of milk taken at each suck is proportional to the area under each deflection. In the later stages of the feed sucks are more closely spaced and the volume of milk obtained with each is smaller

content no changes in intake or sucking patterns were discernible (Woolridge et al, 1980). Moreover, in a study in which babies were reattached to either the second breast or the breast on which they had just finished feeding, the latencies for attachment were not significantly different. This suggests that the fat content of milk played little part in their willingness to continue feeding (Drewett, 1982).

Nevertheless, although instantaneous effects may not be demonstrable, babies could conceivably adapt to *long term* alterations in the composition of milk by taking a greater or a lesser volume. Observation of bottle fed babies fed a low or a high calorie formula would support this suggestion (Fomon et al, 1975), but a further understanding in the case of the breast fed baby requires the development of techniques for measuring both the volume *and* the composition of milk taken by individual infants.

Measuring the dietary intake of the individual breast fed baby

Two methods of measuring the *volume* of milk which the breast fed baby takes have already been mentioned: test-weighing and the ultrasound flowmeter. A third method has been proposed: the use of deuterium oxide (D_2O), a stable, naturally occurring isotope of water. The method can be used to measure the water turnover of the baby alone (Coward et al, 1979) so that the breast milk intake can be deduced if the baby receives no other fluid. Alternatively, the isotope may be given to the mother and the milk intake of mixed-fed babies be calculated from measurements of the D_2O enrichment of both milk and infant saliva (Coward et al, 1982). The method should be used to measure average daily intake over a period of 14 days and, being non-invasive, seems attractive for field studies. However, the ability of the method to measure the intakes of *individual* babies with precision appears to be limited (Butte et al, 1983) and it is not considered further here.

Volume apart, it is surprising that inter-individual differences in milk *composition* have received little attention. Fat concentration is the chief determinant of the milk's energy content and may vary between individuals and within individuals during the feed, between feeds and at different stages of lactation (Hytten, 1954).

The major obstacle is obtaining a sample representative of the milk which the baby has consumed during the feed. Total expression of the breasts at a single feed (Department of Health and Social Security, 1977) might be inferred to produce a sample with a spuriously high fat content because, as indicated above, the baby does not empty the breasts of hindmilk in the way that a pump does. Expression of sample at the beginning and the end of the feed has been proposed (Prentice et al, 1981), but a different approach has been the development of a thin latex nipple shield (Lucas et al, 1980). This is worn during the feed to allow the withdrawal of milk samples via a cannula. Unfortunately, both of the latter alternatives have problems: even when used on the same mother–infant pairs the techniques give highly disparate estimates of fat intake at a feed (Williams et al, 1985).

As yet there are no reliable data about the individual intakes of breast-fed babies; authors have tended to apply fixed values for milk composition (e.g. Whitehead & Paul, 1981). This approach has been adopted to quantify the dietary intake of *populations* of breast fed infants in many parts of the world to formulate guidelines on the optimal age for weaning. While much has been learnt, it is vital to emphasise that we do not yet appreciate the applicability of these generalisations to individual babies.

WEANING

Although the term 'weaning' has many definitions, it is used here to indicate the introduction of foods other than milk into the infant's diet. The reasoning which underlies current recommendations for the timing of this step is complex and has been extensively reviewed in recent years (Underwood & Hofvander, 1982; Whitehead, 1985). A brief review of observations central to the discussion follows.

When and why do mothers introduce non-milk foods?

The weaning practices of mothers in rural and urbanised societies in many parts of the world were documented in the 1981 report of the World Health Organization (WHO), *Collaborative Study on Breast-feeding* (WHO, 1981). By 2–3 months of age 1/4 to 2/3 of infants in most non-industrialised societies were receiving regular food supplements, as were 1/4 of Swedish infants. By 6–7 months almost *all* infants were receiving foods other than breast milk with the striking exception of those born to urban poor and rural mothers in India. (It is noteworthy that these two groups of infants also showed poor growth performance, being well below the third percentile of the WHO weight charts at 9–12 months of age.) Mothers apparently introduced weaning foods for similar reasons in all societies studied: 'insufficient milk', 'hungry' and 'crying' being the common reasons given. British mothers behaved similarly: in 1980, 55% introduced supplementary foods by the time the infant reached 3 months of age, but this was a striking change from the 85% who did so in 1975 (Martin & Monk, 1982), a response perhaps accounted for by mothers' current fears in relation to infant obesity and allergy.

Although age at weaning may be similar in different parts of the world, Whitehead (1985) has pointed out that there are important differences in attitudes to the role of weaning foods. In the industrialised societies mothers tend to view weaning foods as supplements or replacements for breast feeds whereas in developing countries they are treated as complements to prolonged breast feeding and milk output is maintained. The early introduction of supplementary foods also reduces basal prolactin levels through curtailing suckling duration and frequency; this has the further effect of re-establishing ovulation (Howie et al, 1981b).

How can objective recommendations about the optimum timing of weaning be made? The current approach is to base estimates of energy requirements on the energy intakes of breast fed infants born to well nourished mothers (Whitehead & Paul, 1981), adopting the growth of such infants as a standard for less privileged populations.

The infant's dietary requirements

Waterlow and Thomson (1979), by calculating the intake of the average breast fed infant, have indicated that energy deficiency relative to World Health

Organization (WHO)/Food and Agricultural Organization (FAO) 1973 standards (WHO/FAO, 1973) may arise at approximately 3 months of age. It is at about this age that infant growth 'faltering' becomes apparent in many developing countries, but argument persists as to whether the two events are causally related.

Noting the incompatibility between these estimates of needs for breast milk and the observed intakes of breast milk of infants born even to well nourished mothers, Whitehead and Paul (1981) re-examined the energy intakes of fully and partly breast fed infants growing satisfactorily by National Center for Health Statistics (NCHS) growth standards (Hamill et al, 1979). Their data, and a re-examination of data from a variety of studies (Whitehead et al, 1981), have suggested that WHO/FAO estimates constitute a considerable over-estimate of the infant's energy requirements.

If the average energy content of human milk is taken as 69 calories per decilitre (cal/dl) (Department of Health and Social Security, 1977), the requirement for breast milk of a male infant growing along the 50th centile of NCHS standards can be estimated as 800 millilitres (ml) at 2 months of age, 930 ml at 3 months of age and 1020 ml at 6 months of age. Taking into account the observed ranges for 24-hour milk intake of infants in the United Kingdom, USA and Sweden, exclusive breast feeding could satisfy the *average* infant's energy requirement for the first four to six months (Whitehead, 1985). As stated above, it remains a considerable problem to determine the relevance of these findings to *individual* infants because the normal range of 24-hour milk intakes has been wide in all series studied (the upper limit can be at least twice the lower) and variation in the energy content of the milk of different mothers is still an unknown quantity. Moreover, it would seem reasonable to suppose that energy requirements will vary too.

Growth of the breast fed infant

Setting aside the problems of determining the infant's dietary intake, an equally important advance has been the definition of the normal growth trajectory of the breast fed infant. The data used to compile current growth charts were collected at least 20 years ago at a time when infant feeding practices differed from those of today; how does the early growth pattern of breast fed infants today match the standards in common use?

Whitehead and Paul (1984) have pointed out that, if age and percentage weight-for-age (with respect to the 50th centile of the NCHS standard) are plotted for the first year of life, fully breast fed infants show an apparent acceleration in weight gain during the first three months of life. This is in turn followed by a deceleration such that by 6 months of age the infant tends to return to his birth centile. Their analysis of data from the United Kingdom, USA, Finland and the Gambia shows similar *patterns* in varied locations, *suggesting* this to be the natural early growth course of the breast fed infant. It appears that deceleration after 3 months of age is observed even in those breast fed infants who have begun supplements, but there is some suggestion from the Finnish data of Saarinen and Siimes (1979) that bottle fed infants behave differently, maintaining rapid gain into the second six months of infancy.

Although these data refer to NCHS charts, at this age Tanner weight standards (on which Gairdner-Pearson weight charts are based) are similar. Quoting Tanner, Whitehead and Paul (1984) argue that such standards may be inappropriate for making judgments about the adequacy or otherwise of breast feeding before 6 months of age. It could be added also that early rapid growth of breast fed infants detected using such charts should not be taken as an indication of 'overfeeding'.

THE RELATIONSHIP BETWEEN EARLY FEEDING PRACTICES AND LATER DISEASE

It is popularly believed that breast fed infants are less likely to become obese as children and adults and are less likely to develop allergic disease. In recent years these topics have continued to excite controversy and an attempt to summarise current knowledge therefore follows.

Obesity

'Excessive weight gain in the first six months' was stated by Eid (1970) to be a precursor of obesity in childhood. At a similar time both Taitz (1971) and Shukla et al (1972) drew attention to the prevalence of 'overweight' in infancy, particularly among bottle fed infants. Since these studies were carried out infant feeding practices have changed in many important respects: the incidence of breast-feeding has risen, supplementary foods are started later and artificial formulae have been modified to the low solute 'humanised' types in current use. Thus, although these studies directed concern at the possibility of a relationship between early feeding and obesity, little can be inferred from their findings, which is of relevance to a discussion of the relative benefits of breast or bottle feeding today.

Because they refer to a defined population (South Yorkshire) the studies of Taitz (1971, 1978; Taitz & Lukmanji, 1981) are valuable in documenting the effects which these changes have made on early weight gain. Although the weight velocities of breast fed infants did not significantly change over the years 1971–77, those of artificially fed infants fell significantly with the adoption of low calorie/low solute feeding regimens (Taitz, 1978) so that, by 1977, breast and bottle fed infants gained weight at similar rates (Taitz & Lukmanji, 1981). These findings correspond with those of de Swiet et al (1977), who examined weight gain until 6 months of age but could find no differences attributable to the mode of feeding or introduction of supplementary foods.

Whatever the relationship between mode of feeding and early weight gain may be, Poskitt and Cole (1978) concluded, by following up the infants studied by Shukla et al (1972) at the age of 5, that familial factors appeared to exert more influence on childhood body size. Thus, taking into account concerns over the applicability of weight charts in current use, the diagnosis 'overfeeding' is possibly too frequently applied today.

Allergy

The proposition that exclusive breast feeding to a certain age constitutes prophylaxis to the development of allergic disease is attractive and a certain amount of inductive proof has been raised in its favour. Animal studies (Udall et al, 1981) have indicated that natural, in contrast to artificial, feeding reduces the systemic uptake of antigen instilled into the alimentary tract. It is also known that colostrum induces hypertrophy and hyperplasia of the immature mucosa in the beagle pup (Heird et al, 1984). Walker (1985) has suggested that such changes may be important in the development of a mucosal barrier to antigen penetration.

Breast feeding can be envisaged to offer further protection through permitting the passive transfer of secretory immunoglobulin A (sIgA) from mother to baby. The immunological specificity of sIgA in breast milk is known to be determined by those antigens which are prevalent within the mother's bowel (Goldblum et al, 1975), and activity against common food antigens has been detected (Cruz et al, 1981). The newborn infant is deficient in sIgA (Burgio et al, 1980) and seems dependent on that in breast milk for protection at mucosal surfaces. It has been speculated that sIgA plays a part by sequestering food antigens in the bowel lumen preventing uptake and sensitisation (Walker, 1975). Some support for this suggestion lies in the demonstration that the serum IgA titres of 3 month old infants who subsequently developed allergic disease were lower than those of infants who did not (Taylor et al, 1973).

Unfortunately, however, attempts to demonstrate a protective effect of breast feeding using an observational approach have proved far from unanimous in their conclusions; one study has even demonstrated an increased incidence of eczema in those who were breast fed (Golding et al, 1982). A recent review of published studies (Burr, 1983) noted their several methodological flaws, but, setting aside the possibility that differences in study design may account for their varied outcome, further work on immunological aspects of breast feeding offers alternative explanations. It has been observed that babies may become sensitised to food antigens even during exclusive breast feeding (Warner, 1980). Indeed, allergic manifestations can appear at the first feed of cow's milk or formula — in one study of infants showing cow's milk hypersensitivity, 31% did so (Ford et al, 1983). The appearance of specific IgE before known exposure to the food in question has also been described (Hattevig et al, 1984). The presence of intact food antigens in breast milk (Kilshaw & Cant, 1984) may go some way to explaining this, but the possibility of intrauterine exposure to food antigens has also been raised (Kuroume et al, 1976). We also have little understanding of the relationship between antigen dose and response; low doses of antigen could be more damaging than larger doses which may induce tolerance (Jarrett, 1977).

There is no doubt that much remains to be learnt about the role of breast feeding in the prophylaxis of allergic disease, but it is probably wisest for the present to adopt the view that, although its role is unproven, a good deal of circumstantial evidence exists in its favour. Is there any justification for substituting a soya based formula when a mother with a family history of atopy does not breast feed? It is important to distinguish here between the *therapeutic* potential of these formulae in proven cow's milk protein sensitivity and the speculation that they have a role in *prophylaxis*. The dearth of proof for the latter proposition has been much discussed (Taitz, 1982; Burr, 1983; Cant, 1984). Moreover, one would not expect any benefit on immunological grounds, since any effect which breast milk may have is not likely to be based solely on its hypoallergenicity but on antigen exclusion effected through sIgA and other factors. Soya formulae, in any case, appear to have antigenicities as powerful as those based on cow's milk protein (Eastham et al, 1978). Goat's milk is even less suitable as it is nutritionally hazardous to infants below 6 months of age on account of its solute load (Taitz & Armitage, 1984).

A further question relevant to allergy and the breast fed infant is the relationship between maternal diet and infant colic. The first double-blind crossover study (Evans et al, 1981) to examine this problem could demonstrate no significant difference in the frequency of attacks between periods in which the mothers ingested cow's milk and those in which they received placebo (soya based) milk drinks. Jakobssen and Lindberg (1983), however, also using a double-blind crossover design, succeeded in showing a significant reduction in the frequency of colic when cow's milk protein was eliminated from the mother's diet. Three reasons may account for the difference in outcome observed: firstly, Evans et al may have studied too small a sample (20 infants) but, secondly, Jakobssen and Lindberg (1983) selected for study those infants and mothers who had shown some response to a prior open challenge with cow's milk. Additionally, Evans et al (1981) used soya milk as a placebo, and infants could have been as sensitive to this as to cow's milk. In short, there is, therefore, some evidence that maternal dietary antigens may cause colic in the breast fed infant, but, bearing in mind that the effect of antigen avoidance was demonstrable only in a group of selected infants, it could be unreasonable to regard this as a common problem among breast fed infants in general. 'Colic' is a label sometimes misapplied to persistent crying related to feeding difficulties which require supervision.

Finally, how and when should the potentially allergic infant be weaned? Although two Finnish studies (Kajosaari & Saarinen, 1983; Saarinen et al, 1979) have suggested that exclusive breast feeding to 6 months may be beneficial, neither employed blind assessment of the infant's allergic state. There are, therefore, no conclusive grounds for proposing a particular age. Furthermore, there is debate about the way in which different foods should be introduced; it may merely be that late introduction postpones the development of allergy (Saarinen & Kajosaari, 1980), though this view may be oversimplified (Soothill, 1980). Nevertheless, from a practical standpoint it would seem sensible to introduce foods on a stepwise basis, if only to identify those which cause problems. A protocol directed at this aim has recently been proposed (Cant & Bailes, 1984).

CONCLUSIONS

It is clear that, whichever aspect of infant feeding is chosen — breast milk transfer, weaning, induction of allergy — we still have much to learn about the reasons for differing individual responses. In this context it is important to understand that the best we can offer are guidelines; 'rules' could be dangerous for there are few certainties.

REFERENCES

Bowen-Jones A, Thompson C, Drewett R F 1982 Milk flow and sucking rates during breast-feeding. Developmental Medicine and Child Neurology 24: 626–633

Burgio C R, Lanzavecchia A, Plebani A, Jayakar S, Ugazio A G 1980 Ontogeny of secretory immunity: levels of secretory IgA and natural antibodies in saliva. Pediatric Research 14: 1111–1114

Burr M L 1983 Does infant feeding affect the risk of allergy? Archives of Disease in Childhood 58: 561–565

Butte N F, Garza C, Smith E O, Nicholls B L 1983 Evaluation of the deuterium dilution technique against the test-weighing procedure for the determination of breast milk intake. American Journal of Clinical Nutrition 37: 996–1003

Cant A J 1984 Diet and the prevention of childhood allergic disease. Human Nutrition: Applied Nutrition 38A: 455–468

Cant A J, Bailes J A 1984 How should we feed the potentially allergic infant? Human Nutrition: Applied Nutrition 38A: 474–476

Coward W A, Sawyer M B, Whitehead R G, Prentice A M, Evans J 1979 New method for measuring milk intake in breast-fed babies. Lancet ii: 13–14

Coward W A, Cole T J, Sawyer M B, Prentice A M, Orr-Ewing A K 1982 Breast-milk intake measurement in mixed-fed infants by administration of deuterium oxide to their mothers. Human Nutrition: Clinical Nutrition 36C: 141–148

Cruz J R, Garcia B, Urrutia J J, Carlsson B, Hanson L A 1981 Food antibodies in milk from Guatemalan women. Journal of Pediatrics 99: 600–602

Department of Health and Social Security 1977 The composition of mature human milk. Report on Health and Social Subjects 12. HMSO, London

De Swiet M, Fayers P, Cooper L 1977 Effect of feeding habit on weight in infancy. Lancet i: 892–894

Drewett R F 1982 Returning to the suckled breast: a further test of Hall's hypothesis. Early Human Development 6: 161–163

Drewett R F, Woolridge M W 1981 Milk taken by human babies from the first and second breast. Physiology and Behaviour 26: 327–329

Drewett R F, Woolridge M W, Greasley V, et al 1984 Evaluating breast-milk intake by test-weighing: a portable electronic balance suitable for community and field studies. Early Human Development 10: 123–126

Eastham E J, Lichauco T, Grady M I, Walker W A 1978 Antigenicity of infant formulas: role of immature intestine on intestinal permeability. Journal of Pediatrics 93: 561–564

Eid E E 1970 Follow up study of physical growth of children who had excessive weight gain in the first six months of life. British Medical Journal ii: 74–76

Evans R W, Ferguson D M, Allardyce R A, Taylor B 1981 Maternal diet and infantile colic in breast-fed infants. Lancet i: 1340–1342

Fomon S J, Filer L J, Thomas L N, Anderson T A, Nelson S E 1975 Influence of formula concentration on caloric intake and growth of normal infants. Acta Paediatrica Scandinavica 64: 172–181

Ford R P K, Hill D J, Hosking C S 1983 Cow's milk hypersensitivity: immediate and delayed onset clinical patterns. Archives of Disease in Childhood 58: 856–862

Goldblum R M, Ahlstedt S, Carlsson B 1975 Antibody forming cells in human colostrum after oral immunisation. Nature 257: 797–798

Golding J, Butler N R, Taylor B 1982 Breastfeeding and eczema/asthma. Lancet i: 623

Hall B 1975 Changing composition of human milk and early development of an appetite control. Lancet i: 779–781

Hamill P V V, Drizd T A, Johnson C L, Reed R B, Roche A F, Moore W M 1979 Physical growth: National Center for Health Statistics percentiles. American Journal of Clinical Nutrition 32: 607–629

Hattevig G, Kjellman B, Johannsen S G O, Bjorksten B 1984 Clinical symptoms and IgE responses to common food proteins in atopic and healthy children. Clinical Allergy 14: 551–559

Heird W C, Schwartz S M, Hansen I H 1984 Colostrum induced enteric mucosal growth in beagle puppies. Pediatric Research 18: 512–515

Houston M J, Howie P W 1981 Home support for the breast-feeding mother. Midwife, Health Visitor and Community Nurse 17: 378–382

Howie P W, Houston M J, Cook A, Smart L, McArdle T, McNeilly A S 1981a How long should a breast feed last? Early Human Development 5: 71–77

Howie P W, McNeilly A S, Houston M J, Cook A, Boyle H 1981b Effect of supplementary food on suckling patterns and ovarian activity during lactation. British Medical Journal 283: 757–759

Hytten F E 1954 Clinical and chemical studies in human lactation. British Medical Journal i: 175–181, 249–254

Jakobssen I, Lindberg T 1982 Cows' milk proteins cause infantile colic in breast-fed infants: a double blind crossover study. Pediatrics 71: 268–271

Jarret E E 1977 Activation of IgE regulatory mechanisms by transmucosal absorption of antigens. Lancet ii: 223–225

Kajosaari M, Saarinen U M 1983 Prophylaxis of atopic disease by six months solid food elimination. Acta Paediatrica Scandinavica 71: 815–819

Kilshaw P J, Cant A J 1984 The passage of maternal dietary proteins into human breast milk. International Archives of Allergy and Applied Immunology 75: 8–15

Kuroume T, Oguri M, Matsumura T, et al 1976 Milk sensitivity and soybean sensitivity in the production of eczematous manifestations in breast-fed infants with particular reference to intra-uterine sensitisation. Annals of Allergy 37: 41–46

Lucas A, Lucas P J, Baum J D 1979 Pattern of milk flow in breast-fed infants. Lancet ii: 57–58

Lucas A, Lucas P J, Baum J D 1980 The nipple shield sampling system: a device for measuring the dietary intake of breast-fed infants. Early Human Development 4: 365–372

Martin J, Monk J 1982 Infant feeding 1980. Office of Population Censuses and Surveys, HMSO, London

Poskitt E M E, Cole T J 1978 Nature, nurture and childhood overweight. British Medical Journal i: 603–605

Prentice A, Prentice A M, Whitehead R G 1981 Breast milk fat concentrations of rural African women. British Journal of Nutrition 45: 483–494

Saarinen U M, Kajosaari M, Backman A, Siimes M A 1979 Prolonged breast feeding as prophylaxis for atopic disease. Lancet ii: 163–166

Saarinen U M, Kajosaari M 1980 Does dietary elimination in infancy prevent or only postpone food allergy? Lancet i: 166–167

Saarinen U M, Siimes M A 1979 Role of prolonged breast-feeding in infant growth. Acta Paediatrica Scandinavica 68: 245–250

Shukla A, Forsyth H A, Anderson C M, Marwah S M 1972 Infantile overnutrition in the first year of life: a field study in Dudley, Worcestershire. British Medical Journal iv: 507–515

Soothill J F 1980 Dietary antigen avoidance: postponement or prevention? Lancet i: 604

Taitz L S 1971 Infantile overnutrition among artificially fed infants in the Sheffield region. British Medical Journal i: 315–316

Taitz L S 1978 Solute and calorie loading in young infants: short and long term effects. Archives of Disease in Childhood 53: 697–700

Taitz L S 1982 Soy feeding in infancy. Archives of Disease in Childhood 57: 814–815

Taitz L S, Armitage B L 1984 Goats' milk for infants and children. British Medical Journal 288: 428–429

Taitz L S, Lukmanji Z 1981 Alterations in feeding patterns and rates of weight gain in South Yorkshire infants. Human Biology 53: 313–320

Taylor B, Norman A P, Orgel H A, Stokes C R, Turner M W, Soothill J F 1973 Transient IgA deficiency and the pathogenesis of infantile atopy. Lancet ii: 111–113

Udall J N, Pang K, Fritze L, Kleinman R, Walker W A 1981 Development of a gastrointestinal mucosal barrier. II. The effect of natural versus artificial feeding on intestinal permeability to macromolecules. Pediatric Research 15: 245–249

Underwood B A, Hofvander Y 1982 Appropriate timing for complementary feeding of the breast-fed infant. Acta Paediatrica Scandinavica (Supplement) 292: 1–32

Walker W A 1975 Antigen absorption from the small intesting and gastrointestinal disease. Pediatric Clinics of North America 22: 731–746

Walker W A 1985 Absorption of protein and protein fragments in the developing intestine: role of immunologic/allergic reactions. Pediatrics (Supplement) 75: 167–171

Warner J O 1980 Food allergy in fully breast-fed infants. Clinical Allergy 10: 133–136

Waterlow J C, Thomson A M 1979 Observations on the adequacy of breast feeding. Lancet ii: 238–242

Whitehead R G 1985 The human weaning process. Pediatrics (Supplement) 75: 189–193

Whitehead R G, Paul A A 1981 Infant growth and human milk requirements. Lancet ii: 161–163

Whitehead R G, Paul A A, Cole T J 1981 A critical analysis of measured food energy intakes during infancy and early childhood in comparison with current international recommendations. Journal of Human Nutrition 35: 339–348

Whitehead R G, Paul A A 1984 Growth charts and the assessment of infant feeding practices in the western world and in developing countries. Early Human Development 9: 187–207

Whitfield M F, Kay R, Stevens S 1982 The validity of routine clinical test-weighing. Archives of Disease in Childhood 56: 919–921

Williams A F, Akinkugbe F M, Baum J D 1985 A comparison of two methods of milk sampling for calculating the fat intake of breast-fed infants. Human Nutritions, Clinical Nutrition 39c: 193–202

Wolff P H 1968 The serial organisation of sucking in the young infant. Pediatrics 42: 943–956

Woolridge M W, Baum J D, Drewett R F 1980 Does a change in the composition of milk affect sucking patterns and milk intake? Lancet ii: 1292–1294

Woolridge M W, Baum J D, Drewett R F 1982a Individual patterns of milk transfer during breast-feeding. Early Human Development 7: 265–272

Woolridge M W, How T V, Drewett R F, Rolfe P, Baum J D 1982b The continuous measurement of milk intake at a feed in breast-fed babies. Early Human Development 6: 365–373

World Health Organization 1981 Contemporary patterns of breast-feeding: report on the WHO collaborative study on breast-feeding. WHO, Geneva

World Health Organization/Food and Agriculture Organization 1973 Energy and protein requirements. World Health Organization technical reports series 522. WHO, Geneva

Immunisation — where do we go from here?

INTRODUCTION

Immunisation policy in Britain is based on the recommendations of the Joint Committee on Vaccination and Immunisation. In 1984, this body published a new document entitled *Immunisation Against Infectious Disease*, in which it reaffirmed earlier advice concerning the protection of infants and children. For these groups routine vaccination is recommended against diphtheria, poliomyelitis, tetanus, whooping cough, tuberculosis, measles and rubella. The response to this official advice may be measured in terms of vaccine acceptance rates, and these are shown in Table 5.1. It is clear that in some areas considerable success has been achieved. Thus, levels of take-up for diphtheria, poliomyelitis and tetanus vaccines have recently attained new peaks with around 85% of children born in Britain in 1981 completing these vaccination programmes by the end of 1983. In the latter year, only 14 cases of these three diseases were officially notified in England and Wales.

At the other extreme, acceptance of whooping cough vaccine remains relatively low. This has not always been the case — almost eight out of every 10 children born in 1971 or 1972 received the vaccine over the course of the subsequent two years (Table 5.1). But, in 1974, a paper (Kulenkampff et al, 1974) was published which drew attention to 36 children admitted to London's Hospital for Sick Children with severe neurological illnesses: in 33 of the cases pertussis vaccine was reported to have been received during the seven days preceding the onset of symptoms. The report and the growing debate within the medical profession about the vaccine's safety were given extensive coverage by the national press and television. This publicity generated widespread anxiety among parents and take-up of the vaccine fell dramatically: only three out of every 10 children born in 1976 had been immunised two years later. Following this decline, two major epidemics of whooping cough were experienced — one in 1977–79 with more than 100 000 cases and 36 deaths (UK data); the other in 1982, during which almost 66 000 cases were notified along with 14 deaths (figures for England and Wales).

Table 5.1 shows that whooping cough vaccine acceptance rates have in fact been climbing, albeit rather slowly, since the second half of the 1970s. This

Table 5.1 Vaccination of children in Great Britain

% of Children born in vaccinated by end of	1971, 1973	1972, 1974	1973, 1975	1974, 1976	1975, 1977	1976, 1978	1977, 1979	1978, 1980	1979, 1981	1980, 1982	1981, 1983
Diphtheria	81	80	73	74	77	78	79	81	82	84	85
Whooping cough	78	77	60	39	41	32	35	41	46	52	59
Poliomyelitis	80	79	73	74	77	78	79	81	82	83	84
Tetanus	81	80	73	74	77	78	79	81	82	84	85
Measles	53	52	45	46	48	48	49	52	54	56	60

No of school children vaccinated in (thousands)	1973	1974	1975	1976	1977	1978	1979	1980	1981	1982	1983
Rubella (girls only)	295	288	298	344	328	345	405	372	367	371	371*
Tuberculosis	679	646	684	730	757	676	660	725	678	639	568†

*Data for Scotland relate to year ended 30 June 1983
†England and Wales only
Source: DHSS; Scottish Health Service, Common Services Agency; Welsh Office

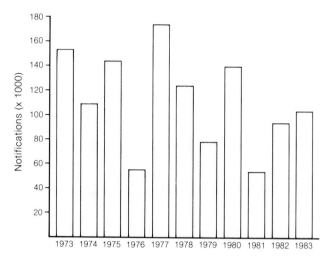

Fig. 5.1 Notification of measles in England and Wales, 1973–83 (Source: Office of Population Censuses and Surveys, with permission)

trend reflects, inter alia, gradual restoration of confidence in the effectiveness of vaccination (the latter being demonstrated by the outbreak of the two epidemics) and reassurances regarding the vaccine's safety (Alderslade et al, 1981). Yet acceptance rates — currently just short of 60% — still have a long way to go if epidemics are not to become a consistently recurring threat to the health of future generations of infants and children.*

Immunisation against measles and rubella is a further source of contemporary concern. In both instances, vaccine take-up rates fall disappointingly short of the desired targets, leading to the occurrence of unnecessary morbidity and mortality. This paper focuses on these two diseases with the objective of identifying how shortfalls in vaccine acceptance might be remedied.

MEASLES

Measles is a highly contagious viral disease which can be a significant cause of morbidity. From a follow up study of nearly 9 000 cases of measles notified during the last quarter of 1976, Miller (1978) has reported that 4% of episodes may be regarded as severe and a further 44% as moderately severe. Complications are experienced in approximately 10% of cases and usually take the form of either otitis media (46%) or respiratory illness (40%).

Measles may also cause death — most frequently as a result of bronchopneumonia, followed by encephalitis. From an analysis of mortality data for England and Wales over the period 1970–83, Miller (1985) calculated

*For a comprehensive discussion of the whooping cough controversy the reader's attention is drawn to the essay by Euan Ross which appeared in the first volume of *Progress in Child Health*.

an overall (and largely unchanging) ratio of deaths to measles notifications of 1.5 per 10 000 (Table 5.2). For infants under 1 year, however, the ratio was more than three times higher, at 4.8, while for children aged 1–2 years it was 2.3. Furthermore, the study dispelled any notion that measles mortality is confined to those already suffering ill-health or permanent physical/mental impairment. Fifty-three per cent of the 270 deaths over the period 1970–83 occurred in individuals with no pre-existing condition, and among the 42 deaths under 1 year of age, three-quarters involved infants without any pre-existing illness.

Table 5.2 Deaths from measles in previously normal and previously abnormal persons, England and Wales, 1970–83

Year	Total measles deaths	Ratio/10 000 notifications	Previously normal No (%)	Previously abnormal No
1970	39	1.3	24 (62)	15
1971	25	1.9	17 (68)	8
1972	29	2.0	18 (62)	11
1973	27	1.8	18 (67)	9
1974	19	1.7	12 (63)	7
1975	13	0.9	10 (77)	3
1976	11	2.0	4 (36)	7
1977	18	1.0	5 (28)	13
1978	13	1.0	6 (46)	7
1979	14	1.8	7 (50)	7
1980	23	1.6	8 (35)	15
1981	12	2.3	3 (25)	9
1982	10	1.1	3 (30)	7
1983	17	1.6	9 (50)	8
	270	1.5	144 (53)	126

Source: Miller, 1985

A substantial proportion of measles related morbidity and mortality is potentially avoidable. Since 1968 a vaccine has been available which is effective — administration during the second year of life provides 95% protection — and safe — post-vaccination central nervous system complications occur about once for every million doses given (Lancet editorial, 1983). Yet take-up of measles vaccine has been disappointing. Table 5.1 shows that despite a recent trend towards increasing acceptance, only 60% of children in Britain are currently vaccinated against measles. (This figure is, of course, an average which disguises the fact that vaccine take-up by district ranged from 28% to 85% in 1983 (Noah, 1984a).) Against this background epidemics have continued to occur and official notifications have yet to drop below 50 000 per annum (Fig. 5.1). Indeed, the annual average for 1980–83 exceeded 97 500 in England and Wales, and measles claimed an average of almost 18 lives per year over this period (data from the Office of Population Censuses and Surveys).

Recent trends in the United States differ sharply from those experienced in the United Kingdom. Between 1977 and 1979 a National Childhood Immunisation Initiative was launched in an attempt to reduce the large number of American children who remained susceptible to one or more of the preventable childhood infections. Within this overall objective a more specific target of eliminating the transmission of indigenous measles was established in 1978. This goal required the attainment of near universal immunisation rates, and this has been achieved — since 1982, 97% of children entering school for the first time have shown immunity to measles. As a result, notified cases fell from 57 345 in 1977 to just 1436 in 1983. Consequently, cases per 100 000 total population in England and Wales are almost 350 times the number in the United States.

Explaining the UK performance

No one factor in isolation is sufficient to explain the huge disparity between the performances of the two nations. The existence of laws in the United States requiring proof of immunity — that is, written documentation showing the date of vaccination on or after the first birthday or a history of measles diagnosed by a physician — as a condition of school entry is clearly of major significance. At the same time, important 'negative' factors have been operating in Britain. Measles has tended, for example, to be regarded as a relatively trivial episode of ill-health and an almost inevitable experience of early childhood. A recent study of parental attitudes (Blair et al, 1985) found that only 20% of the respondents 'named serious problems caused by measles that corresponded with the problems that health professionals were aiming to prevent by immunisation'. Furthermore, over half of the sample thought that immunisation was only sometimes or never effective. Misunderstanding in these respects has undoubtedly served to limit the take-up of vaccination.

Many other factors have contributed a similar effect. Difficulties early in the vaccine's history concerning efficacy and side effects, for example, may have exerted an adverse long term impact on its reputation. Vaccination may be thought unnecessary because of an apparent history of measles during the first year of life. Yet such 'inaction' may frequently be inappropriate; Adjaye et al (1983) reported that two-thirds of a sample of 53 children believed to have suffered measles during their first 12 months proved on serological investigation to be vulnerable to the disease. Confusion surrounding the contraindications to vaccination coupled with a degree of overcaution, perhaps heightened if not caused by the whooping cough controversy, also seem likely to have depressed acceptance rates for measles vaccine. (In this context Middleton (1983) has argued that contraindications are fewer in number than is frequently presumed and lead in fact to the exclusion of only 5% of potential recipients.)

One final obstacle to the achievement of substantially higher take-up rates for measles vaccine stems from the fact that vaccination is delayed until the second year of life. At this stage child clinic attendances are considerably fewer in number and thus so too are the opportunities either to administer protection or to advise on the latter's benefits. Half of the parents in the study by Blair et al (1985) could not recall having talked to a health professional about immunisation.

RUBELLA

Rubella is generally a mild childhood infectious disease that is self-limiting and has few serious complications. Indeed, symptoms are often so fleeting as not to be recognised clinically (Joint Committee on Vaccination and Immunisation, 1984). However, if rubella is contracted during pregnancy there is a risk, which is substantially greater during the first trimester than at subsequent stages, that the infant may be born with defects. These congenital abnormalities typically include heart problems, impaired hearing and cataracts. It is therefore essential that women who may become pregnant are protected against the disease. In Britain this objective is pursued via a policy of selective immunisation advising vaccination for all girls between their 10th and 14th birthdays. In addition, it is recommended that all seronegative women of child-bearing age should be offered protection, provided they are not pregnant.

The nature of the policy followed in Britain since 1970 (when vaccine first became licensed for use) is such that an unambiguous assessment of its efficacy is not yet possible. Nevertheless, investigations of the immunological status of young females generally suggest a favourable impact. A survey among university students and young adult blood donors found that between 94% and 97% of women born in 1956 or more recently (that is those eligible for rubella vaccine at school) had antibodies against rubella (Clarke et al, 1983). The corresponding range for males in the same age groups was 80% to 88%. Assuming equal exposure of males and females to rubella, this suggests an average net gain due to vaccine of about 12%.

Despite these encouraging findings, the principal objective of the vaccination programme, the elimination of congenital rubella syndrome (CRS), has still to be accomplished. Suspected cases of congenital rubella are notified under the National Congenital Rubella Surveillance Programme to one of two centres serving the north and south of the country, and recent data are shown in Figure 5.2. Following the peak year of 1973 when 85 affected children were born, there was a reasonably steady decline in incidence until 1977. Widespread rubella epidemics then raised the number of confirmed cases to 50 in 1978 and 74 in 1979. The subsequent two years were epidemic free, but moderate outbreaks were again experienced in 1982 and 1983. Currently available data indicate new registrations of confirmed or suspected congenital rubella for these two years totalling 21 and 25 respectively. These figures are, however, only provisional because additional cases of hearing loss as a manifestation of intrauterine rubella infection may yet be reported. Never-

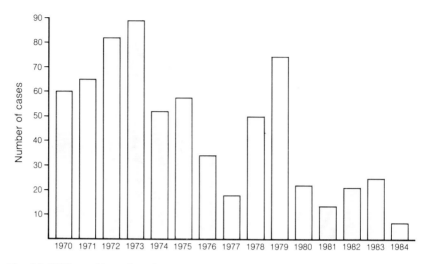

Fig. 5.2 Children with confirmed or suspected congenital rubella by year of birth (Smithells et al, 1985, with permission)

theless, it has been suggested that final outturn registrations for 1982 and 1983 may well be fewer than those for 1978 and 1979 (Smithells et al, 1985).

Whatever the outcome of these recent moderate epidemics of rubella, one fact remains clear: vaccination policy is not at the present time being implemented sufficiently rigorously to ensure the elimination of CRS. Overall data indicate that 84% of females were vaccinated by the age of 14 years in 1982. This proportion was a significant improvement on the 68% recorded for 1975, but considerable efforts will be required to achieve the 95% target set by the DHSS. Furthermore, there is evidence of inadequacy in the execution of the second strand of British rubella policy: one quarter of elective abortions for rubella contracted in pregnancy are in women having their second child (Le Fanu, 1984).

WAYS FORWARD

Measles

The government has set a goal of reaching a measles immunisation take-up level in children in the second year of life of 90% by 1990 (Patten, 1984). This figure may be regarded as very ambitious given the present take-up rate and the fact that the target exceeds by several percentage points the acceptance levels for the most successful elements of contemporary vaccination policy. Nevertheless, take-up by at least 80% of the relevant population is necessary if measles incidence is to be reduced 'to levels at which it is no longer a public health problem' (Noah, 1984b). In order to attain this threshold — which is still modest compared with the achievement of the United States — initiatives will be required that are capable of improving present acceptance by no less than 33%.

The analysis by Blair et al (1985) of parental understanding of the potential dangers of measles and of the benefits of immunisation revealed misconception and doubt on a significant scale. There is therefore a clear need to improve awareness and in this respect campaigns organised on a local basis may be especially valuable. A successful example of this type of initiative is provided by the recent measles vaccination project conducted by North Bedfordshire District Health Authority (Ryan, 1984). The campaign ran for six months during the autumn and winter of 1983–84, reaching general practitioners, health visitors and schools as well as attracting interest from the local press, radio and television. The number of measles vaccinations carried out between October and February was more than twice the figure during the corresponding period 12 months earlier and notifications were 86% fewer.

At the same time 'promotional' initiatives might also be profitably targetted at health care professionals involved in vaccination. A survey of general practitioners, clinical medical officers and health visitors in Coventry by Middleton and Pollock (1984) found considerable differences in the practice of measles immunisation. And other commentators have suggested that family doctors are not giving enough active encouragement to parents to have their children vaccinated against measles. Such observations reflect, in part at least, a tendency to underestimate the potential hazards of the disease.

Uncertainty regarding vaccine contraindications has been identified as another factor contributing to the observed inconsistency in the implementation of measles vaccination, and this has in fact been highlighted once again in a recent survey published by Bath District Health Promotion Unit (1984). The Unit found, for example, that 16% of general practitioners were unwilling to vaccinate any child with an allergy to hen's eggs even though DHSS guidelines state that, excluding cases of severe hypersensitivity, this is no longer a contraindication; and in a comparison of DHSS recommendations with information contained in the British National Formulary and supplied by manufacturers, Hull and Nicoll (1984) found that for neither pertussis nor measles vaccine were the three sources in agreement on contraindications and special considerations. There is therefore a clear need, as Hull and Nicoll have argued, to remove these unnecessary obstacles by ensuring that written guidelines are simple, straightforward and in accord.

Finally, the achievement of higher vaccination levels necessitates effective monitoring systems to ensure that all individuals who become eligible for immunisation are offered protection and to provide follow up for those who fail to respond. Such facilities might be expected to prove especially valuable in the case of measles vaccination because of the delay in administration until the second year of life. In Coventry, Middleton and Pollock (1984) have reported that the take-up rate for measles vaccine is only 48%, yet their analysis of immunisation consent forms indicated that 90% of parents express a willingness to have their children protected against disease.

In this respect, well designed computer-based systems which maintain a continuously updated record of those eligible for immunisation and ensure that appointments are issued would appear to offer substantial advantages. The benefits of computer assistance in measles have been described by Bussey and Harris (1979), and the increasing use by health authorities of the immunisation call-up module developed by the Child Health Computing Committee is thus an encouraging development (Rigby, 1983). At the same time, however, it is of course essential that such computer systems operate efficiently: one of the factors discovered to be discouraging higher take-up of measles vaccine in Bedfordshire was 'a block in the programme ... whereby the regional computer failed to call up children for vaccination who had not completed earlier courses such as the basic three-in-one' (Ryan, 1984).

Rubella

The failure, as yet, of rubella vaccination policy to lead to the elimination of congenital rubella syndrome has led some commentators to suggest that the UK approach should be abandoned in favour of that employed in the United States. The latter, by vaccinating *all* infants at the age of 12 to 15 months seeks to interrupt the transmission of rubella as well as to provide females with protection lasting throughout the years of childbearing potential.

A recent report from the US suggests that CRS might now be at or close to record low levels (Morbidity and Mortality Weekly Report, 1984). Protagonists of the British rubella vaccination policy maintain, however, that there is no case for a switch to the United States approach. First, it was in any event predicted at the start of the British programme that the central objective of reducing the incidence of CRS would be delayed until well into the 1980s — that is, until substantial numbers of immunised school girls have entered the childbearing age range. Thus in Britain in 1980, 60% of the 725 024 live births were to mothers who were aged 25 years or more and had consequently not been included in the school rubella vaccination programme. If it is assumed that the maternal age distribution of live births in 1980 persists into the immediate future then it will not be until 1990 that 94% of live births will be to mothers who would have been eligible for immunisation during their school days.

Second, the British approach means that 70% or more of women attain child-bearing age having acquired immunity via natural infection. Furthermore, the policy has the additional advantage that the continued existence of wild virus in the community allows for booster re-infections which may be important in maintaining long term immunity (Badenoch, 1984). In contrast, the United States depends on vaccine-induced immunity and there is still some uncertainty with regard to the duration of protection gained in this way (Dudgeon, 1983). In addition, computer simulations constructed by Knox (1980) to evaluate the outcome of different rubella vaccination strategies revealed that very small rates of decay in vaccine immunity would have a considerably more damaging impact on the efficacy of a US style policy than on the type employed in Britain.

Finally, the success of the US policy hinges on the eradication of the reservoir of infection in the community; it is thus dependent on extremely high vaccination take-up rates. Data for the early 1980s show that 96% of children entering school in the United States had been vaccinated against rubella (Anderson & May, 1983). As in the case of measles, this achievement reflects in large part the fact that vaccination is a pre-requisite of school entry. Without the introduction of compulsion into British policy, it is unlikely that a vaccination programme aimed at all pre-school children would achieve the necessary levels of coverage; certainly British experience to date with measles vaccine provides little encouragement in this respect. Consequently, Nelson and Peckham (1983) have expressed the belief that 'a change to the American rubella policy could run the risk of increasing the incidence of congenital rubella in this country'.

In view of these considerations, it has been argued that it is perfectly consistent for a particular vaccination strategy to be appropriate to one country but not to another and that the priority in Britain must be to raise the effectiveness of the established vaccination programme. Given this objective, a national publicity initiative is underway to encourage immunisation take-up. It seems likely, however, that few women are unaware of or fail to understand the problem of rubella (Zealley, 1984). Instead, the removal of shortcomings in the administration system provides the key to increasing vaccination rates. Black (1984), for example, has reported that a simple change in the requirements governing the return of vaccination consent forms raised the vaccine acceptance rate among Oxford school girls from 86% to 93%. Modification of the contraindication criteria facilitated a further increase to almost 96%.

Efficiency in administration is also an essential pre-requisite for the successful execution of the second element of rubella vaccination policy — that is, the protection of susceptible women who have already reached child-bearing age. All women attending for antenatal advice, for example, should be tested for immunity to rubella and every effort made to ensure that the vaccine is administered post partum to those found to be seronegative (Joint Committee on Vaccination and Immunisation, 1984). There is evidence, however, that this opportunity is not being fully exploited. Miller et al (1982), in a study of the consequences of maternal rubella, found that two-thirds of the 1016 women contracting the disease during pregnancy were multiparous.

Considerable scope also exists outside this particular setting for protecting those women who have bypassed the school girl immunisation programme. Hospital occupational health departments, for example, could play a useful part in identifying susceptible individuals among prospective employees and offering them vaccination (Jachuck et al, 1985). It has been argued, however, that general practice provides the ideal setting for screening and that perhaps the most cost-effective option would be to incorporate the necessary procedures, where appropriate, into the consultation process (Rowlands &

Bethal, 1982). Given, in addition, the contribution of family planning clinics, it is clear that several agencies are, and could become more, involved in reducing the susceptibility of women of child-bearing age to rubella.

CONCLUSION

Vaccination is a highly effective means of minimising the morbidity and mortality attributable to measles and rubella (White et al, 1985). It is also associated with substantial economic benefits. Focusing on measles, vaccination has been shown to generate financial savings via reductions in disease treatment costs (McConnell & Tohani, 1984) and to liberate resources for use elsewhere in the health service (Binnie, 1984). Formal economic assessment of vaccination programmes may utilise a number of approaches: benefit-risk analysis, benefit-cost analysis and cost-effectiveness analysis. In addition, differences between independently conducted studies in the nature of their underlying assumptions, their comprehensiveness and of course in the specific type of vaccination strategy under consideration may yield seemingly inconsistent findings. Nevertheless, in a recent review Koplan (1985) has commented, from analyses based on United States data, that 'measles and rubella vaccines have been shown to have benefits that far outweigh risks and costs; they both save money and decrease morbidity, mortality and suffering. The benefit cost ratio of measles is 15:1 and rubella is 13:1'.

In this country, however, current immunisation levels fall short of the desired targets — substantially so in the case of measles. In sharp contrast, the United States has almost universal take-up rates for these two vaccines, and this is largely the consequence of laws requiring proof of immunity as a condition of school entry. Similar intervention — specifically, legislation requiring parents actively to opt out of the vaccination system should they so wish (Campbell, 1984) — has been urged for the UK but, in the foreseeable future at least, is unlikely to be adopted in a nation where 'the freedom to be ill is valued so highly' (Middleton, 1983). Consequently, progress depends, inter alia, on the creation of greater understanding of the hazards of disease and of the benefits associated with immunisation and on improved efficiency in the execution of the vaccination service. There is evidence that some areas of the country are already achieving vaccine acceptance rates significantly in excess of the national average. These successes stem from initiatives in organisation and awareness campaigns and frequently reflect the enthusiasm of local paediatricians, community physicians and other health care professionals. It is the extension of such endeavours, each designed to meet the special challenges of specific communities, that offers perhaps the brightest prospects for reducing the unnecessary morbidity associated with measles and rubella in Britain today.

REFERENCES

Adjaye N, Azad A, Foster M, Marshall W C, Dunn H 1983 Measles serology in children with a history of measles in early life. British Medical Journal 286: 1478

Alderslade R, Bellman M H, Rawson N S B, Ross E M, Miller D L 1981 The National Childhood Encephalopathy Study. In: Whooping Cough. HMSO, London, p. 79–169

Anderson R M, May R M 1983 Vaccination against rubella and measles: quantitative investigations of different policies. Journal of Hygiene [Cambridge] 90: 259–325

Badenoch J 1984 Rubella immunisation: whose baby? British Medical Journal 288: 564–565

Bath District Health Promotion Unit 1984 GPs opinions on measles vaccination (September)

Binnie G A 1984 Measles immunisation: profit and loss in a general practice. British Medical Journal 289: 1275–1276

Black N 1984 Quoted in Le Fanu J 1984 Medical News 7 June: 20–21

Blair S, Shave N, McKay J 1985 Measles matters, but do parents know? British Medical Journal 290: 623–24

Bussey A L, Harris A S 1979 Computers and the effectiveness of the measles vaccine campaign in England and Wales. Community Medicine 1: 29–35

Campbell A 1984 Quoted in Doctor 26 July: 3

Clarke M, Seagroatt V, Schild G C, et al 1983 Surveys of rubella antibodies in young adults and children. Lancet i: 667–669

Dudgeon J A 1983 Immunisation policies. British Medical Journal 286: 1511

Hull D, Nicoll A 1984 Immunisation misinformation. Lancet ii: 1215–1216

Jachuck S J, Bound C L, Jones C E 1985 Role of the occupational health service in screening and increasing the uptake of rubella immunisation. British Medical Journal 290: 119–120

Joint Committee on Vaccination and Immunisation 1984 Immunisation against infectious disease. HMSO, London

Knox E G 1980 Strategy for rubella vaccination. International Journal of Epidemiology 9: 13–23

Koplan J P 1985 Benefits, risks and costs of immunisation programmes. In: Evered D, Whelan J (eds) The Value of Preventive Medicine. Ciba Foundation, London, p. 55–68

Kulenkampff M, Schwartzman J S, Wilson J 1974 Neurological complications of pertussis inoculation. Archives of Disease in Childhood 49: 46–49

Lancet editorial 1983 Failure to vaccinate Lancet ii: 1343–1344

Le Fanu J 1984 The best way to boost immunisation rates? Medical News 7 June: 20–21

McConnell W W M, Tohani V K 1984 Measles in the Southern Health Board — implications for resources. British Medical Journal 289: 293–296

Middleton J D 1983 Measles — case for a strategy on vaccination. Pulse (3 December)

Middleton J D, Pollock G T 1984 Measles immunisation levels. Lancet i: 167–168

Miller C L 1978 Severity of notified measles. British Medical Journal i: 1253–1255

Miller C L 1985 Deaths from measles in England and Wales, 1970–83. British Medical Journal 290: 443–444

Miller E, Cradock-Watson J E, Pollock T M 1982 Consequences of confirmed maternal rubella at successive stages of pregnancy. Lancet ii: 781–784

Morbidity and Mortality Weekly Report 1984 Rubella and congenital rubella — United States 1983. MMWR 33: 237–242

Nelson D B, Peckham C S 1983 Immunisation policies. British Medical Journal 286: 1818

Noah N D 1984a What can we do about measles? British Medical Journal 289: 1476

Noah N D 1984b Failure to vaccinate. Lancet i: 51

Patten J 1984 Vaccination. Hansard written answers (30 July): Col. 99–100

Rigby M 1983 The Health Services (12 August)

Rowlands S, Bethel R G H 1982 Rubella screening: organisation and incentive. Journal of the Royal College of General Practitioners 32: 491–94

Ryan R P 1984 Measles vaccination: the 1983 Bedfordshire campaign. Health Education Journal 43: 112–14

Smithells R W, Sheppard S, Holzel H, Dickson A 1985 National Congenital Rubella Surveillance Programme 1 July 1971–30 June 1984. British Medical Journal 291: 40–41

White C C, Koplan J P, Orenstein W A (1985) Benefits, risks and costs of immunisation for measles, mumps and rubella. American Journal of Public Health 75: In Press.

Zealley H 1984 Quoted in Le Fanu 1984

The care of siblings of sudden infant death syndrome babies

There are two main considerations in the management of a baby born to parents who have previously suffered a sudden infant death (SID). The first is the parents' anxiety for the safety of their new baby and their anxiety about how they will cope with a new baby. The second is the actual, slight increase in risk of sudden death in a sibling of a SID (Irgens et al, 1984).

PARENTAL ANXIETY

Beckwith (1970) has defined sudden infant death syndrome (SIDS) as 'the sudden death of any infant of young child, which is unexpected by history and in which a thorough postmortem examination fails to demonstrate an adequate cause for death'. SIDS is a useful term for parents as it enables them to express what has occurred, 'My child died of sudden infant death syndrome', but it does not, and by definition cannot, explain why their baby died. The death of any child is hard to accept, but it is that much more difficult for parents whose apparently well child dies without explanation.

Feelings of guilt are a common component of grief. Parents who lose a child are particularly susceptible to feelings of guilt because the child was dependent on them for his or her daily care. If the child dies without any apparent warning and of no identifiable cause, the parents are left worried that their care was inadequate and that in some way they have failed their child. Despite reassurance from professionals, these fears can be very persistent. Advice on child rearing is prolific so that whatever decisions parents made about the rearing of their baby, they will be able to find acceptable alternatives which in retrospect may seem preferable. The introduction of solid food, essential to every child's normal development, is a typical example of the every day decisions that a parent must make: Is my child ready for solid food? What food do I introduce? How often? How much? I have spoken to over 200 couples about the care of their subsequent baby and few have not expressed doubt about their management of their previous baby. This loss of confidence in their own ability and judgment forms a large aspect of their anxiety, and, while the urge to have another baby is strong, they are often frightened by the responsibility it will place on them. This is particularly apparent in parents who

72

lose their first baby but it is not peculiar to them. Parents cannot give a subsequent child the same amount of undivided attention that it was possible to give to their first child, and this difference can be another source of guilt when the second child dies.

In addition to this loss of confidence in themselves, parents have an altered expectancy in the survival of another baby. They fear their baby may die despite the best care he or she can receive because the cause of these deaths is unknown and therefore no measures can guarantee to prevent a repetition. The fear of a second loss can affect their bonding with the new baby as they are reluctant to form too close an attachment in case of further loss.

INCREASED RISK TO SIBLING

Most of the studies that have estimated risk of recurrence of SIDS in a sibling have looked at retrospective data. Peterson et al (1980) estimated that a sibling is at 10 times greater risk than the normal population risk of 1 in 500 live births. They invited parents who had had a SID to complete a questionnaire. From these returns they found that, of 1194 families, 11 had experienced a repetition of SIDS in the next born child, an incidence of 1.9%. This may be an overestimation of the actual risk because the sample was self-selected.

In Northern Ireland, Frogatt et al (1971) looked at the occurrence of SIDS in families prior to the index case; they found an incidence of between 1.1% and 1.6%.

A prospective study should offer the most reliable information on the risk to a subsequent sibling. One prospective study has been undertaken in Norway, by Irgens et al (1984). Of the 826 162 infants born between 1967 and 1980, 1062 died of SIDS (1.3 per 1000 live births). Five deaths occurred as the second case in a family. The risk of recurrence for the next born sibling was 5.6 per 1000 live births or about fourfold. The normal incidence of SIDS is higher in England and Wales than in Norway: 2.1 per 1000 live births in 1982. Therefore it would seem from this study that the risk to a subsequent sibling in England and Wales may be 1 in 125.

MANAGEMENT OF THE PARENTS AND BABY

There is no method that can guarantee the prevention of SIDS, but much is known about its epidemiology (Table 6.1). There are several factors associated with a higher incidence of SIDS which it is possible to influence. The association of risk is statistical and there is no evidence that influencing these factors can alter the prognosis. However, it does seem to give parents confidence if these points are discussed and they can then decide whether to take action.

Further interventions can be taken after the baby has been born which have been shown to be acceptable to parents but are as yet unproven in preventing SIDS. These measures include ways of monitoring the infant at home as well as

Table 6.1   Epidemiological factors associated with an increased risk of SIDS

Young maternal age
Short interpregnancy interval
Maternal smoking
Multiple pregnancy
Low birth weight
Intention to breast feed
Winter months
Age 2–4 weeks
Male
Lower socio-economic class

more general surveillance methods and increased availability of professional help.

Counselling

Parents' anxiety about the survival of a new infant can be allayed to a certain extent by careful and patient explanation of SIDS and the factors influencing SIDS at a level appropriate to the parents' understanding. Explanation of the epidemiological factors that can be modified may help the parents feel that they can take positive steps to improve the intrauterine and postnatal environment favourably for their baby. However, it must be realised that parents may not find these precautions easy to institute.

Ideally, the parents need to be advised prior to conception. It is desirable that they are counselled by a person suitably knowledgable about SIDS, such as a paediatrician, after the death of their baby. Parents will usually need to be seen at least twice. On the first occasion the counsellor should have access to the postmortem report. Although the report may not in fact provide much useful information to the doctor, the parents will have high expectations that it will be helpful and therefore it is essential for the counsellor to be prepared to discuss the information contained as well as the current understanding of SIDS and to answer the parents' questions. The parents need to be given an opportunity to talk about the events leading up to their baby's death. It is unlikely that they will be ready to discuss in detail the care of a subsequent baby. Many parents, however, will wish to conceive again within a few months, and they should be offered the opportunity to return to discuss the measures that can be taken and the practical help that is available.

The following aspects can be considered when counselling:

1. Inter-pregnancy interval

A short inter-pregnancy interval is associated with an increase in risk, as is a young maternal age (Carpenter et al, 1977). Therefore, in terms of optimal conditions for the pregnancy, conception could be delayed for at least one year after the birth of the previous child, and this may be more important for the young mother under 20 years of age, particularly if she has other children. The mother needs time to recover from the previous pregnancy and the puerperium and she also needs time to grieve for her baby. Babies who reach 2–4 months of age in the winter months are at higher risk of sudden death than those babies who reach the same age in the summer (Carpenter & Gardner, 1982). There could therefore be advantages in timing conception for a spring or summer birth. However, the situation is complex. Parents often have a strong desire to conceive another child quickly. A couple who have lost their first baby have also lost their newly acquired roles as mother and father. This loss may be more poignant for the woman who left full time employment during her pregnancy and therefore cannot easily retrieve her previous identity. The parents must be made to realise that another child cannot replace the child that has died, but only the parents themselves can decide when emotionally they are ready to have another child and the time needed will be different for different couples.

2. Smoking

Lewak et al (1979) found maternal smoking during pregnancy increased risk of SIDS twofold for 1–19 cigarettes smoked per day and by fourfold if 20 or more cigarettes were smoked per day. It would seem advisable that maternal smoking is reduced and preferably abandoned. As mothers who smoke during pregnancy will almost certainly continue to smoke after the baby is born, it is virtually impossible to determine the individual effects on the baby. It would seem sensible to eliminate the possible risks from passive smoking and to keep a baby in a smoke-free environment. Where adults smoke in the household, this could be restricted to rooms not used by the baby.

3. Prematurity and low birth weight

Many studies, including those of Lewak et al (1979) and Jorgensen et al (1982), have shown an increased risk of SIDS in infants born prematurely or with a low birth weight. Mothers with a previous history of SIDS can therefore be advised of the need to attend for antenatal care early in their pregnancy and regularly thereafter so that fetal growth can be monitored and poor growth identified, allowing for possible intervention.

4. Breast feeding

The multicentre study of post-neonatal mortality (Knowelden et al, 1984) revealed a significant difference between the duration of breast feeding in the cases and in the controls. Thirty-three per cent of the matched controls breast fed for a minimum of 12 weeks compared with only 14% of all the cases and 19% of the cases who died unexpectedly (for cases living at least 12 weeks). Carpenter et al (1977) found that just the intention to breast feed is a favourable factor, perhaps reflecting attitudes underlying the decision which will manifest themselves in other ways that are also beneficial to the survival of the baby. However, while it seems advisable to encourage mothers who have previously suffered a SID to breast feed their next baby, breast feeding in itself does not offer any guaranteed prevention. In the multicentre study of post-neonatal mortality, breast feeding was attempted in 46 of 151 cases who died unexpectedly and 48 of the cases who died unexpectedly after 12 weeks were breast fed for four to 11 weeks. Discretion in counselling is therefore needed to avoid mothers suffering further guilt if breast feeding later fails for any reason.

5. Overheating

Stanton (1984) suggests overheating may be an important factor in some SIDs. Pyrexia may trigger apnoea in the young infant, rather than the febrile convulsion of the older child. Parents can be made aware of the possible dangers of overheating. Health visitors are in an ideal position, when visiting in the home, to give practical advice about appropriate clothing for the baby and suitable room temperatures. The use of a room thermometer can be helpful.

6. Recognition of symptoms

Several studies (Watson et al, 1981; Knowelden et al, 1984) have shown that parents do not always recognise the severity of symptoms shown by their infants and do not always know when to seek appropriate medical advice. A baby can die with no cause apparent at necroscopy and yet have some warning signs such as unusual drowsiness, altered cry or refusal of feeds. This is an area where the health visitor can teach parents about the significance of babies' symptoms during her regular contact in the home. The Foundation for the Study of Infant Death (FSID) publishes a Green Card which offers simple advice on 'When to consult a doctor about your baby'.

More detailed symptom charts have been supplied to parents who have previously suffered a SID and who participate in the Infant Home Surveillance Research Project, funded by FSID (Emery et al, 1985). These charts list 31 items varying from snuffles, coughs and diarrhoea to behavioural changes including 'not himself or herself today'. The chart lasts one week and each day the parents are encouraged to work through the list marking any signs that are observed. In the pilot study of this project it was found that the chart assisted the parents in making a daily assessment of their baby's health and, in particular, alerted them to changes. The charts were used in conjunction with weekly visits from their health visitor, who was asked to discuss the chart with the mother. The parents were also advised to seek help the same day that they were concerned about any presenting symptoms.

It is important that any changes in health noticed in a subsequent baby that the parents bring to a doctor are not dismissed without proper attention. I have found that these parents are often embarrassed about their anxieties and are worried about being a nuisance to their doctor, which is a concern that should be dispelled. Examples of the symptom charts are now available from FSID.

7. Increased visits by the health visitor

Scoring systems in use in Sheffield and other centres (Carpenter et al, 1983) to identify babies at high risk of unexpected death have directed health visiting time to possibly vulnerable babies. Sudden death has decreased since the introduction of the scheme in Sheffield, though whether this is related to the increased time spent with families by the health visitor is difficult to establish. Regular visiting enables the development of close understanding between the health visitor and the mother, which in turn facilitates the exchange of advice.

Apnoea monitors

For over a decade, apnoea monitors have been issued to certain parents for use at home with a young infant, usually to parents who have had a previous SIDS or whose baby has been found non-breathing and has been resuscitated ('near miss' episode). The main premise behind the use of the monitor is that it will alert the parents to a respiratory crisis giving an opportunity for intervention.

Our knowledge as to the events which occur when a baby dies of SIDS is limited. Much research has been undertaken looking for failures of respiratory control and respiratory and cardiac irregularities. The incidence of prolonged apnoea, both central (where breathing movements and airflow are absent) and obstructive (where only airflow is absent) as well as periodic breathing (respirations alternating with apnoea), has been studied in infants deemed to be at high risk of SIDS. Much of this work has been undertaken in babies who have undergone a 'near miss' episode. Guilleminault et al (1979) found a higher incidence of apnoea in their 'near miss' cases as opposed to the normal control infants. Kelly and Shannon (1979) similarly found periodic breathing in excess amounts in their 'near miss' cases. A prospective study of breathing movements in normal infants has been undertaken by a multicentred team coordinated by D P Southall (Southall et al, 1983). Twenty-nine infants subsequently suffered SIDS, and none of their recordings showed prolonged central apnoea. It remains possible that these events develop later, prior to death, but the results throw doubt on the significance of prolonged apnoea found after a 'near miss' event. The apnoea may be a result of the crisis, not the cause. This study did not look for obstructive apnoea, which has been found in 'near miss' infants by Guilleminault et al (1979) and Warburton et al (1977).

Disadvantages of apnoea monitoring

The monitors currently available that are suitable for home use are inadequate (Milner, 1985): first, they do not detect obstructive apnoea; second, in the absence of breathing movements they may be triggered by the cardiac pulse;

and, third, they give excessive false alarms. In summary then, they cannot necessarily be relied on to detect the crisis for which they are issued.

Cases of babies dying despite the use of an apnoea monitor have been documented (Lewak, 1975; Duffty & Bryan, 1982). Equally, however, there have been numerous cases reported where parents have felt it was necessary to apply vigorous stimulation after an alarm in order to rouse their baby (MacKay et al, 1984; Tudehope & Cleghorn, 1984).

The use of an apnoea monitor can have disruptive effects on normal family life (Black et al, 1978), though most parents are prepared to tolerate the disturbances. The problems include remaining within hearing of the alarm — not always easy above the noise of electrical appliances in common use in the home — the anxieties caused by false alarms, mechanical failure of the monitor and the availability of suitable babysitters.

Advantages of apnoea monitoring

Apnoea monitors that are provided within the context of an adequate support system are very acceptable to a large number of parents who have suffered a SIDS (MacKay et al, 1984). Typically, their baby's death will have been silent, and they are readily able to believe that their baby 'just stopped breathing', in which case the use of a monitor to identify a respiratory crisis will have great appeal. I have spoken to parents who have wanted to use an apnoea monitor and who are able to accept that the monitor may not be able to prevent a further death. For them the attraction lies in the opportunity it gives not only to attempt resuscitation but also to be with their baby when a crisis is occurring. Of course, they also feel that a monitor tells them when a crisis has not occurred, so that they can approach the cot with confidence rather than trepidation when the alarm has not rung. Most monitors also 'tick' with each movement detected, which provides further reassurance. Parents also are comforted by the monitor in that it is a professional acknowledgement of the concern they have for their baby.

Support system

There have been several papers about experiences of issuing monitors for use in the home (MacKay et al, 1984; Black et al, 1978; Emery et al, 1985). While these identify problems, including the cost and extensive support service that a monitoring programme involves, they all suggest that, with the appropriate support, monitors can help parents and are well received by those parents who want to use them. Monitors should not be issued to parents without thorough instruction on their operation and how to respond to the alarm, including resuscitation techniques. It is also advisable that a record is kept after each alarm giving details of the baby's condition and the action taken by the parents. Technical support is needed in the event of the breakdown of the monitor. This is not an insignificant problem, and whenever there is doubt about the monitor it needs to be changed or the baby admitted to hospital. The sudden loss of a monitor through monitor failure can be devastating to parents.

Weighing

There is evidence that some SIDS babies have not been growing normally prior to death (Gadson & Emery, 1976). The Infant Home Surveillance Research Project (Emery et al, 1985) compared two methods of surveillance of subsequent siblings of cot deaths. A random allocation was made between weighing scales and apnoea monitors and the equipment drawn was used at home by the parents with support from the family's health visitor, general practitioner and paediatrician.

Those parents receiving scales, weighed their baby each day on beam-balance scales. Each week the weights were plotted on to the Sheffield weight chart (Copyright FSID) (Fig. 6.1) by their health visitor. Assessment of growth was made in terms of channel widths. Only 5% of infants can be expected to cross one channel width within two weeks or two channel widths within eight weeks. The charts allow for normal variation in growth but also provide criteria for identifying unusual changes in weight gain. In babies over 1 week old, these changes were closely associated with periods of ill-health or feeding difficulties (Table 6.2). This method of surveillance was well accepted by the parents. Its appeal lay partly in its familiarity; most parents are familiar with scales and

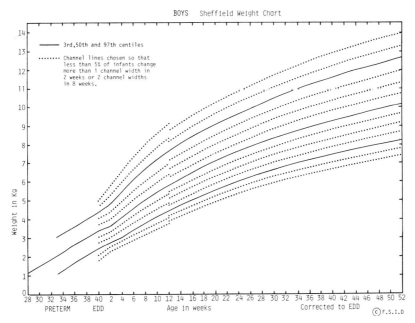

Fig. 6.1 Sheffield weight chart for boys (reduced version), reproduced by permission of FSID

Table 6.2 Conditions associated with unusual changes in weight gain (identified by channel changes on the Sheffield weight chart) in 17 babies from a sample of 50 babies weighed daily from birth to 6 months old

Associated conditions	Channel change	
	1	2
Infections	7	5
Feeding difficulties	2	0
Nothing specific	1	2

weighing items. Also, parents liked the idea that the system might give early warning of problems developing in their baby.

Increased visits by health visitor

Health visitors have much to offer these families. There is particular value in visiting the parents at home where they are likely to be most relaxed and thus able to express fears and be receptive to advice. Parents who participated in the Infant Home Surveillance Research Project were visited at least once a week by their health visitor in addition to any clinic attendances they made. The majority of the parents found this form of help very valuable, in particular because it meant regular contact which they did not have to seek out for themselves. They found the health visitor able to develop their confidence as parents and able not only to offer advice but also to listen to their many anxieties about their baby and his or her management. A symptom chart was kept by the parents on which they could mark any symptoms shown by the baby each day. This was shown to the health visitor, who was thus easily made aware of any changes in the baby's health since her last visit providing a focus point for discussion. The use of the symptom chart appeared to facilitate the easy development of a working relationship between the health visitor and parents. The health visitor is well placed to act as a liaison between the general practitioner and the paediatric team, facilitating appropriate contact.

Case conference

In Sheffield and some other places, the practice has been developed of holding case conferences after all post-perinatal deaths (Taylor & Emery, 1982). The conference is attended by the family doctor, health visitor and paediatrician. The conferences were convened to investigate the deaths in terms of whether the death had been 'preventable' or 'inevitable'. From these discussions those attending have also been able jointly to plan how the parents might best be helped in the event that they have another baby.

SUMMARY

Parents who have previously suffered a SIDS need special care when they have another baby. They are naturally anxious for their baby and about their own ability to cope, especially during the first few months of the baby's life. The risk of recurrence of SIDS is not high but it is slightly higher than for the normal population. Several measures can be instituted to help the parents; perhaps the most important are time and understanding care from health professionals.

REFERENCES

Beckwith J B 1970 Discussion of terminology and definition of sudden infant death syndrome. In: Bergman A B, Beckwith J B, Ray C G (eds) Proceedings of the Second International Conference on Cause of Sudden Infant Death. University of Washington Press, Seattle, p. 14–22
Black L, Hersher L, Steinschneider A 1978 Impact of the apnoea monitor on family life. Pediatrics 62: 681–685
Carpenter R G, Gardner A, McWeeny P M, Emery J L 1977 Multistage scoring system for identifying infants at risk of unexpected death. Archives of Disease in Childhood 52: 606–612
Carpenter R G, Gardner A 1982 Variations in unexpected death rates relating to age, sex and season. In: Studies in Sudden Infant Deaths. HMSO, London
Carpenter R G, Gardner A, Jepson M, et al 1983 Prevention of unexpected infant death. Evaluation of the first seven years of the Sheffield intervention programme. Lancet i: 723–727
Duffty P, Bryan M H 1982 Home apnea monitoring in 'near miss' sudden infant death syndrome (SIDS) and in siblings of SIDS victims. Pediatrics 70: 69–74
Emery J L, Waite A J, Carpenter R G, Limerick S R, Blake D 1985 Apnoea monitors compared with weighing scales for siblings after cot death. Archives of Disease in Childhood 60: 1055–1060
Frogatt P, Lynas M, MacKenzie G 1971 Epidemiology of sudden unexpected death in infants ('cot death') in Northern Ireland. British Journal of Preventive Social Medicine 25: 119–134
Gadson D R, Emery J L 1976 Fatty change in brain of perinatal and unexpected deaths. Archives of Disease in Childhood 51: 42–48
Guilleminault C, Ariagno R, Korobkin R, et al 1979 Mixed and obstructive sleep apnea and near miss for sudden infant death syndrome 2. Comparison of near miss and normal control infants by age. Pediatrics 64: 882–891
Irgens L M, Skjaerven R, Peterson D R 1984 Prospective assessment of recurrence of risk in sudden infant death syndrome siblings. Journal of Pediatrics 104: 349–351
Jorgensen T, Biering-Sorensen F, Hilden J 1982 Sudden infant death in Copenhagen 1956–1971. IV. Infant development. Acta Paediatrica Scandinavica 71: 183–189
Kelly D H, Shannon D C 1979 Periodic breathing in infants with near-miss sudden infant death syndrome. Pediatrics 63: 355–360
Knowelden J, Keeling J, Nicholl J P 1984 A multicentre study of post-neonatal mortality. HMSO, London
Lewak N 1975 Sudden infant death syndrome in a hospitalized infant on an apnea monitor. Pediatrics 56: 296–298
Lewak N, Van den Berg B J, Beckwith J B 1979 Sudden infant death syndrome risk factors. Prospective data review. Clinical Pediatrics 18: 404–411
MacKay M, Abrem E, Silva F A, MacFadyen U M, Williams A, Simpson H 1984 Home monitoring for central apnoea. Archives of Disease in Childhood 59: 136–142
Milner A D 1985 Apnoea monitors and sudden infant death. Archives of Disease in Childhood 60: 76–80
Peterson D R, Chinn N M, Fisher L D 1980 The sudden infant death syndrome: repetitions in families. Journal of Pediatrics 97: 265–267
Southall D P, Richards J M, De Swite N, et al 1983 Identification of infants destined to die unexpectedly during infancy: evaluation of predictive importance of prolonged apnoea and disorders of cardiac rhythm or conduction. British Medical Journal 286: 1092–1096
Stanton A N 1984 Overheating and cot death. Lancet ii: 1199–1201
Taylor E M, Emery J L 1982 Two-year study of the causes of postperinatal deaths classified in terms of preventability. Archives of Disease in Childhood 57: 668–673

Tudehope D I, Cleghorn G 1984 Home monitoring for infants at risk of the sudden infant death syndrome. Australian Journal of Paediatrics 20: 137–140

Warburton D, Stark A R, Taeusch H W 1977 Apnea monitor failure in infants with upper airway obstruction. Pediatrics 60: 742–744

Watson E, Gardner A, Carpenter R G 1981 An epidemiological and sociological study of unexpected death in infancy in nine areas of southern England. II. Symptoms and patterns of care. Medicine, Science & The Law 21: 89–98

Failure to thrive: an old problem revisited

INTRODUCTION AND HISTORY

Failure to thrive (FTT) has been a clinical problem that has plagued generations of physicians and other child care providers. Only within the last few decades, however, have clinicians and researchers come to recognise the condition as involving physiological, psychological and psychosocial disturbances. Thus, the implications for diagnosis and treatment of FTT have expanded and become more broad based. The purpose of this chapter is to provide the historical background for the topic of FTT and to present some of the theory and controversy surrounding the subject. In addition, I will try to elucidate the various ways of categorising FTT. Finally, I will suggest a somewhat different approach towards the conceptualisation of FTT and provide a rational and comprehensive approach towards diagnosis and management.

Although children have been abused and neglected for centuries (Cupoli et al, 1980), it was not until the end of the 19th and the beginning of the 20th centuries that the medical profession began to take a more active interest in such issues. Social thinkers and the body politic had, however, been raising questions about the exploitation and neglect of children during the previous 50 years (Radbill, 1968; Ross, 1980; Radbill, 1980). One of the earliest reports in the paediatric literature of children not growing was provided by Holt in 1899, in which he described children who 'ceased to thrive' (Smith & Berenberg, 1970). In 1908 Chapin described a group of 'atrophic infants' who were sick and ailing and who came from poor home circumstances. He advocated the non-institutional care of these children and the use of foster homes in the country where they could be nurtured and where good nutrition could be provided. He, indeed, was one of the first to see the relationship between the home environment, poor nutrition, illness and the child's poor growth and lack of well-being.

In the medical profession these ideas lay dormant for some 30 years until Spitz's work, in which he described 'anaclitic depression', malnutrition and growth failure in institutionalised children to which he applied the term 'hospitalism' (Spitz, 1945, 1946; Spitz & Wolf, 1946). In this work he made a link between the child's lack of well-being and the lack of adequate caretaking. Bakwin (1949) expressed grave concern about emotional deprivation among hospitalised children. Talbot et al (1947) made a significant contribution to the understanding of FTT with their exploration of the interface between emotional, nutritional and endocrine disturbances in children with unexplained growth failure. He and his coworkers established the link between poor growth and deprivation and inadequate caloric intake. They also identified psychosocial dysfunction in these children's families and so applied the concept of failure to thrive in institutions to FTT in the home. They suggested that as a result of nutritional deprivation these children might be secreting subnormal amounts of growth hormone. Thus, a link between psychosocial disturbance, inadequate caloric intake, endocrine disturbances and growth failure was postulated. This was some of the work that laid the foundation for broadening the perspectives of later workers who explored the role of the caretaker, as well as the effect of the physical and emotional environment, on the growing child both in the home and in institutions (Barbero & Shaheen, 1967; Chase & Martin, 1970; Coleman & Provence, 1957; Glaser et al, 1968; Leonard et al, 1966; Patton & Gardner, 1962).

MODELS OF FAILURE TO THRIVE

Many workers have tended to place the aetiology of FTT into two distinct categories: organic and non-organic. On the one hand it is considered that the child who has an organic (structural, genetic, metabolic, infectious, neurologic, etc.) cause for his/her poor growth fails to thrive as a result of the disease process. Although it is generally agreed that illness during childhood is psychologically stressful for the child and the family, most believe that it is the pathological organic process that leads to the failure to thrive rather than the psychological stress. On the other hand, children who fail to thrive without a clearly identifiable organic (non-organic) cause are frequently felt to be neglected by their caretakers so that their failure to thrive is explained by inadequate nutrition as well as inadequate and/or inappropriate stimulation and nurturing. In short, they are viewed as abused and neglected (Kempe et al, 1980). Thus, a dichotomy is presented. FTT is either the result of an organic disturbance or of psychosocial dysfunction.

Silverman and Roy (1983) have taken a somewhat different approach to the classification of FTT. They have identified three growth patterns found among children with FTT. Pattern I consists of subnormal head circumference with weight and height proportionately reduced. Pattern II involves a normal or enlarged head circumference with weight only slightly reduced or at times proportionate to height. In pattern III there is a normal head circumference with weight reduced out of proportion to height (Fig. 7.1).

Pattern I children frequently have central nervous system disorders, congenital malformations, dysmorphic syndromes or chromosomal abnormalities. There may also have been a history of prenatal or perinatal insult such

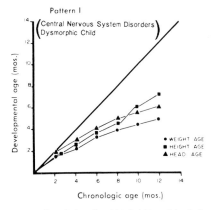

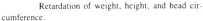

Retardation of weight, height, and head circumference.

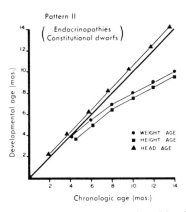

Retardation of height greater than weight and normal head circumference.

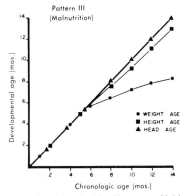

Fig. 7.1 Three patterns of growth retardation (Taken from Silverman & Roy, 1983)

Retardation of weight with near normal height and head growth.

as congenital infection or birth asphyxia resulting in central nervous system injury.

The second pattern of growth disturbance is frequently associated with a variety of dwarfism syndromes, endocrine and metabolic disturbances and constitutional factors. Gastrointestinal problems or other chronic illnesses can also be seen with this pattern of growth failure and need to be taken into consideration in the assessment of the child who may appear to be typical of the second pattern (Palmer, 1982).

The third pattern, which is the most common, is usually associated with inadequate caloric intake. This may be related to underlying gastrointestinal disorders or to any other chronic illness in which there is inadequate nutrition. Also included in this group are children who have no underlying organic basis for their failure to thrive.

All these models, although of heuristic value, appear too simple and unidimensional. One of the arguments presented in this chapter is that FTT is multidimensional and that the categories are not clear-cut but in reality are frequently blurred and fused. One of the advantages of this lack of precision and lack of clarity is that it forces one to evaluate the child and family from many different perspectives. However, this lack of precision can be disquieting. One way of relieving this uneasiness would be to use the term 'growth failure' for the child with primarily organic disease and the term 'failure to thrive' for the child with no underlying organic disease. This differentiation of nomeclature has, to some extent, already occurred (Goldbloom, 1982).

'FTT IS A SYMPTOM, NOT A DISEASE'

In considering FTT or growth failure one must continually bear in mind that these are not diagnoses. Rather, they are signs and symptoms of some underlying condition or circumstance whose nature needs to be identified. Furthermore, FTT is not a single entity and does not have a single cause, even in the same patient. Indeed, there may be several factors contributing to the failure to thrive, not the least of which may be the child himself. Therefore, the task is first to diagnose the cause(s) of the condition(s) or circumstance(s) leading to the FTT or growth failure and then to institute treatment followed by an assessment of the effectiveness of that treatment. Before one can embark on this task, however, one must have a description or definition of the symptom. There have been a number of definitions of FTT which have included children whose weight has been consistently below the third centile or whose weight is 80% of the ideal weight for their age (Accardo, 1982). In this chapter, however, a child who is failing to thrive is defined as one who crosses the percentile curves of weight by two standard deviations or who has a persistent deviation below his/her own established growth curve (Cupoli et al, 1980). There is, however, an aspect other than weight gain that I believe should also be considered. The definition in *Chamber's 20th Century Dictionary* of the word 'thrive' is, 'to grow: to grow healthily and vigorously: . . . to flourish'. There is more to thriving or failing to thrive than mere weight gain or lack thereof. There is a lack of 'well being', psychologically as well as physically. Thus, both the child's physical and psychological well-being must be considered in the definition and ultimately the evaluation of failure to thrive.

In the following sections I would like to present three groups of children with FTT or growth failure: (1) those with primarily organic causes for their FTT; (2) those with primarily non-organic causes; and (3) those with a combination of organic and psychological factors leading to their poor weight gain, growth failure and lack of well-being.

ORGANIC FAILURE TO THRIVE

Bearing this definition in mind, let us then return to the dichotomy between organic versus non-organic FTT. It has been well documented that ongoing illness involving any physiological or biochemical system can result in growth failure. Thus, children with heart disease, metabolic and endocrine disorders, neurological disease or dysfunction, chronic pulmonary or renal disease, chronic infection with or without immunological, oncological or haemotological disease, structural or functional gastrointestinal disorder, birth defects and children of very low birth weight with major sequelae all can suffer from growth failure (Accardo, 1982). When these conditions are present it is frequently a relatively straightforward process to make the diagnosis. All too often there are obvious signs and symptoms as well as laboratory findings that lead the clinician to the correct diagnosis. Treatment and cure may be difficult, but diagnosis or at least categorisation can be easily accomplished.

It is not the purpose of this chapter to delineate all the known organic causes of growth failure. What should be noted though, is that there is a reported variable incidence of organic versus non-organic causes for growth failure. Some authors indicate that the most common causes for FTT or growth failure are non-organic (Sills, 1978), while others indicate that there can be a relatively high incidence of FTT associated with organic disease (Hannaway, 1970; Berwick et al, 1982). These differences, I would hazard to say, reflect the various institutions reporting FTT and perhaps the authors' particular biases and the patient population (Mitchell et al, 1980).

NON-ORGANIC FAILURE TO THRIVE

Let us now turn to the majority of children with non-organic failure to thrive (NFTT). Among this group of children one encounters the family which is highly dysfunctional, often neglectful and abusive and where the parents have a history of being abused themselves (Steele, 1980). The relationship between the parents themselves is disturbed; they are unable to reach out for help and have little access to meaningful support systems.

The parents, most frequently the mother, are individuals with a poor self-image. They are frequently immature, depressed and unable to respond to the child's needs to the extent that they often provide inadequate nurturance and inadequate nutrition (Whitten et al, 1969). The father is often out of the home or is disengaged from the life of the family. At times the roles of the parent and child may be reversed, with the mother being the needy, dependent one and the baby being expected to fulfil the nurturing role. An interesting typology has been provided by Evans et al (1972), based on their research with families in which children were failing to thrive. They described three different family types that may be helpful in predicting the prognosis for families with children having NFTT. Group I was made up of families living under good conditions and providing good physical care for the child. Mother had had a severe loss within four months of the birth of the child and was acutely and severely depressed. The relationship with the child was strained and the mother was unsure of herself. However, the hospital course went quite smoothly with the mother being involved with the hospital staff and the outcome for all concerned was good. Group II consisted of families who were chronically depressed in which the child or children were just one more chronic problem. These families lived under highly deprived circumstances in which the mother-child interaction was very strained and in which the prognosis was guarded unless exceptional intervention was provided. Group III was the most extremely deprived group and had the highest potential for physical abuse. Living conditions might be good but the child was neglected and the mother was extremely hostile and angry. The child was perceived as 'bad' and was handled in an abrupt and angry fashion. The hospital course was stormy and the prognosis very poor.

Pollitt et al (1975), rather than looking at families per se, have focused on mothers of children with NFTT. As a result of their study they concluded that these mothers tended to relate less often to their children, tended to use physical punishment more frequently and so had less of an opportunity to establish a meaningful synchrony with their child. This may have been triggered by the child's particular idiosyncrasies or the mother's own particular stressful childhood.

Egeland et al (1980) have noted that mothers whose children fail to thrive are frequently anxious, lack competence and confidence in their caretaking abilities and have poor interactions with their children. Those studied had less understanding and awareness of the difficulties and demands involved in being a parent and tended to be more aggressive, hostile and defensive when under stress.

No matter what the adult disturbance, one must always bear in mind that the child has a role in what is obviously a disordered transactional relationship (Kotelchuck, 1980) and that role and its nature must be identified. There has been a tendency for workers to focus on the mother's deficiencies (and those in the family constellation including fathers) as well as the abusive environment when addressing children with non-organic FTT. These parents have frequently been viewed pejoratively without taking into consideration the total interaction. Usually the disturbance lies within the parent and may be projected on to the child. There may, however, also be some profound environmental and developmental stresses that result in the provision of inadequate nutrition and nurturance. On the other hand, Chatoor and Egan (1983) have identified a group of children whose FTT generally occurs in the course of the second part of the first year, during the developmental phase of separation–individuation. The child attempts to define himself/herself and to separate from the mother by refusing to eat, which has the opposite effect of involving the mother more deeply in the feeding process and so creating feeding as the battleground for the process of separation–individuation. Under these circumstances one may indeed encounter family stress and dysfunction, but it is not the same as abusive, depressing and isolated circumstances described above. Here the child becomes engaged along with the parent in the evolution and maintenance of the failure to thrive. Aside from identifying another aetiology for failure to thrive this group serves to highlight the role the child may play in the unfolding of the FTT, be it under neglectful circumstances or as part of a developmental conflict.

There is another form of non-organic failure to thrive that must be noted, although it is not encountered with great frequency. This is the FTT associated with deprivation dwarfism described by Powell et al (1967a, 1967b) and reaffirmed by Green et al (1984). In this entity the child presents with hypopituitarism. There are endocrine abnormalities along with very severe behaviour disturbances. Neither the endocrine abnormalities nor the behavioural disturbances resolve until the child is removed from the abusive neglecting home. Moreover, even if the child is treated with replacement therapy there is no increase in growth or resolution of the other endocrine abnormalities until the patient is removed from the insulting environment.

In reviewing these various ways of classifying FTT and growth failure, what emerges is that historically a rather rigid and unidimensional approach has been taken with this symptom. The child has either an organic or a non-organic cause for the FTT. FTT is viewed as an 'either/or' phenomenon rather than as the result of multiple interacting forces. Prototypes are presented which may be helpful at a superficial level but which obscure the complexity, multidimensionality and transactional nature of FTT. A narrow approach towards diagnosis and management are fostered, and the fact that environmental and psychological factors must be considered in the face of organic illness (Goldbloom, 1982; Homer & Ludwig, 1981) is frequently ignored and vice versa.

Despite this historical predilection for dichotomous thinking, several authors have arrived at several different and creative ways of viewing failure to thrive, at least in the category of NFTT. (1) One such way is to include it in the spectrum of feeding disorders, as does Woolston (1983), and then, using a classification similar to the one derived by Evans et al (1972) to elucidate and delineate further what may be differing subcategories of dysfunction in the child, the parent and the parent–child interaction. (2) As has been noted above, there is the view that non-organic FTT is the result of inadequate mothering. Rutter (1979) has reviewed the arguments supporting this view and has noted that, although distortions in the early mother–child relationship can have long term adverse developmental and psychological sequelae, there is also a resiliency on the infant's part, allowing it to recover from these early adverse circumstances. Moreover, he has pointed out that deprivation involves a heterogeneous group of adversities which operate through different psychological mechanisms. Early separation, abnormal bonding (i.e. the child perceived as evil, deviant or does not fulfil the parent's needs or expectations) and inappropriate nurturance, all play a part in the child's growth and development. (3) Skuse (1985) has taken the view that undernutrition is the underlying factor for these children's failure to thrive, but undernutrition can certainly be influenced by a host of differing variables and maladaptive behaviours that exist within the child, the parent and the family. (4) Kotelchuck (1980) in his review of non-organic FTT, takes a very broad view of the problem and emphasises the heterogeneity of the population. He and Skuse agree that under some circumstances NFTT may result from inadequate and neglectful parenting. However, this is by no means always the case. Indeed, he emphasises the role the child may play in the genesis and perpetuation of the FTT. He also raises the question that if one uses a child-oriented model of FTT the question is still left open as to whether the underlying cause is social or biomedical or some combination of these factors.

In the light of the above discussion, I would like to suggest a third category of children with failure to thrive who have an organic as well as a psychological basis for their poor growth (Goldson et al, 1985a, 1985b). Indeed, this group of children may represent the majority of patients seen in hospitals with the symptom of FTT. This is a group of patients who *do* have organic illness but who also have underlying psychological disturbances that may antedate their illness or arise during the course of their illness. These psychological dynsfunctions may arise as a result of environmental stresses, family characteristics or may be a function of the child's particular temperamental makeup and response to stress (Thomas & Chess, 1977). The existence of these psychological factors in many circumstances may alter the course of the organic illness. This group of children can be divided into roughly three categories. The first category consists of children with subtle neuromotor problems who have difficulty eating because of their oral-motor disturbances. The parents and professionals frequently misinterpret the difficulty in eating as being food refusal on the child's part with the caretaker subsequently forcing the child to eat. The child then indeed refuses to eat, fails to gain weight and the parent is accused of being either incompetent or negligent. The child frequently is irritable, resists the food (bottle or breast) and generally is behaviourally and physiologically disorganised.

The second category of children refuse to eat because of an aversive experience during eating. Such children may have allergic reactions during eating or have gastro-oesophageal reflux. Other children in this category may have required prolonged parenteral nutrition and so never have had the normal experience of eating (Geertsma et al, 1985). Consequently, once they are physiologically able to eat they may refuse to do so.

Finally, there are a number of children with organic problems who respond to the stress of their illness and the stresses in their environment (home or hospital) by refusing to eat even after their organic illness has resolved.

There is then a third category of children who have significant psychiatric disorders, such as rumination or self-induced gagging resulting in vomiting, who lose control over themselves and progress to a state of severe protein–energy malnutrition and profound failure to thrive.

In summary, one can divide children who do not gain weight as they would be expected to into three different groups. First, there is the child with an underlying organic disorder whose growth failure is the result of the pathological process. Second, there is the child with no organic basis for his/her failure to thrive who rather fails to grow as a result of inadequate nutrition either because of neglect or a dysfunctional environment or because of a developmental conflict which results in food refusal. Finally, there is a group of children who have organic disease which is complicated by their own psychological characteristics and eating-related responses to stress and illness. That is, they refuse to eat within the context of an acute or chronic illness and frequently continue their food refusal even after the organic issues have been resolved.

IMPLICATIONS FOR THE TREATMENT AND MANAGEMENT OF FAILURE TO THRIVE

Let us for a moment set aside these a priori groups and start with the premise that growth failure or failure to thrive is the result of the interaction between the child's organic disturbance, his psychological make-up and responses, and the environment in which he finds himself. That is to say, whenever a child fails to thrive one must take into consideration all three broad areas. This then suggests that, for example, a child with cardiac disease with a resulting growth failure can also have psychological and environmental dysfunction influencing the course of the illness. This would also hold for children with primary gastroenterological or allergic disorders, or any organic illness for that matter. On the other hand, the child who is significantly malnourished as a result of parental neglect or of food refusal or rumination may also have a significant organic problem which has to be resolved along with the psychological and environmental ones. In a word, among the tasks for the clinician is the need to recognise that all these aspects of the child's world — the organic, the psychological and the environmental — influence the condition and that, as part of the diagnosis, the relative importance or weight of each of these factors has to be determined. If one accepts this formulation, then the approach taken must be broad based, interdisciplinary and comprehensive. Starting with fixed ideas or a priori diagnoses is not productive and may even delay the diagnosis and the institution of treatment. The evaluation of the child with FTT must therefore include the concurrent assessment of the organic, the psychological, and the psychosocial and, the diagnosis of non-organic FTT should not be made by exclusion. On the contrary, just as one would make a positive diagnosis of failure to thrive as a result of renal disease, so one can make the diagnosis of FTT as a result of psychosocial dysfunction with inadequate nutrition, affirmatively.

Although such terms as non-organic and organic FTT have been employed, the goal of the approach advocated in this chapter, be it in an inpatient or outpatient setting, has been to take a broad, unprejudiced view regarding causality, from the outset of the evaluation. As noted above, there are children who fail to thrive because of organic or non-organic factors or as a result of a combination of organic and psychological factors. However, no matter what the 'major' aetiology may be, other factors certainly play a part, and it is as important to identify them as it is to identify the predominant factor. In the following discussion let us tease apart the three broad factors that can play a part in initiating and perpetuating FTT.

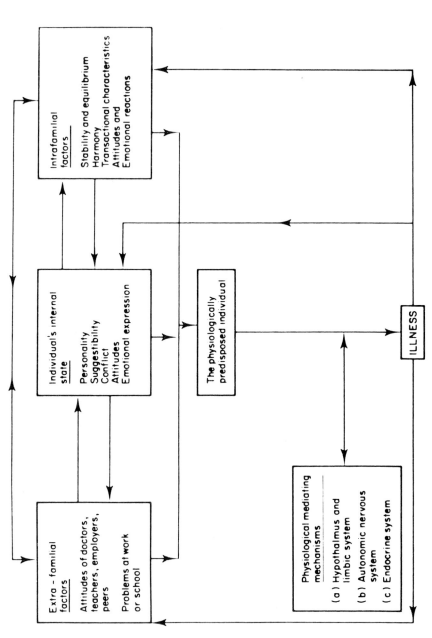

Fig. 7.2 Model for the interaction between the physiological, psychological and environmental factors and their role in the generation of illness. (Taken from Lask, 1982)

The initiation and perpetuation of FTT

One of the aspects that must be addressed in the evaluation of FTT or growth failure is the organic component. It has been stated in the literature (Sills, 1978; Berwick et al, 1982) that the yield of extensive laboratory investigations is not very great in ascertaining the causes of FTT. This is certainly true, although it may depend on the institution and its population. Nevertheless, an extensive laboratory evaluation taken with a 'shot gun' approach is rarely helpful, is expensive and can be harmful for the child. Instead, after a comprehensive history and physical examination have been obtained some basic laboratory studies should be done. These should include a complete blood count, urinanalysis and culture, blood urea nitrogen, serum electrolytes, stool examination including ova and parasites and liver function studies. With these few tests one can rule out some of the most common organic causes for failure to thrive as well as get a baseline level of the child's physiological status. Obviously, if there are abnormal findings one would then pursue further investigations. However, if the laboratory findings are normal there is no need to obtain further studies 'just for completeness's sake' or 'to rule out' other more esoteric disorders.

Concurrent with the organic investigations, psychosocial and psychological assessments should also be performed. A comprehensive evaluation of the family should be obtained looking at items such as: the family history, style of family functioning, family structure, the parental perception of the child, past and present stresses and the family's response to stress, parental interactions, parent-child interactions, family support systems and coping strategies. See Figure 7.2 for a conceptualisation of the various factors involved in the generation of illness.

Children who fail to thrive or who have sustained growth failure have arrived at this condition over a period of time and have usually had considerable impact on the family, and one is not going to be able to understand all that has transpired in one hurried interview. Time and parental trust and confidence are needed if one is to arrive at an understanding of the psychosocial condition and then be able to put it into a meaningful context with respect to the child's failure to thrive. This applies to failure to thrive or growth failure irrespective of the underlying aetiology or aetiologies.

The third factor in the diagnostic equation is the child. Here again a broad approach must be taken. Aside from physiological disturbances, what are the child's developmental and behavioural characteristics? How do they influence his/her caretakers? What do they tell us about the child's role in initiating, influencing and even maintaining the condition of poor growth or failure to thrive? One of the first things one would want to know is what is the child's developmental level of functioning. Using any number of standardised developmental scales or psychometric tests, one can determine this level as well as identify the child's strengths and weaknesses. Another aspect of the assessment of the child would be of his behaviour. Children with non-organic FTT have been described as being hypotonic with abnormal posturing. They tend to be apathetic, passive and irritable, yet cry very little and have decreased vocalisations. They have poor appetites and histories of feeding problems, do not cuddle, have poor eye contact and relate poorly to their physical and emotional environments (Bullard et al, 1967; Krieger & Sargent, 1967; Powell & Low, 1983). Taking the time to observe the child interacting with strangers or familiar persons, adults or peers can be helpful in understanding some of the child's interactive capacities and coping strategies. This, in turn, may lead to more insights into the child's past and present experiences and shed some light on diagnosis as well as helping with intervention strategies. The point to be made is that it is important to arrive at some knowledge of how the child relates to his/her world.

Another of the general issues for the child failing to grow or to thrive is that of eating. Is the child being offered enough appropriate food in a relaxed, comfortable, interactive setting? Is the process of receiving food and eating a pleasurable experience from both a physical and an interactional viewpoint? Does the caretaker enjoy feeding the child or is there conflict? Is the child able to suck or chew and swallow? Is the child refusing to eat and why? What are the aversive experiences that have led to this negative behaviour? If any or a combination of these circumstances is the case, what are the reasons for the disturbance in eating? What elicits the child's behaviour and how can that behaviour be extinguished?

In order to answer these questions a feeding assessment is of the utmost importance. This should include not only an evaluation of the child's oral-motor functioning but also of his/her behavioural interaction both with the primary caretaker and with a professional skilled in the care and feeding or children.

MANAGEMENT OF THE CHILD WITH FAILURE TO THRIVE AND THE FAMILY

The management of the child with FTT and working with the family are usually difficult. Some families have sought the help of many physicians with little success in diagnosis and so are frustrated and angry. Others have been neglectful of the child and so there is a question of the adequacy of parenting and questions of abuse. In virtually all circumstances there is stress and anxiety. Thus, if one is to succeed in arriving at a diagnosis of FTT and successfully managing the problem at least three conditions have to be met.

First, the approach towards diagnosis and management must be inter-disciplinary. No one discipline has all of the knowledge and expertise to diagnose and treat the child with failure to thrive. It then follows that the diagnosis and treatment must include different disciplines with flexible and individualised approaches. This, however, does not mean that each discipline goes about its own evaluation independently. Instead, a team with one member being designated the coordinator must establish a plan of action which is agreed upon. Furthermore, it must be decided who will provide information to the parents and how it will be delivered. The family must be protected from 'too many cooks, who may spoil the broth' and create confusion.

Second, the physical setting in which the family and child are cared for and assessed should be conducive to a more natural parent–child interaction. Admission to a busy acute-care ward is not the way to diagnose and manage the child and family with FTT. Indeed, many patients can be managed on an outpatient basis. However, if a child is not desperately ill but still requires inpatient management, care should be provided in a family-oriented, relaxed setting where nurses and other health care professionals can get to know the child and parents well and work with them in a consistent, unhurried manner.

Third, the approach of the staff, be it in the inpatient or in the ambulatory care setting must be non-judgmental and non-accusatory. Parents of children with FTT have low enough self-esteem and such a sense of guilt that they do not need to have these feelings reinforced by censorious professionals. The parent should be welcomed into the hospital or clinic setting and encouraged to participate in the care of the child. Ideally, the parent should become an ally in the quest to identify and clarify the child's and the family's difficulties. However, this may not always be possible.

In any discussion of failure to thrive one must address strategies for intervention. If the child is severely malnourished one must obviously treat the medical condition and only then the family. If the major factors are psychosocial, these must be addressed so as to ensure the child's safety. If the major factors are developmental, they must be dealt with from that perspective, meeting the child's and the family's needs. There is no one way to manage the child and family with FTT, and one must rather look at and balance the interacting forces and arrive at a treatment programme that is comprehensive and effective. But, what is effective?

MEASUREMENT OF PROGRESS

At a superficial level, whether or not the child gains weight, makes developmental progress (if he/she was delayed) and begins to thrive are one set of criteria. How the family progresses and is able to function is another. If the child has a chronic metabolic disease and the family is unable to adapt to the child's needs and remains dysfunctional, treatment and improvement of the metabolic disorder alone does not signify success. It is only when the child and the family have been managed so that they are both functional, that one can speak of effective treatment.

In order to determine effectiveness one must establish and provide a system for ongoing follow up. Again, this should be done from an interdisciplinary and interactional viewpoint using those disciplines that have played the predominant parts in diagnosis and treatment. Criteria for improvement — physiological, psychological and psychosocial — should be established, agreed upon and fulfilled in order for one to determine whether or not treatment has been successful.

PROGNOSIS

In considering children with growth failure or FTT one inevitably must examine their overall prognosis. There is no clear-cut consensus as to how these children and their families fare in the long term. Some authors have talked about children with FTT who have also sustained non-accidental trauma. Others have studied the outcome for children who are malnourished as a result of extreme poverty. There has been some discussion about children with specific organic problems that have resulted in growth failure.

For those children suffering from non-organic FTT some have described a grim long term outcome while others have noted that with appropriate intervention these children may do well (Glaser et al, 1968; Mitchell et al, 1980), but it has been noted that children with severe protein-calorie malnutrition, whose deficits are not corrected early, do not do well, especially in the area of cognition (Chase & Martin, 1970; Carvioto et al, 1966; Grantham-McGregor et al, 1982; Oates et al, 1985). Children with major organic problems also have variable outcomes.

There is therefore a somewhat grim picture painted for the untreated child with FTT, but, rather than dwelling on this, let us take a somewhat different approach. If we accept the conceptualisation of failure to thrive as the result of the interaction between organic, psychological and psychosocial factors it becomes apparent that each child, depending on his or her particular circumstances, temperament and response to intervention will have a different outcome. The emphasis therefore should be to encourage early identification and comprehensive assessment with a broad based approach towards treatment as the best means of achieving the best result for these children and their families.

SUMMARY AND CONCLUSIONS

In this chapter I have tried, first, to provide a historical backdrop for the topic of failure to thrive and to present some of the theory and controversy surrounding the subject; second, to elucidate the various categories of failure to thrive or growth failure and also address their limitations; and, finally, to suggest a somewhat different approach toward the conceptualisation of failure to thrive and provide a rational and comprehensive approach towards diagnosis and treatment.

The child who fails to thrive or sustains growth failure does so as the result of the interaction of many factors. His or her condition is not unidimensional but rather multidimensional in scope. Moreover, it must be viewed in the context of the child's individual psychological makeup and within the family context. This makes the diagnosis and management all the more difficult since it is not only the child, with his or her organic or psychological problems, that must be treated, but also the family. However, a broad based approach decreases the risk of missing the underlying aetiology or aetiologies and the chances of a successful outcome will be improved. The accurate, efficient and comprehensive diagnosis and management of the child who fails to thrive is one of the major challenges that confronts the practitioner caring for children today.

ACKNOWLEDGEMENTS

I would like to express my appreciation to Drs L. Kotelchuck, H. Cantwell and J. LaCrosse and to Ms T. Schiavone for their critical review of the manuscript and their helpful criticisms and suggestions.

REFERENCES

Accardo P J 1982a Growth and development: an interactional context for failure to thrive. In: Accardo P J (ed) Failure to Thrive in Infancy and Early Childhood: a Multidisciplinary Team Approach. University Park Press, Baltimore, p. 3–18
Accardo P J 1982b Failure to Thrive in Infancy and Early Childhood:a Multidisciplinary Team Approach. University Park Press, Baltimore
Bakwin 1949 Emotional deprivation in children. Journal of Pediatrics 35: 512
Barbero G C, Shaheen E 1967 Environmental failure to thrive: a clinical view. Journal of Pediatrics 71: 639–644
Berwick D M, Levy J C, Kleinerman R 1982 Failure to thrive: diagnostic yield of hospitalization. Archives of Disease in Childhood 57: 347–351
Bullard D M, Glaser H H, Heagarty M C, Pivchik E C 1967 Failure to thrive in the 'neglected' child. American Journal of Orthopsychiatry 37: 680–690
Chapin D H 1908 A plan for dealing with atrophic infants and children. Archives of Pediatrics 25: 491–496
Chase H P, Martin H P 1970 Undernutrition and child development. New England Journal of Medicine 282: 933–939
Chatoor I, Egan J 1983 Non-organic failure to thrive and dwarfism due to food refusal: a separation disorder. Journal of the American Academy of Child Psychiatry 22: 294–301
Coleman R W, Provence S 1957 Environmental retardation (hospitalism) in infants living in families. Pediatrics 19: 255–292
Cravioto J, Delicardie E R, Birch H G 1966 Nutrition, growth and neurointegrative development: an experimental and ecologic study. Pediatrics (Supplement 2) 38: 321–333
Cupoli J M, Hallock J A, Barness L A 1980 Failure to thrive. Current Problems in Pediatrics 10: 1–43
Egeland B, Beitenbucher M, Rosenberg D 1980 Prospective study of the significance of life stress in the etiology of child abuse. Journal of Consultative and Clinical Psychology 45: 195–205
Evans S L, Reinhart J B, Succop R A 1972 Failure to thrive: a study of 45 children and their families. Journal of the American Academy of Child Psychiatry 11: 440–457
Geertsma M A, Hyams J S, Pelletier J M, Reiter S 1985 Feeding resistance after parenteral hyperalimentation. American Journal of Diseases of Children 139: 255–256
Glaser H H, Heagarty M C, Bullard D M Jr, Pivchik B A 1968 Physical and psychological development of children with early failure to thrive. Journal of Pediatrics 73: 690–698
Goldbloom R R 1982 Failure to thrive. Pediatric Clinics of North America 29: 151–166
Goldson E, Milla F J, Bentovim A 1985a Failure to thrive: a transactional issue. Family Systems Medicine 3: 205–213
Goldson E, Bentovim A, Milla P J 1985b Failure to thrive: another approach. Clinical Research 33: 110A
Grantham-McGregor S M, Powell C, Stewart M, Schofield W N 1982 Longitudinal study of growth and development of young Jamaican children recovering from severe protein-energy malnutrition. Developmental Medicine and Child Neurology 24: 321–331
Green W H, Campbell M, David R 1984 Psychological dwarfism: a critical review of the evidence. Journal of the American Academy of Child Psychiatry 23: 39–40

Hannaway P J 1970 Failure to thrive: a study of 100 infants and children. Clinical Pediatrics 9: 96–99

Homer C, Ludwig S 1981 Categorization of etiology of failure to thrive. American Journal of Diseases of Children 135: 848–851

Kempe R S, Cutler C, Dean J 1980 The infant with failure-to-thrive. In: Kempe C H, Helfer R E (eds) The Battered Child. 3rd ed, revised and expanded. University of Chicago Press, Chicago, London, p. 163–182

Kotelchuck M 1980 Non-organic failure to thrive: the status of interactional and environmental etiologic theories. Advances in Behavioural Pediatrics 1: 29–51

Krieger I, Sargent D A 1967 A postural sign in the sensory deprivation syndrome in infants. Journal of Pediatrics 70: 332–337

Lask B 1982 Physical illness and the family. In: Bentovim A, Barnes G G, Cooklin A (eds) Family Therapy: Complementary Frameworks of Theory and Practice. Vol 2. Grune and Stratton, New York, p. 441–461

Leonard M F, Rhymes J P, Solnit A J 1966 Failure to thrive in infants: a family problem. American Journal of Diseases of Children 3: 600–612

Mitchell W G, Gorrel R W, Greenberg R A 1980 Failure-to-thrive: a study in a primary care setting. Epidemiology and follow- up. Pediatrics 65: 971–977

Oates R K, Peacock A, Forrest D 1985 Long-term effects of nonorganic failure to thrive. Pediatrics 75: 36–40

Palmer F B 1982 Gastroenterology. In: Accardo P J (ed) Failure to Thrive in Infancy and Early Childhood: a Multidisciplinary Team Approach. University Park Press, Baltimore, p. 153–167

Patton R G, Gardner I 1962 Influence of family environment on growth: the syndrome of 'maternal deprivation'. Pediatrics 30: 957–962

Pollitt E, Eichler A W, Chan C-K 1975 Psychosocial development and behavior of mothers of failure-to-thrive children. American Journal of Orthopsychiatry 45: 525–537

Powell G F, Brasel J A, Blizzard R M 1967a Emotional deprivation and growth retardation simulating idiopathic hypopituitarism. I. Clinical evaluation of the syndrome. New England Journal of Medicine 276: 1272–1278

Powell G F, Brasel J A, Blizzard R M 1967b Emotional deprivation and growth retardation simulating idiopathic hypopituitariam. II. Endocrinologic evaluation of the syndrome. New England Journal of Medicine 276: 1279–1283

Powell D F, Low J 1983 Behavior in nonorganic failure to thrive. Journal of Developmental and Behavioral Pediatrics 4: 26–33

Radbill S X 1968 A history of child abuse and infanticide. In: Helfer R E, Kempte C H (eds) The Battered Child. The University of Chicago Press, Chicago, London

Radbill S X 1980 Children in a world of violence: a history of child abuse. In: Kempe C H, Helfer R E (eds) The Battered Child. 3rd ed. The University of Chicago Press, Chicago, London, p. 3–20

Ross C J 1980 The lessons of the past: defining and controling child abuse in the United States. In:
Gerbner G, Ross C J, Zigler E (eds) an Agenda for Action. Oxford University Press, New York,
Oxford, p. 63–81

Rutter M 1979 Maternal deprivation, 1972–1978: new findings, new concepts, new approaches.
Child Development 50: 283–305

Sills R H 1978 Failure to thrive: the role of the clinical and laboratory evaluation.
American Journal of Diseases of Children 132: 967–969

Silverman A, Roy C C 1983 Pediatric Clinical Gastroenterology, Chapter 1. The C.V. Mosby Company, St. Louis, Toronto, London, p. 3–9

Skuse D. Non-organic failure to thrive: a reappraisal. Archives of Disease in Childhood 60: 173–178

Smith C A, Berenberg W 1970 The concept of failure to thrive. Pediatrics 46: 661–662

Spitz R A 1945 Hospitalism. Psychoanalytic Study of the Child 1: 53–74

Spitz R A 1946 Hospitalism: a follow-up report. Psychoanalytic Study of the Child 2: 113–117

Spitz R A, Wolf K M 1946 Anaclitic depression. Psychoanalytic Study of the Child 2: 313–342

Steele B 1980 Psychodynamic factors in child abuse. In: Kempe C H, Helfer R E (eds) The Battered Child. 3rd ed. University of Chicago Press, Chicago, London, p. 49–85

Talbot N B, Sobel E H, Burke B S, et al 1947 Dwarfism in healthy children: its possible relation to emotional, nutritional and endocrine disturbances. New England Journal of Medicine 236: 783–793

Thomas A, Chess S 1977 Temperament and Development. Brunner$Mazel, New York

Whitten C F, Pettit M G, Fischoff J 1969 Evidence that growth failure from maternal deprivation is secondary to undereating. Journal of the American Medical Association 209: 1675–1682

Woolston J L 1983 Eating disorders in infancy and early childhood. Journal of the American Academy of Child Psychiatry 22: 114–121

The National Child Health Computer System

INTRODUCTION

It is a frequently overlooked truism that advances in clinical techniques are of benefit only if they are effectively delivered to the consumer. Similarly, developments in preventive medicine achieve their full potential only if they are delivered to the highest risk population. It is also well established that there is a social class gradient to the uptake of preventive health services, not least those for children, and that this uptake is negatively correlated with risk of developmental delay or other problems. Furthermore, there is considerable experience that at the upper end of the social class spectrum there is, on occasion, a failure or unwillingness to recognise a developmental problem, so that the seeking of professional help is unnecessarily delayed. In order that children should not suffer through the failures of adult behaviour, there is, therefore, a particular ethical responsibility on the providers and managers of preventive child health services to ensure that there is not only equal access, but also effective equal opportunity of uptake for all children.

Early applications

It was in 1962 that West Sussex County Council Health Department introduced a computer system for scheduling immunisation appointments for pre-school children and recording the outcome. The basic philosophy of that system still holds true in the current national system. The central feature is the creation of a population register of name, address, date of birth and general practitioner for newborn children and those moving into the authority. From this, parents are invited to indicate the treatment centre they wish to attend for immunisation and the antigens they wish their child to receive. The computer program then generates appropriate appointments linking together the needs of children and the availability of sessions in a forthcoming period. The detail, though, has become much more sophisticated as both computing abilities and clinical requirements have become more refined.

The original West Sussex system was shown to be effective, and was described at the time by Galloway (1963). Subsequently, its costs and benefits were analysed, and the system was shown by Saunders (1970) to be justified on economic grounds alone.

As a result, closely related systems were designed by a number of other health authorities, particularly those in shire counties. Whereas such local systems were able to accommodate local needs, the design was often piecemeal, with little compatibility between systems, creating particular problems when records were transferred or staff moved. Moreover, the authorities which found it easiest to finance such local developments were inevitably those in more affluent areas, which by definition were likely to include a lower proportion of high risk children. Indeed, as a result the initial analyses showing higher immunisation uptake rates in areas with computer systems (as published by Bussey and Holmes, 1978) were challenged on the grounds that they merely reflected social class structures. Though much more difficult to standardise for this dimension, a further study by Bussey and Harris (1979) demonstrated that, as far as measles vaccination was concerned, authorities with computer appointment systems had a higher uptake rate even when allowing for demographic factors.

Meanwhile, a number of authorities followed the logic through and realised that the same principles ought to be applied to pre-school developmental screening and to school health services. These applications are more complex to design, however, because of the wider variety of clinical practice and the need to record much more than a date of attendance and the procedure applied. Consequently, the number of local developments of pre-school health and school health systems was much lower, and even more restricted to the larger county authorities. Nevertheless, a study by Chesham et al (1975) has shown the same uptake benefits to apply.

THE NATIONAL SYSTEM

The concept

Though there was concern about the proliferation of unstandardised local systems, and about their inequitable distribution, it was the imminence of the 1974 National Health Service (NHS) reorganisation which created the impetus to design a national system. It must be recalled that until 1974 community health services, including preventive services for children, were the responsibility of local government. From April 1974 these local authority health departments became part of the new area health authorities. The Department of Health and Social Security (DHSS) was concerned that as part of the change over, local authorities might terminate access to their computers for systems which were no longer their responsibility. As few of the local systems were suitable for transfer to computers owned by the NHS at the time, there was a threat of cessation of service. The DHSS therefore commissioned the National Computer Centre to assess the requirements and determine the design for a national system to be available for any authority finding itself in that position.

The principles

Though the immediate motivation was to protect existing computer-based services, the potential creation of a national system also gave rise to a number of opportunities which have been grasped. In particular, these relate to standardisation of documentation, so that records transferred can be readily interpreted by the receiving authority. Similarly, with widespread use of one system, staff training is simplified and can to a larger degree be incorporated into basic professional training. However, the dangers of standardisation were also noted and have been avoided. There is no standard health care schedule within the national system, only standardised documents and data definitions — so each participating authority determines its own local schedule according to local needs and local consultation. Furthermore, though the system is normally operated on regional health authority computers, each district health authority is autonomous in its use of the system and has sole control over the activity and the data. Finally, the 'national' concept applies only to the availability of the computer programs — there is no national exchange of data and indeed this is not possible. This is a major asset in reassuring both the public and professional users that there is no possibility of sinister use of the records, control being local, but it does produce a need (as yet unfulfilled) to agree on a means of sharing *statistical* data if evaluative use is to be made of the service-based data.

The National Computer Centre, as part of their study, recommended the 'sun-satellite' concept, whereby a Child Register Module is focal to the operation of the system, with three separately designed 'satellite' modules for delivery of immunisation, pre-school health and school health. This leaves any health authority with a choice as to which combination of modules to operate, though within the system each child will have one comprehensive medical record.

The National Computer Centre proceeded to specify the system necessary for the Child Register and Immunisation Module, and the resultant specification was passed to the NHS for implementation. The then Welsh Health Technical Services Organisation, now reconstituted as the Welsh Health Common Services Authority, was selected as the centre of responsibility and produced the first programs to the supplied specification. The initial part of the system had to be released without full pilot operation.

CHILD REGISTER

The Child Register is created from information on each Notification of Birth, which by statute is completed for each newborn baby. A well established system already exists whereby information about any child born in an authority other than his or her authority of residence is passed on by the authority where the birth occurs. Information on the Child Register includes all the identification information necessary to generate appointments and to supply appropriate information to the child's general practitioner and health visitor. Information about each birth is also exchanged with the Registrar of Births. For operational and security reasons, the child register information about each child is kept separate from the medical file, being linked by a unique number.

This unique number is also used to identify the child whenever information is input on to the computer record, and it therefore appears on all appropriate documents. This number is comprised of: health authority code; Soundex Code based on the surname, date of birth and sex; a suffix used if two records would otherwise have an identical key and two check digits. The Soundex Code is based on a principle which is designed to overcome alternative spellings of surnames and converts the surname to a four-character code. The check digits are arithmetically derived from the remainder of the key and render it virtually impossible to enter information on to the wrong child's record by making an error in the remaining part of the key.

From the Child Register a full index is readily created, either on paper or on microfiche. This gives the child health office an index of all children, together with key information indicating the stages of health care delivery they have reached.

The accuracy and comprehensiveness of the child register is, however, dependent on the gathering of information. While notification of new births is generally accurate, the NHS is still without a formal and regular mechanism of notifying population movement. This system, like any other, is therefore very dependent on the knowledge and good local contacts of field staff, particularly health visitors. In addition, links with family practitioner committees may lead to an exchange of registration information, but this is of course dependent on the family changing its general practitioner registration.

IMMUNISATION MODULE

Facilities

In broad terms, the Immunisation Module works on the well tried principle of creating an immunisation record for each child on receipt of an immunisation consent. When it was first introduced, the system adopted the then normal principle of this document obtaining legal consent to prophylaxis, as a pre-requisite to appointments being issued. Subsequently, concern has been expressed about the appropriateness of this approach, not only because of the possibility of an uninformed consent being given in a period of postnatal euphoria, but also because of the need to get formally signed revisions to consent should subsequent information about the child or about clinical circumstances mean that the original consent is inappropriate. An alternative approach is now therefore available, whereby the initial consent is merely one to receive appointments, and the legal consent is obtained at the clinic at the time of commencement of each course of immunisation. While overcoming the former problems, this latter procedure does raise alternative issues, particularly the need for the parent or legal guardian and not a relative or friend to attend with the child. Each authority adopting the system therefore now has the choice of which consent pattern, and therefore which commensurate documentation, to use throughout its area.

As well as consent to immunisation or to receive appointments, the initial document also collects the parent's choice of immunisation centre. In implementing authorities, all community clinics normally take part within the system, and the opportunity exists for any general practitioner to take part too. Standard instructions are recorded for each immunisation centre concerning the frequency and duration of sessions. From this the computer system, on a weekly or fortnightly cycle, calculates which centres will hold sessions during the forthcoming period and which children recorded as attending that centre will fall due for immunisation. In priority order, appointments are then created, appointment cards raised and lists sent to the centres indicating which children have been scheduled. Each centre decides its own session frequencies and has a choice of appointment methods. At the session the professional staff record the antigens received, and for children who do not attend they show whether an excuse was received. When these lists are returned to the computer centre each child's record is updated. For non-attenders a further appointment will be issued for the next session, except that when a child has failed to attend twice without excuse the record is suspended and a notification produced to the appropriate health visitor so that the case can be followed up individually. Information can be recorded about unscheduled attenders, and item of service payment due to general practitioners is automatically calculated and notifed to the Family Practitioner Committee.

Batch numbers

It might be assumed that one important advantage of a computer system would be to record individual antigen batch numbers so that adverse reactions could be reported meaningfully and recipients of suspect batches quickly traced. Unfortunately, this has not yet proved possible because each manufacturer uses a different means of identifying batches and many of the codes are not readily computer compatible. Under the circumstances, to enter batch numbers into the system without an assurance that they could be reliably retrieved when needed would be unsafe, and therefore at present they are not recorded; instead, the source documents have to be retained. A further attempt at obtaining national agreement to a computer-compatible coding system is now in hand following the recommendations of the Steering Group on Health Services Information, published by the DHSS (Department of Health and Social Security, 1984a).

Resolution of initial limitations

An important lesson was learned when the initial version of the Child Register and Immunisation Module was released. This concerned the variety of health service practice and the consequent need to run full field trials to ensure that user requirements are met. Because the specifications for the early parts of the system were produced by computer scientists following discussion with a limited number of health authorities, when authorities came to adopt the system they found a number of considerable limitations to efficient use in their own localities, such as the computing convention that a month is a four week period, whereas in community clinic terms a monthly session relates to the calendar month. Because of anomalies such as these, it was felt essential to refine the Child Register and Immunisation Module before developing further parts of this system. Moreover, to ensure full NHS representation, the DHSS established a national committee, the Standard Immunisation System Development Steering Committe, with two nominated representatives from each region, together with professional representation, with executive power to specify to the centre of responsibility the amendments which were necessary. This approach proved slow but thorough, and by 1977 a series of developments had been completed to improve the system. This developed version of the system is now utilised by 60% of health authorities in England and Wales, and with completion of the other modules it is known that other authorities will be adopting it shortly.

CHILD HEALTH COMPUTING COMMITTEE

The lessons of obtaining representative input to design having been learned, and the initial limitations of the Immunisation Module having been rectified, in 1977 the Department of Health and Social Security arranged for the Standard Immunisation System Development Steering Committee to be superseded by the Child Health Computing Committee (CHCC). This new committee had the responsibility of supervising the maintenance of the existing modules and of developing the two further modules. Regional representation was reduced to one member and key professional bodies, including the British Paediatric Association, the Royal College of Obstetricians and Gynaecologists and the General Medical Services Committee, were included, together with the Office of Population Censuses and Surveys and representatives of Scotland and Northern Ireland. Under the aegis of this committee the design of the basic functions of the system has been completed.

PRE-SCHOOL MODULE

Basis of design

The objectives of this module are to use the same child register to schedule and record developmental surveillance. However, not only is this a much larger task than immunisation scheduling, but there is not the same level of national agreement as to what information should be recorded or the types of procedure which should be included. The design of this module therefore started from first principles, seeking to define the objectives of the module and the data items necessary and to learn from the experience of the systems then in action. The result was a detailed system specification which was agreed and published by the Child Health Computing Committee in 1979.

This system specification proposed using very much the same approach to the actual appointment scheduling aspects as is used for immunisation, including the choice by the parent of the centre to be attended, the determination by the centre of the schedule to be used and the identification to health visitors of persistent defaulters. However, because there is less agreement about appropriate schedules, each authority can simultaneously operate three different ones with the individual examination centre choosing which to operate. Again there is opportunity for general practitioners to participate.

Information recorded

It is with regard to the information recorded for each child that this Module varies most from the Immunisation Module. Broadly speaking, there are three dimensions to the outcome of examination which are recorded. The first relates to a summary of the examination outcome, the second to significant diagnoses and the third to other significant information about the child, particularly the need for additional special recall examinations. Moreover, because the examination itself is influenced by previous information, the examining doctor or nurse receives in advance an individual record form which contains identification and neonatal information, together with the results of up to two previous examinations.

Outcome

The basic outcome of each examination is recorded as height, weight and assessment of up to 10 functional fields. Seven of these fields, such as vision and hearing, are pre-labelled so as to ensure continuity of information when children move. However, three remain unlabelled, with the opportunity for each participating health authority to make its own use of these, the decision as to the allocations being made when the authority first implements the Module. The actual codes to be used against each functional field have been redefined in the light of field trials and now form a classification indicating whether the child is satisfactory in each respect, has a problem highlighted by the examination, will be further observed, is already receiving treatment or was referred as a result of the examination. However, the system itself does not define the tests to be used or the parameters within these tests, or indeed the profession of the examiner. These decisions are among those made when an authority first implements the Module, together with whether all functional fields will be examined at each age.

Diagnosis

Recording of diagnoses for each child is by means of the British Paediatric Association Supplement to the International Classification of Diseases (ICD). Only significant diagnoses are recorded, not intercurrent illnesses. The computer programs contain a library of ICD codes so that, while the information is stored on the individual record by ICD code number only, on medical examination forms it can be printed out in clear language. Each diagnosis can also be flagged to indicate that it is of significance for the dental treatment of the child, and it can also be indicated that a diagnosis is no longer active but remains of significance within the child's medical history. Here too experience of trial operation has led to refinements of detail.

Additional information

Thirdly, additional information can be recorded at each examination. Of most significance is that a child should receive a special recall prior to the next examination, either by a doctor or by a member of another profession. Entry of this information on to a medical examination form will not only add the information to the child's record but will ensure the creation of an appointment at the appropriate time. This makes the system infinitely flexible to suit the needs of the individual child, to complement its flexibility to the needs of the individual authority. With the implementation of the Education Act 1981, the Module can also record whether the child has been referred for a multi-disciplinary assessment under the Act and in broad terms the outcome of that assessment, particularly whether a statement under the Act has been issued and whether the child has special requirements in school.

The Module is also intended to record the information on the Neo-Natal Discharge Form. This document was designed by the Child Health Computing Committee at the request of the DHSS, to be used as part of the system or free-standing in its own right. Where it is used, the information provides an invaluable start to the child's sequential record.

Testing and launching

The computer programs for the module were completed on time in mid-1981 by the Welsh Health Technical Services Organisation. The Child Health

Computing Committee had already made the policy decision that full field trials would be undertaken before the Module was released, and objectives and the protocol for these trials had been agreed and volunteer authorities identified. The target programme was for a six month period of training and preparation for implementation, for trials to operate for the first half of 1982 and for the evaluation thereof to be completed and published by the end of the year.

At this stage, however, the British Medical Association (BMA) expressed anxiety about the release of the system in the absence of data protection legislation because of the sensitive information quite appropriately recorded. Despite initial discussions, the BMA declined to remove their opposition until there had been scrutiny both of the computer programs and of the intended operating environment. With regard to the computer programs, it was agreed exceptionally to release to professional experts nominated by the BMA the detailed technical information on the system, so that the programs could be verified as performing the functions specified in an appropriate and technically safe manner. This scrutiny proved the technical operation to be fully satisfactory. With regard to the operating environment, the attention of the BMA was drawn to the Confidentiality and Security Protocol prepared by the Child Health Computing Committee, which itself was based on ethical principles agreed with the BMA and endorsed by the Secretary of State for Social Services, as described later in this chapter. After due consideration, the Central Ethical Committee of the BMA agreed that the trials should proceed but with independent professional observers in each trial locality. This in fact added a valuable dimension to the trials, and the observers were provided by both the BMA and the Health Visitors' Association (HVA).

The trials therefore commenced six months later than intended, in July 1982, and with a slight reduction on the intended six month preparatory period. Three localities were chosen — Brent in the North West Thames Region, Mid-Glamorgan in South Wales, and Tameside in Greater Manchester. These were selected to ensure a wide geographical and demographic coverage; Mid-Glamorgan implemented the Module separately in two of its six geographical units.

After the six month trial phase, during which every function of the system was operated, field visits were paid to each authority, and field staff given the opportunity to meet the evaluation team in community health localities convenient to them. From this, and the subsequent workshops which analysed the responses, came valuable information which led to some refinement of the system, particular form design, and to some areas for longer term development. The resultant report was adopted by the Child Health Computing Committee (1983) and issued to all health authorities, and a summary was also published by Rigby (1983). With BMA and HVA endorsement following implementation of the pre-release amendments, the Module was made available for any health authority to use with effect from January 1984, and by mid 1985 10% of authorities had already adopted it.

SCHOOL HEALTH MODULE

Design

During this period, the School Health Module was being designed. As with the Pre-school Module, because of the lack of formal national agreement as to the detailed procedures of the school health service, design was undertaken from first principles. Early on, the approach was adopted that the module should in fact consist of a series of sub-functions covering such fundamental activities as medical examination, immunisation, dental inspection, vision and hearing screening and nurse surveillance interviews, with each participating authority deciding which sub-functions to use. It was agreed that each participating authority should have the choice of issuing appointments and invitations by post to home addresses, or via schools. Finally, because of the importance of fitting in with constraints in schools it was agreed that scheduling would not normally be automatic on age, but would require the health professional involved to notify the dates when they were attending any particular school, at which stage the computer system would indicate all children due for appointment.

Health information

The resultant system outline was published by the Child Health Computing Committee in 1981. It first sought an extension to the Child Register to create a register of school children by means of a form to be used by schools when notifying education authorities of a change in the school register. A medical examination form was designed very similar to that for pre-school health, and screening lists broadly similar to pre-school immunisation lists but recording pass and fail or non-attendance for specified vision and hearing tests were also developed. Similarly, a dental inspection clinic list was devised. With regard to immunisation itself, it was recognised that the courses due during the school years are single-dose courses and are sufficiently spaced in time that separate consent needs to be obtained for each one. It was therefore agreed that rather than a consent form and clinic list approach, a separate comprehensive consent and recording form for each dose was more appropriate; this also gave opportunity to print out the full immunisation history to date for information and verification when each new consent was due.

Education advice

A major extension of the activity in the school health service is the sharing of key non-diagnostic case management information with school teachers, for instance indicating that a child with hearing loss needs to sit near the teacher. Such information is important to help schools in their task of ensuring that each child reaches his or her full potential; some information is important for the physical safety of the child and possibly of other pupils. At the same time, strict control needs to be kept of such information sharing. This is accommodated within the School Health Module by the ability to print out a record card for the school containing key management messages about the individual child; the inclusion of such messages is only at the specific instruction of the examining doctor and is therefore considered to be ethically sound. It is the responsibility of the doctor to decide what information to pass and whether to have appropriate discussions with the parents. Moreover, such written information is only a basic safety net and does not replace direct discussion between the doctor and the head teacher.

Trials

The Child Health Computing Committee had again resolved that the Module should not be released without adequate field testing. With the programs due to be completed in mid 1983, agreement of the BMA and HVA was obtained to trials commencing with school entrants in September 1983, with the trials continuing until Easter 1984. On this occasion the BMA provided observers from both general practice and community medicine. The request for volunteer authorities was this time heavily over subscribed, and to get the widest pattern of school health practice as well as demography four authorities were selected — Mid-Glamorgan, Pontefract, Shropshire and South Bedfordshire. The first of these provided continuity with the Pre-school Module trials, though the primary school children involved were too old to have been included within the pre-school trials. Only in Shropshire were the boundaries of the trial area co-terminus with that of the education authority.

Manual records

It was also felt that implementation of the School Health Module might produce significant simplification of manual records for healthy children, which in most authorities are raised at primary school entry but comparatively seldom added to after the initial medical examination. Participating authorities were invited to decide what was likely to be the best solution locally and then to evaluate this as part of the trials.

Valuable feedback

Bearing in mind the much greater degree of change to existing working practices and record keeping produced by the School Health Module, the trials passed comparatively smoothly. Partway through, it was agreed to extend the operative period until May 1984 without allowing the ultimate reporting date to slip. This was in order to accommodate a wider range of recall activities which were found to occur primarily during the summer term.

In the event, most reaction during the trials was caused by the two areas which had received least attention at the design stage because they seemed most straightforward. These were child registration and dental inspection. With regard to child registration, school clerical staff were invaluable in highlighting a number of areas where the main Child Health System was not as comprehensive as it might have been, particularly with regard to recording alternative surnames which did not necessarily represent permanent changes and regularly used familiar forenames which did not replace the officially registered forenames. In the light of these valuable suggestions the Child Register of the whole of the Child Health System has been expanded.

Education statistics School staff also pointed out that with scope for additional statistical fields for education use, the School Health Module Child Register would meet most education authority requirements. Such statistical fields have now been added for this purpose, in the belief that the sharing of one register will give added incentive to ensure maintenance of its accuracy, as well as simplifying clerical tasks. Comments on form design have also been adopted.

Dental functions Reactions from the dental profession showed that, because dentists normally examine the whole of a school population at one visit, full benefit would not be obtained from the dental functions until the whole population of a school was covered. Moreover, there were variations in professional view as to what information should be routinely recorded, some dentists wanting a simple outcome of inspection while others aimed for dental epidemiology details. There was also subsequent discussion with the Dental Services Statistics Group as to whether the type of treatment needed or the reason for the treatment was the more appropriate item to record. In view of these professional variations, the dental functions of the module have been expanded, but with a number of alternatives, so that each participating authority's district dental officer can determine how to use the system in any particular authority.

Medical and screening functions The medical inspection and vision and hearing surveillance functions of the system were found to be generally satisfactory except that the staff involved wished them to be more far reaching. In particular, at design stage it was felt appropriate to record only broad screening results, with referral to doctors of children with unsatisfactory results being seen as a professional function to be undertaken directly. In the light of the trials, participating staff felt that the system should not record pass or fail but the actual clinical results of the hearing and the vision tests, and that having done so the referral to the doctor of less serious problems could be through the system, thus eliminating paper work and reducing the risk of referrals being overlooked. Therefore, appropriate pre-release enhancements have been built in, and the medical examination form will now print out previous vision and hearing results as well as the previous two medical results.

Similarly, doctors sought extension to the information and the functions recorded at the medical examination. Future recalls can be booked not only for the same examiner but also for other examiners, and other locations can be specified as well as being scheduled either by exact time interval or at the next medical visit to the school. Doctors in the trials also suggested that diagnoses recorded should be flagged to indicate which ones should be the particular subject of attention at the re-examination.

Release of the Module

The trials again concluded with two day visits to each authority, where field staff of both education and health authorities had the opportunity to meet the evaluation team. In general, the trials were felt to have gone well, and the computer programs were released for general use from September 1985 following the pre-release development indicated above. The evaluation report itself was approved by the Child Health Computing Committee in 1984 and circulated early in 1985, and a separate summary has been published by Rigby (1985).

Compared with the Pre-school Module, however, the outcome of the evaluation, while being as positive in demonstrating the practicality and the benefits of the module, nevertheless was not all embracing and without reservation. In view of the complexity and age range of the school health service and the involvement of two quite separate services, this is not surprising.

First, unlike pre-school health, in a comparatively short trial period neither all functions of the computer system nor all potential applications could be tested. Therefore as yet some specific functions, such as BCG immunisation and the school leaver routines, have not been generally released and will be subject to individual piloting when authorities are ready to use them. Moreover, some means of operating, such as conducting primary school entry medical examinations in community clinics with postal appointments prior to school admission, can be accommodated within the system but were not used by any of the trial localities.

Secondly, there is the likely need to review manual record systems, where some of the trial authorities felt there was value in maintaining ongoing manual records for all school children, while others felt that a transparent filing wallet labelled with an adhesive label generated by the computer could adequately store the completed computer medical examination form as the sole record for a healthy child together with any referral letters and subsequent information and that, for a child with more complex problems, a supplementary card could be slotted into that folder. Analysis of the number of children requiring such supplementary information varied several-fold, both between trial authorities and within one authority.

Inter-professional issues

Thirdly, and most significantly, the trials brought into clear focus a number of issues of principle between the health and education services which hitherto have been resolved by custom and practice or by default in individual authorities. Such issues include the degree to which significant management information about a child should be passed round within a school while retaiing its basic confidentiality and, secondly, the balance of ethics between a health authority keeping confidential the medical information imparted to it while at the same time the education authority may have to rely on parents completing an education-designed questionnaire to elicit the same important medical information. These ethical issues are not themselves a product of the computer system but are highlighted by it, and their resolution will give added confidence to the use of the computer system. Consequently, the evaluation report contains a specific paper on these items and the Child Health Computing Committee has initiated a major national debate involving leading representatives of organisations within the two services and their professions to pursue appropriate policies and solutions.

CONFIDENTIALITY AND SECURITY

This last aspect links back to the more general subject of confidentiality and security for the Child Health System. Confidentiality establishes ground rules for the use of the information recorded and legitimately made available within the system; security protects against unauthorised access and also accidental loss of the data. The Child Health Computing Committee, after study by a special working party, in 1979 established its own confidentiality and security protocol to protect the information within the system. This is based on three ethical principles which were agreed with the BMA and specifically endorsed in the House of Commons by the Secretary of State for Social Services, as recorded in Hansard (1978a & b). These principles state that the information is recorded for the continuing health care of the individual child; that its use is restricted to the authors, those clinically responsible for the child and their successors; and that release of identifiable information for research or other purposes may only be with the approval of an appropriate ethical committee. The protocol then gives guidance on how these principles can be achieved in day to day working practice in the context of community health services. The guidance on security covers safe transmission of records, safe storage of records at community office and clinic level and secure practices within computer centres, including the maintenance of duplicate computer files. This protocol was itself subjected to evaluation during the two sets of trials, and subject to some limited refinement with BMA and HVA approval following the pre-school trials, was found to be effective. As with the ethical issues raised during the school module trials, the very need for a confidentiality protocol largely reflects the lack until recently of more formal guidelines; hitherto, practice has varied across the country from the very satisfactory to the unsatisfactory.

More recently, two new factors have emerged. The first is the Data Protection Act 1984, which sets further constraints on computer applications. The full impact of this on particular health service computer application cannot be assessed until the Data Protection Registrar produces all the regulations, but the general principle of statutory control of the use of such data must be welcomed. Secondly, the DHSS has published (1984b) a draft Code on Confidentiality of Personal Health Data. While not yet definitive, this too seeks to ensure that sensitive information is adequately protected.

BENEFITS OF COMPUTER-BASED RECORDS

Quality of care

As computer applications, not least the national Child Health System, require major investment in their initial creation, the trauma of a major change in working practice and record keeping and compliance with statutory controls, the question must therefore be asked as to what the benefits are to justify the upheaval. The first and foremost such benefit must be the quality of care of the individual child. This can be assessed and proved only in aggregate for particular cohorts, but it is for the individual that the service is initially undertaken.

Reference has already been made to the studies which demonstrate higher uptake when computer systems schedule children for procedures due and notify health visitors of individual defaulters. With the Pre-school and School Health Modules this is extended to ensuring that recall appointments are made to match individual need, removing the hazards of such recalls being overlooked, not least when either staff change or the child moves. Furthermore, the use of computer-printed turn-round documents ensures that summary medical information is always to hand at an examination, and that there is rapid transmission of interpretable summary information when a child moves, without the risk of parting with the main case notes until the child's arrival has been confirmed. With the School Health Module this also applies to continuity of key management advice to schools, even though the doctor may change or the child may transfer between schools.

Sharing of information

A further dimension of this benefit to the individual is the sharing of medical information between agencies within the health service. First, an aggregate immunisation history is created for each child. From this, individual immunisation history cards can be supplied to the child's general practitioner ready for insertion straight into the medical record wallet. The outcome of community health medical examinations and screening, including diagnoses recorded and advice passed to schools, can also be printed out in similar format. District dental officers can receive information about individual children whose medical conditions are significant for dental treatment, not only ensuring that individual dental officers are warned of potential hazards, but also enabling those children to be selected for additional preventive techniques.

Hospital paediatricians can request information prior to outpatient consultations, and accident and emergency departments can be supplied with summaries of the tetanus protection of all local children. The system will gain further value as hospitals and general practitioners increasingly add to the record significant information drawn to their attention, such as long term effects of illness or accident.

General practitioners can participate to the degree they wish, both in delivering the service and in exchanging information. Where they undertake preventive services their appointments can be scheduled for them to their specification and item-of-service fees calculated. Even where they do not participate directly, they can receive information relating to their child patients.

Despite the resolutions of the Court Report (Department of Education and Science and the Welsh Office, 1976) and the aspirations of particular groups within the medical and other professions, there will be no speedy resolution to the problems of separate general practice, community health and hospital care for children. Either conflict can continue, with the likelihood that lack of exchanged information will be to the detriment of the child, or complementary methods of working to an agreed pattern specific to the locality and with planned information sharing can be implemented. As discussed by Rigby in 1981, for the foreseeable future there will be roles for all three aspects of services for children. The flexibility and information-sharing aspects of the Child Health System give it great value in forging an integrated local pattern of service through planned interlinkages at little extra cost.

Information for management

The aggregate information from the system in use in any authority will also permit improved management of the service and evaluation of the techniques used, which should further benefit the child population. The information the system can provide is infinitely flexible, but it can, for instance, identify variations in service uptake by localities as small as individual post code areas or by particular practices, or show the outcome of screening examinations by individual clinic centres. This will enable management to deploy health service resources to areas of greatest need or identify localities where the service is not being operated effectively. Using the information in a different way, the efficacy of individual examinations, or tests within examinations, can be studied over a period of time to permit improvements in techniques.

This type of management information use was the prime objective of the Steering Group on Health Services Information. The experience of design, implementation and evaluation of the Child Health System was drawn on by the Steering Group by co-option of the author to the working group preparing the Community Services Report (Department of Health and Social Security 1984a). The Steering Group has expressed a view that adequate management information for preventive child health services can be obtained only by the use of a computerised population register, and the Steering Group specifically identified the Child Health System as a recognised means of collecting their minimum data sets. Now that full data definitions have been obtained from the Steering Group some minor modifications need to be made to the system, but these are in hand.

There is also tremendous scope for epidemiological study. This can aid local management; it can also help evaluate and refine preventive health techniques. Therefore, as well as encouraging local use, the Child Health Computing Committee is seeking suitable ways of coordinating national studies in which user districts may collaborate.

In order to facilitate this management use of the system, the Child Health Computing Committee has already made available a statistical package relating to the Child Register and Immunisation Module. However, rather than centrally determining requirements, during the Pre-school and School Health trials statistical tables intentially were not made available but rather the staff of the trial authorities asked to assess during the trials the use to which they could possibly put the aggregate information. From this was obtained a number of useful proposals, which were put into a further comprehensive statistical package being finalised in Autumn 1985. Continuing developments of this aspect are anticipated in the light of further experience, statistical techniques and user sophistication.

COSTS

Quite rightly, a frequently asked question is what is the cost of operating the system in order to achieve the aforementioned benefits. Unfortunately, this question is impossible to answer centrally. The computer programs themselves are designed through central funding, and a modest charge for maintenance is being levied on each authority using the system. However, the major costs will relate to ongoing computing costs at local level, to postage and stationery costs and to staff time.

Different regions have different policies with regard to recharging for the use of computer facilities, and this will be further influenced by the size of the child register in an authority and by the data capture techniques in operation. These costs can be determined only at local level.

Stationery and postage costs will be dependent on the record keeping systems implemented and on the number of examinations in the schedule. Depending on previous policies, including whether appointments were previously issued, these may represent either an increase or a decrease on previous costs.

The third dimension is even more difficult. The computer system will incur some additional professional staff time because there is some increase in record keeping, together with a need to notify register changes. On the other hand, again depending on previous practice, there should be a decrease in work, such as the keeping of diary files, and in the routine transmission of results to other professionals. Depending on previous practice, there may be more, or less, time spent on examinations and in routine visiting as a result of the schedule which is introduced with the implementation of the system. What informed use of the Child Health System should permit is improved overall preventive service management, so that case loads can be adjusted to need and less valuable activities foregone in those areas proved to produce least benefit. Therefore the cost of the system can be determined only locally. What should ensue, however, is an improvement in deployment of resources and in the longer term in quality or care.

COMPUTER TECHNOLOGY

Considerable interest is expressed in the computing techniques used, often more than in the data items or service objectives of this system. The system was initially designed for operation on ICL (International Computers Ltd) mainframe computers using DME (Dual Machine Environment) operating techniques and with batch input of information. This was because such was the NHS standard in 1974, and a prime objective of the system was that it should be available to any health authority through its regional computer centre. The Child Health Computing Committee has sought to give first priority to completing the design of the system, and the appropriateness of this is demonstrated by the volume of use of the first modules and the increasing uptake of the later modules. However, regional computers and batch data entry do not necessitate transmission of paper records to regional computer centres for recording of the data. Remote data capture and output, normally at community office level, is becoming increasingly common as the NHS develops communications networks. This technique is considered to be highly desirable, both because it saves time and also because it is more secure, and therefore the Child Health Computing Committee strongly supports it. The only reason that it has not been formally built into the system so far is that regions have developed different network techniques and hardware, necessitating local design.

The system is now converted to Virtual Machine Environment (VME) operation, which, apart from increasing computing efficiency, means that it can be used through local terminals for real time interrogation of individual records. In addition, electronic links, such as the automatic generation of birth notification and neonatal discharge data from hospital maternity patient administration systems, are being tested prior to wider release.

The combination of remote data capture and real time interrogation should meet most health professionals' needs. A local computer, and real time updating with its inherent problems of authorisation and verification, though often sought in the first instance, are not essential for this type of application. What concerns the community health service is an ability quickly to interrogate and easily to update records, and this is what can be provided by the current version of the national Child Health System given appropriate communication systems in the regions.

Nevertheless, the Child Health Computing Committee recognises the importance of exploiting the latest technology provided it is proven and generally available. To this end, together with the Welsh Health Technical Services Organisation, in 1984 it asked the Computer Policy Committee (CPC) for guidance as to how the Child Health System should develop in the future. The CPC in turn commissioned management consultants Arthur Andersen and Company, who undertook a study which recommended that the facilities of the system should be developed to apply to other preventive community health services, and that with the development of new techniques the system could be made more transferable between different makes of computer. The CPC is examining these issues, which are seen as being an evolution of the Child Health System and as needing at least four years to develop. The intention is that existing users of the Child Health System will then be able to progress easily to the next generation system, in the same way that users will not see any change from DME to VME operation other than through an increase in the facilities.

TRAINING, SUPPORT AND DEVELOPMENT

Training materials

What the Child Health Computing Committee has fully recognised is the need for training materials and other support if the system is to reach its full potential. Already, 60% of midwives, health visitors and clinic doctors participate in the use of the system, and this proportion will increase. Furthermore, because the system is linked to major national bodies such as the Joint Committee on Vaccination and Immunisation, it will continue to react to new clinical requirements. This produces a responsibility to keep field staff trained and fully informed, though implementation of this process can be undertaken only by individual district health authorities.

During both the Pre-school Module and the School Health Module trials, one of the evaluation objectives was to identify the staff training needs and how these could best be met. As a result, the CHCC commissioned a comprehensive training package for the Pre-school Health Module, with North West Thames Regional Health Authority kindly providing a member of staff to produce this. As well as providing training material and a handbook for the local trainer, it also provides a count down and key to all the stages of implementation through which an authority will have to pass.

The inception of the National Health Service Training Authority has, however, provided a major new ally in educating staff of the service to make efficient and informed use of the Child Health System. The training authority is now represented on the Child Health Computing Committee, and is already making a valuable contribution. A training package has been designed for the School Health Module, this time as a joint venture. Work on guidance on use of the management information facilities has also just been completed, and further developments of support materials are intended.

Development support

Equally important to user authorities should be the support provided by ongoing developments. The need for these will arise from a number of directions — clinical developments, national requirements, user requests and technological opportunities being the main ones. As summarised by the Chairman of the CHCC in a British Medical Journal editorial (Walker, 1983), the regional and professional membership of the Committee gives it a firm base to identify and respond to such requirements.

SUMMARY

The power of the Child Health System, fully available to any district health authority from September 1985, is not yet widely appreciated. It will permit full clinical recording and appointment scheduling for some 20% of an authority's resident population, namely children from birth to school leaving, together with those non-residents who attend clinics or schools within its boundaries. The information recorded will give a summary of each child's history and development, including full immunisation history, all significant diagnoses and a summary of routine and special screening and surveillance. It will create a new epidemiological picture, permit improved overall evaluation and management of the child health services and enable health professionals to concentrate on these children known to have the greatest needs while eliminating the task of routinely checking records.

The ultimate objective, improved health care delivery to the individual and to the child community, has already been proved to the satisfaction of the trial authorities. The indications are that many other authorities are following in their footsteps in seeking the benefits of the full Child Health Computer System.

REFERENCES

Bussey A L, Harris A S 1979 Computers and the effectiveness of the measles vaccination campaign in England and Wales. Community Medicine 1: 29–35
Bussey A L, Holmes B S 1978 Immunisation levels and the computer. Lancet i: 450
Chesham I, Rigby M J, Shelmerdine H R 1975 Paediatric screening. Health and Social Services Journal 85: 293–294
Child Health Computing Committee 1979 Pre school health module — an outline. Welsh Health Technical Services Organisation, Cardiff
Child Health Computing Committee 1981 School health module — an outline. Welsh Health Technical Services Organisation, Cardiff
Child Health Computing Committee 1983 Evaluation report of the trials of the pre-school module. Welsh Health Technical Services Organisation, Cardiff
Child Health Computing Committee 1984 Evaluation report of the trial of the school health module. Welsh Health Technical Services Organisation, Cardiff
Department of Education and Science and Welsh Office 1976: Fit for the future — report of the Committee on Child Health Services (Chairman: Professor S D M Court) HMSO, London
Department of Health and Social Security 1984a Steering Group on health services information (Chairman Mrs E Körner). Fifth Report to the Secretary of State. HMSO, London

Department of Health and Social Security 1984b Draft code on confidentiality of personal health data (DA(84)25). DHSS, London
Galloway T McL 1963 Management of vaccination and immunisation procedures by electronic computer. Medical Officer 109: 232
Hansard 1978a Vol 950: Col 808–809, 26th May
Hansard 1978b Vol 951: Col 280, 9th June
Rigby M J 1981 Child health — a time for better understanding? Health Trends 13: 97–99
Rigby M J 1983 Clean bill of health for module. Health and Social Services Journal 93: 1444–1445
Rigby M J 1985 School care goes hi-tech. Health and Social Services Journal 95: 486–487
Saunders J 1970 Results and costs of a computer-assisted immunisation scheme. British Journal of Social and Preventive Medicine 24: 187–191
Walker C H M 1983 Computing in child health: significant progress. British Medical Journal 287: 1400–1401

Child health records and the computer

INTRODUCTION

In this chapter I shall review the experiences of a North West London health district in the adoption of the Pre-school Module of the National Child Health System described by Michael Rigby in chapter 8. As one of three trial authorities, however, not all of Brent Health Authority's experiences will need to be repeated by other authorities who wish to take on this system now, as many of their findings and recommendations have resulted in modifications of the original system. This chapter will present the picture very much from the paediatrician's viewpoint and will include some mention of alternative systems. As will become apparent, it is not yet possible to make a final judgment of the system, but some of the clear benefits as well as some criticisms are presented, with an indication of the future usefulness of the computer not only for the community child health records of the 'well' population, but also for the integration of these child health services with those for children with special needs and the acute hospital based services. Since the process of planning, training and implementing such a comprehensive computerised Child Health Record System requires a major investment of both time and money, this account will start with what I feel are the compelling reasons why such a system should be introduced.

THE FUTURE OF CHILD HEALTH SURVEILLANCE: UNANSWERED QUESTIONS AND GOVERNMENT DEMANDS

In the last five years there has been a proliferation of reports and correspondence about the community and preventive child health services. At the centre of the debate is the all important question of whether child health surveillance offers any benefits. Do the various surveillance programmes detect — and remedy — any problems that would otherwise have remained unrecognised? Almost more than the all important *content* of the surveillance programmes, the debate which has aroused greatest interest has been on *who* should carry out the various checks — family doctor, a community based child health doctor or the health visitor (Rigby, 1981; GMSC debate, 1984).

In seeking an answer to these questions a major obstacle has been the dearth of facts on which to judge existing services or plan future improvements. The paradox is, however, that all these facts are faithfully collected and recorded by doctors or health visitors in every district health authority in the land. They are recorded onto a range of record systems varying from comprehensive many-paged folders to small or even miniature record cards of almost every colour, but most commonly white, or pink for girls and yellow for boys. Standard DHSS approved forms do exist, but there are many modifications and increasingly individual designs ranging from one GP's simple photocopied aide memoire to the commonly used MCW46, commercial mini records for family practitioners or the Nottingham Childfile — to my knowledge the only major new child health system produced by a university child health department so far.

With the exception of the Nottingham Childfile, the one thing that almost all these systems have in common is their fate. They are stored in filing cabinets. Sometimes they are lost and at other times many partial duplicates are in circulation. For the average health authority with up to 20 000 pre-school children, some 140 000 to 200 000 significant items of information are recorded annually and at the present time the only information that is extracted from these records is that required by the DHSS for completion of form LHS 27/2 (Fig. 9.1) and for statistics on immunisations. Apart from the immunisation uptake totals, these statistics provide absolutely no information about the content and outcome of many thousands of consultations and no indication of the quality of care provided. They do not answer the basic questions of who should do what to whom, when and how often. This type of qualitative analysis is rarely available except as a result of one-off surveys or projects, such as those of Hendrickse (1982) and Davies and Bretman (1985), both from Nottingham, and others such as the Thomas Coram Research Study (Jenkins, 1984). These studies tend to reflect the care provided in above average quality child health clinics rather than that of the country as a whole. In addition, the requirments of the Korner minimum data set are far greater than the current DHSS statistical returns, and there is also a strong belief among paediatricians in community child health (as well as the demands of Griffiths-type managers) that the ability to analyse and evaluate these services is mandatory.

For these reasons among others I am convinced of the need to apply computer technology to child health records in the country as a whole, though, as I will show, the best way to do it and the outcome still remain to be judged.

FIRST CONSIDERATIONS — AND DOUBTS

Brent Health Authority was first asked to participate in the trials of the Pre-school Module of the National Child Health Computer System in 1977. The development of this system as presented in chapter 8 was slow to get going and one of the main reasons for this delay was the question of confidentiality which caused such concern to the British Medical Association and Family

DEPARTMENT OF HEALTH AND SOCIAL SECURITY

COMMUNITY HEALTH SERVICES STATISTICS YEAR ENDED 31 DECEMBER 1984

Form LHS 27/2

District Health Authority
...... BRENT ......

MATERNITY AND CHILD HEALTH
CLINIC SERVICES
1984

PART A.   ANTE-NATAL MOTHERCRAFT AND RELAXATION CLASSES

1.   Number of women who attended classes in 1984

Confinement Booked:	Number of Women who attended Classes
(a) Institution	340
(b) Domiciliary	—
(c) Total	340

2.

Number of attendances during 1984	1092

PART B.   CHILD HEALTH CLINICS
(including clinics provided by voluntary organisations on behalf of the DHA)

(a)   Children attending clinics in 1984

	Year of Birth			Total Number of Children (1)+(2)+(3) (4)
	1984 (1)	1983 (2)	1979-82 (3)	
Number of children who attended clinics	3212	5200	5361	13773

Number of children who attended clinics in 1984: To be recorded as the first visit to the clinic in the calendar year irrespective of whether the child had attended in the previous year(s).

(b)   Attendances by children at clinics during 1984

	Year of Birth			Total Number of Attendances (5)+(6)+(7) (8)
	1984 (5)	1983 (6)	1979-82 (7)	
Number of Attendances by children	19425	16326	8885	44636

All attendances during the calendar year should be recorded including the first visit recorded in Table (a).

(c)   Sessions held by Medical Staff and Health Visitors

Number of Sessions held in 1984 by:				Total number of Sessions (9)+(10)+(11)+(12) (13)
Medical Officers (9)	Health Visitors (10)	GPs employed on sessional basis (11)	Hospital Medical Staff. (12)	
1982	23		—	2005

The actual number of sessions is required not sessions equated to half days.
Column 10:   Record only the number of sessions held by health visitors alone (ie not accompanying a medical officer or GP). Do not include sessions if a health visitor is providing sessions in a GP Surgery for a GP who is not sessionally employed by the DHA.

Column 11:   Include only sessions carried out under contract to the DHA. Do not include sessions held by general practitioners for their own patients.

Fig. 9.1 Department of Health and Social Security form LHS 27/2, part B: child health clinics

Practitioner Committees. This account of Brent's eventual adoption of the system thus starts in 1982 with the planning stages, with the programme actually starting to operate for children born on and after 1 February 1983.

In addition to the reasons outlined above, the invitation to be a trial authority was welcomed as being particularly appropriate for a health district with an exceptionally highly mobile population with very varied social and ethnic characteristics and including substantial areas of social deprivation. The coverage of the child population as far as could be analysed was patchy and in some areas definitely poor. At school entry a small survey showed that 43% of children had untraceable pre-school records and 31% more than three changes of address. The advantages to such a district of the National Child Register and Immunisation Modules of the system had already been experienced, as well as some of the pitfalls and requirements for introducing such record and appointment systems.

Two of these requirements stood out. First, the need for very careful planning and training of the staff who would be using the system and, secondly, the unstated but apparent myth that the 'computer' somehow replaces the need for human intervention in getting children into the clinics. Some months after the inception of the programme a marked dip in the uptake of primary immunisations occurred: this was soon corrected once news of this trend was fed back to the health visitors, who had, it was thought, unconsciously relaxed their normal efforts. It had been generally expected that immunisations were now 'all looked after by the computer'. (Early warning of such a trend would of course have been impossible without the feedback that a computerised record system can provide.)

Brent therefore chose to delay the start of the Pre-school Child Health System by six months beyond the date suggested by the National Child Health Computing Committee, both to ensure thorough planning and training programmes and because it was hoped to influence the committee to make some modifications to the records before starting. It was clearly indicated that trial authorities would have this opportunity.

The large number of pamphlets, user manuals and specimen forms that constituted the package presented to the trial health authority was initially a formidable sight. Although health authorities now considering adopting the system will have the advantage of the modifications that resulted from the trials, it still remains a large amount of paperwork to digest. It does, however, define the tasks and issues with great clarity and in particular identifies extremely important safeguards which must be adopted to ensure confidentiality. This issue remains one which causes public concern, but if the recommendations are adopted the majority of health districts will in all probability end up with greatly improved security. Parents and bodies such as the Community Health Councils should find this satisfactorily reassuring.

The main reservations about the National Child Health Computing Committee package came from the paediatrician sitting on the working party set up to consider it. Some of these reservations remain today, especially regarding the content of the clinical record form. These will be further outlined below, after an account of the main features to be considered when planning, training for and implementing such a project. Whatever reservations there are, however, should be compared with the answer to the all important question — could one or should one set up an independent district system? For the average health authority I feel that the answer is definitely in the negative — or certainly was three years ago — and even now, with increasing availability of microcomputer systems which would allow a locally designed system to be operated there are still many advantages in adopting a national system. This is particularly true now that it is updating the computer technology in such a way that local control and microlink capability will be combined with the resources of regional and national computing development committees.

PLANNING

In Brent a large working party was set up to plan the implementation of the Pre-school Module of the National Child Health system, which included extra representatives from the British Medical Association (BMA) and Health Visitors Association (HVA) who were present as observers at all the trials. Even without these, however, a fully representative working party should meet well in advance of the proposed start of the programme and the suggested constituents are as follow:

Obstetrician
Senior Nurse (Midwifery)
Specialist in Community Medicine (Planning)
Consultant Paediatrician (Community Child Health) *or*
Senior Clinical Medical Officer equivalent
Senior Nurse (Health Visiting)
Relevant Unit Administrator or Deputy
Computer Centre Representative (from Region)

Training Officer (Region or District)
Clinic based future users of system
   Health Visitor
   Clinic Doctor
   Clinic Clerk
Family Practitioner Representative
District Finance Officer

Adequate representation from the clinics themselves — i.e., the users of the system — is of great vaue, as well as the more senior medical, nursing and administrative representatives.

Early input from the Finance Department is essential as the introduction of this system costs money and, without approval of both short term and long term financial implications, the whole exercise will founder. As well as meeting as a group, the various components can usefully meet separately to analyse their own area of functioning in greater detail, but for most training sessions a multi-disciplinary approach was found to be the most effective, working with clinic teams small enough to enable local needs to be met but in every case under the guidance of a good training officer. The training input should continue for some time after the use of the computerised record system has started.

The administrative and clerical aspects of the system and computer technology will not be reviewed in detail. Apart from early technical problems (now solved) this part of the system works well and has a high degree of flexibility, which allows an almost infinite number of appointment systems to cope with local preferences. Inevitably with a batch-mode centralised system, there is an element of delay if changes to a programme are required (usually of two weeks), and this delay can also cause problems of duplication, particularly in a district where English is often not the first language. A small number of babies may thus receive extra immunisations — e.g., from the family practitioner and then at the community clinic — but this is not unique to a district with a computerised record system; the difference is that the computer informs one of the error.   The only serious problem which arose from the actual design of the computer program occurred in the immunisation 'schedule' and was not detected for some time. The inexorably logical computer took note that measles immunisation was preceded by three doses of triple vaccine or Dip/Tet and Polio and thus any child who failed to attend for the second or third of these doses was simply not sent an appointment for the measles. This fault was eventually noticed by an extremely efficient clerical officer in charge of the computer section and not by either a health visitor or clinic doctor!

The remainder of this chapter will be devoted to a review of the more clinical aspects of the planning and use of a computerised child health record, both by and for the clinic medical officer, family doctor or health visitor, and its usefulness to the clinical manager — senior clinical medical officer, consultant paediatrician or specialist in community medicine (child health or planning). The developmental examination record form is not a comprehensive record but a basic coded summary of the findings, previous and present, including significant medical conditions, actual measurements of height and weight, coded assessments of the various parameters of development under assessment, with a facility to include up to three local options, and a recommendation for action in the form of routine re-appointment, referrals, extra appointments and comments. This form does not therefore at present constitute a complete child health record and will need to be completed in addition to the normal records in use in the district clinics or surgery. The computer records cater for appointments scheduled at whatever frequency is requested by the user District as well as for unscheduled attendances and in Brent's experience there was no problem with either the organisational side of this system or with compliance.

The completion of such an extra form at even the busiest of clinics has been accepted without complaint by all clinic staff. This acceptability can be encouraged by taking the opportunity to scrutinise the existing records and, if necessary, re-designing them, both to improve their quality and to make them directly compatible with the computer record form, well before the start of its use.

The commonly used MCW46 and other similar records are often a catalogue of observations of varying significance, with no clear end point and no indication of action to be taken in relation to clinical findings. The clinical methods of surveillance and the limits of normal should be clearly defined, together with the point at which referral should take place. This will convert the ill-organised catalogue described above into a defined screening procedure capable of being coded onto a computerised record form from which valid statistical analyses can then be made. This philosophy is most clearly expounded in the report on the Nottingham City project and other papers by Leon Polnay and his colleagues at the Department of Child Health, Nottingham University (Polnay & Hull, 1985). They have developed an independent and local computerised child health system designed for a personal microcomputer which is operated directly by clinic staff, with access being controlled by a six digit security code. This is a very different system to the National Child Health Computer System, but the basic philosophy of a rigidly defined system of valid child health screening should be applicable to any sytem whether manual or computerised, local or national.

EARLY PROBLEMS AND APPRAISAL OF THE SYSTEM

Partly as a result of the design of the developmental examination record, and partly because of the non-conformity or variation in interpretation of the form by the doctors, there were considerable problems to be sorted out in the early months.

1. The design of the form

As indicated earlier there were strong clinical misgivings about this form from the start, as well as some design faults. These have now mainly been corrected. The design of the Neonatal Discharge Form was of such complexity, with the inclusion of such a plethora of obstetric and neonatal data, that it was almost universally rejected. It has now — three years later — been redesigned and trials are just about to commence. Thus the section for recording neonatal details on the examination record form has been rendered useless, and clinic staff have to rely on the pre-existing maternity discharge form.

The developmental examination record summarises the outcome of the usual range of clinical examinations made in child health surveillance, but in my view there is one grave omission. There is no facility for recording head circumference measurements either in the neonatal section or in the current examination, and centiles are not included along with absolute measurements of height and weight. Growth is obviously best recorded on an appropriate chart, but if the developmental examination record is to be of use both epidemiologically and as a tool for monitoring the standard of examination, a complete record of growth is required, especially in the first year of life.

2. The system of coding the findings

In the original version of the form one was required to classify children as being satisfactory or *unsatisfactory*. The current version still uses regrettably old fashioned terminology. The codings are shown below:

First version: Second version:

S = Satisfactory   S = Satisfactory
H = Handicapped but   I = Impairment
       still satisfactory   R = Referral
U = Unsatisfactory   C = Check
D = Doubtful   O = Observation
                                        T = Treated
                                        N = Not examined

(In the latest version for school health, impairment is replaced by problem and check is omitted.)

From this it will be seen that there are other ambiguities in the interpretation of 'Check' versus 'Observation' and also the meaning of 'Treated'. Currently, users are left to define these terms for themselves or omit any one of them. This requires the provision of explanatory notes so as to ensure uniformity of interpretation. However, as a result of extensive correspondence with the Statistics and Information Sub-committee, as well as the input of a developmental paediatrician to the School Health Module, this section is being suitably revised.

Training

The developmental examination record sections for recording medically and dentally significant conditions and indicating special educational needs are all useful; though, regarding the latter, the detailed classification made possible here, is not often required in the first tier well baby clinic situation. Considerable training input is required to ensure that suitable entries are made under 'Significant Medical Conditions' by the doctors. This is also true for the ICD coding of these conditions, particularly if it is carried out by a clerical officer. In the early months of using the records a great mass of clinical trivia was entered by the doctors or they made inadequate definitions of medical conditions that *were* significant.

Education of both the doctors and coder is therefore essential and, if ICD coding is to be a clerical task, regular access to a paediatrician is required for obtaining answers to queries.

THE RESULTS

The main attractions of a computerised form of clinical record are the output of statistical and epidemiological data that can be obtained and being able to monitor the input of those carrying out the clinical examinations. At the time of writing, however, there has still been no output or feedback of any sort from the National Child Pre-school Module for North West Thames. This was in spite of the fact that suggested programmes for analysis were circulated at the outset.

This frustrating delay results from many problems, both national and regional, and from financial problems. They should end in September 1985 with the introduction of the latest phase of the development of the computing system as outlined by Walker (1983), but somewhat later than the dates then forecast. The results that follow have therefore been compiled *manually* from the completed *computer* record forms. With the immunisation forms, however, detailed feedback has been available for some time, and a sample of this is presented to show the potential usefulness of the computerised Child Health Record System (Table 9.1). These detailed uptake figures can easily be compiled on a quarterly basis either for the whole health district or broken down for each clinic or GP surgery.

Table 9.1   Immunisation uptake, mid-1985, by children born in 1982

Clinic	Number eligible		Percentage uptake		
	M	F	Dip/Tet/Polio*	Pertussis	Measles
O.T.H.	74	63	94.2	84.7	84.7
C.A.H.C.	103	113	88.4	75.5	80.6
M.P.C.	69	73	85.2	73.2	77.5
P.R.C.	101	74	84.0	68.6	72.0
S.L.C.	77	81	82.9	69.6	67.7
P.C.C.	166	145	76.8	58.2	61.7
C.P.H.C.	174	161	69.0	57.7	56.1

Dip/Tet/Polio = Diphtheria/Tetanus/Polio
*Figures normally provided separately for each component, but values identical in examples given here. (Table compiled from regular computer printout)

Data broken down in the latter way are especially useful in enabling one to draw up a league table of performance and to examine the differing procedures or organisation that may be contributing to the high or low overall uptake figures. This can then be used to effect an improvement at the bottom of the league. The ability to compare and set specific targets for individual clinics to achieve is a valuable management tool that has demonstrable results. The feedback can be made individually to a single health visitor or clinic medical officer as well as on a wider scale, for example by a newsletter sent to all clinic staff; medical, nursing and clerical. An informed and motivated clerk receptionist has a very definite contribution to make in preventive child health.

Even without any output programme yet in operation, the computerised child health record system has provided a new insight into the quality, as well as the quantity, of child health surveillance programmes in Brent health clinics. This includes the limited number of family practitioners who are also participating. All records on which any abnormality is recorded can easily be extracted during coding and inspected weekly, giving the consultant paediatrician or Senior Clinical Medical Officer an instant 'keyhole' view of the work of each doctor or health visitor, thus enabling immediate communication to take place about any point of concern or discrepancy that needs further action. A picture soon emerges of the 'champion' (or most indecisive) 'squint detector' for example, or the doctor who keeps recalling children for repeat hearing tests but seldom refers any of them to the audiology clinic.

A partial analysis of total returns for a quarterly period is also very simple using the computer examination record forms. It is somewhat ironic though to have to use the human or manual method of analysis rather than the computer programme for which they were designed. As Table 9.2 shows, even this relatively simple type of analysis is vastly more illuminating than the basic DHSS statistics previously shown, and obviously far greater potential for cross correlations will be possible once the computer programs are in operation. We were also able to show the gradual increase in uptake from one quarter to the next which took place as the use of the system progressed (Table 9.3), with the fall in uptake in the fourth quarter. This resulted from the start, in that quarter, of developmental checks for the 18 month age group, thus confirming the

Table 9.2   Analysis of findings during one quarter, 1984

	Age		
	6 weeks (n = 572)	8 months (n = 539)	18 months (n = 134)
Locomotion	3	12	5
Manipulation	2	6	3
Vision	2	3	1
Hearing	2	21	4
Speech	—	1	5
Behaviour	2	1	1
Physical	16	14	—
Head circumference	3	6	—
Squint	6	16	2
Total problems	36	80	21
Rate	1/15	1/6.7	1/6.4

Table 9.3   Child health clinic attendances during 1984

	Quarter			
	1st	2nd	3rd	4th
Unscheduled	423	518	523	586
Scheduled	748	894	934	1032
Total	1171	1412	1457	1618
Per month	390	471	489	539
% uptake	69	84	87	64

generally held impression that after the age of 8 months attendance at the clinics fell sharply.

A definite change in policy has been influenced by these two basic evaluations since they showed a relatively high incidence of medical problems in the first two age groups compared with the 18 month check, as well as the poor attendance at the latter age. This gave added weight to the view that a domiciliary assessment by health visitors at 18 months would both be medically justified and improve uptake. The procedure is now under evaluation and was extremely easy to organise by making appropriate changes in the computer controlled appointment system — replacing clinic appointments scheduled for a particular day or week by monthly lists of eligible 18 month olds for each health visitor, after ensuring that they were all well trained for this role.

To summarise the results so far: they do provide a potential for analysis, monitoring and evaluation, providing facts on which to base decisions for change and improvements, which is an immense improvement on previous manually held records. It is still not possible to validate the results or, for example, to distinguish reliably between true and false positive findings (let alone the false negatives). Some suggestions for a more verifiable output as well as indications of the wider potential of the system are set out in the final section.

THE FUTURE OF CHILD HEALTH RECORDS AND THE COMPUTER

One of the problems of the National Child Health Computing System — or any other system — is that, while it remains part of a dual system — i.e., manual plus computer records — it can never provide a complete and valid analysis of the outcome of child health surveillance. So long as there is the possibility of recording findings, and especially referrals or action taken, on non-computerised records at unscheduled attendances, a great deal of information will never reach the computer. Thus an initial failure of a hearing test may be recorded on the computer record form, but subsequent repeat tests may not, so that the outcome is lost to analysis. No amount of exhortation always to use the computer record forms for all repeat screening tests, can guarantee compliance. Therefore the National Child Health Computing System must not simply supplement local manual clinic records, *it should entirely replace them.*

This does not mean to say that there should be no other, plain language notes made of a child's attainments — or a parent's problems and worries — and there is in fact a strong case for having some such backup notes. They should, however, be the property of the child's parents and not some official pseudoconfidential clinic based record. A great many doubts are expressed about the ability of parents to keep their child's records, but they can manage this in France — and St Thomas's 'Golden Book' was greatly valued by parents in London as was the *Nottingham Baby Book* in Nottingham (Polnay, 1984). I doubt whether parents are any more prone to lose records than any district child health clinic, provided the design of the records is such that they will be valued by the parents. When discussing parent-held records, problems are raised about how to record subjective judgments of the examiner about quality of parenting for example or even actual suspicion of child abuse, but these problems are surely not insurmountable. The necessity to express shared concerns about such problems would greatly improve the doctor–parent relationship, and there is always the possibility of telephoning or writing to the social worker in addition.

In order to answer the questions raised about the validity of child health surveillance therefore, the National Pre-school Child Health System could provide the essential data for evaluation if it was modified to allow sufficient examination details to be recorded so that it would then constitute the only clinic record for the child, apart from a well designed and attractive parent-held record. Such a modification could be planned jointly as part of a nationally agreed policy of child health surveillance, as suggested by Macfarlane and Pillay (1984) in their paper about pre-school health services, and again in the newsletter of the Community Paediatric Group of the BPA (Macfarlane, 1985).

There will be many who will argue against such a national policy backed up by a national record form, objecting to its uniformity or the simplified content, but surely it is far better to have a basic validated screening programme than a wide variety of procedures that can be demonstrated to be seriously deficient in detecting problems as well as raising anxieties in parents of perfectly healthy babies (Holt, 1984)? Such a national programme would not preclude, but would rather encourage, research developments and improvements in screening methods, and with the imminent availability of the National School Health Record system it could be extended throughout the entire age range. In addition to providing a validated record of the outcome of child health surveillance programmes, the computerised Child Health Record System should of course be linked with compatible hospital record systems and records of children with special needs or, for example, mental handicap registers. It is also essential that this record should be linked with or should contain data from the immunisation records also held on a national computer system, including any adverse reactions. Ross (1984) stated that much of the difficulty with pertussis vaccine could be avoided if proper computerised vaccination data were stored on a national basis. This is another cogent reason for a national computer-held record form in addition to enabling one, at long last, to judge the outcome and effectiveness of child health surveillance throughout the country.

The potential of a national computerised child health record system could thus reach far ahead of the often stereotyped and inaccessible child health records which it would replace. Far from perpetuating a basic lowest common denominator type of philosophy, it could provide the foundation for an improved system of child health surveillance and preventive service, linked with services providing for both the actute needs and the more long lasting special needs of children in Britain from the 1980s onwards into the 21st century.

REFERENCES

Davies L M, Bretman M D 1985 What do community health doctors do? Survey of their work in the child health service in Nottinghamshire. British Medical Journal 290: 1604–1606
Hendrickse W A 1982 How effective are our child health clinics? British Medical Journal 284: 575–577
Holt K 1984 Interviewed for article GP child screening project hits setback, General Practitioner 18 May 1984
GMSC debate 1984 on Paediatric surveillance reprinted in British Medical Journal 288: 1702–3
Jenkins S 1984 The functions of child health clinics, J A Macfarlane (Ed) Progress in Child Health Vol 1, Churchill Livingstone, ch 17
Macfarlane A 1985 A national child health surveillance programme — to be or not to be? Community Paediatric Group spring newsletter
Macfarlane J A, Pillay U 1984 Who does what, and how much in the pre-school child health services in England, British Medical Journal 289: 851–852
Polnay L 1984 The community paediatric team — an approach to child health services in a deprived inner city area Progress in Child Health Vol 1, Churchill Livingstone, ch. 16 (also personal communications)
Rigby M J 1981 Child Health — a time for better understanding? Health Trends 13: 97–99
Ross E M 1984 Whooping cough vaccine reviewed Progress in Child Health Vol 1, Churchill Livingstone, ch. 7
Walker C H M 1983 Computing in child health: significant progress British Medical Journal 287: 1400–1401

Disruptive behaviour in school

Classroom disruption is a daily challenge to teachers. It is one for which most have been poorly prepared. A class repeatedly punctuated by disruptive incidents is not one in which a curriculum, however carefully devised, can be well pursued. Even pupils, contrary perhaps to popular conception, rank the most important characteristic of a teacher as the ability to control the class (Gannoway, 1976).

Any investigation of disruption and its associated factors needs to take into account that disruption varies from class to class depending on the teacher, time, activity and other factors. The basic unit of study is the disruptive incident, not the pupil or teacher. Nevertheless, there are teachers who suffer above average disruption (Hargreaves et al, 1975; Marsh et al, 1978), and there are pupils who are frequently disruptive with many teachers and in many school contexts (Galloway et al, 1982) and over a long period (Farrington, 1978). So, while it must always be remembered that disruption is a complex, situationally dependent and interactive phenomenon with multiple causation, it has been valuable to study the children who are pervasively and persistently disruptive, and the schools and teachers who seem more disrupted than others.

A general and now familiar picture emerges of the background character-istics of these pupils, their schools and home contexts. Disruptive pupils as a group tend to have lower IQ, poor academic attainment, lower socioeconomic class and a relatively high prevalence of 'neurological' problems and to come from broken homes, or homes where there is marital discord, and from families with financial or housing difficulties. They also tend to suffer harsh and/or inconsistent discipline at home from fathers who often have a criminal or psychiatric history (Shepherd et al, 1971; Rutter et al, 1975; Farrington, 1978; Graham & Rutter, 1968; Galloway et al, 1982; Sturge, 1983; Frude, 1984).

In addition, schools differ in their rates of disruption and delinquency more than the characteristics of their pupil intake would predict (Power et al, 1967; Rutter et al, 1979; Galloway, 1980). Some of the factors of school organisation and ethos which correlate with *low* rates of disruption/deliquency are: emphasis on reward rather than punishment, immediacy of action on indiscipline, turning a blind eye to some rule breaking, not encroaching on pupils' out of school activities, teachers being approachable about pupils' personal problems, involving pupils in leadership activities, punctuality of teachers, well prepared lessons and a democratic organisation of teachers (Power, 1972; Reynolds, 1975; Rutter et al, 1979; Frude, 1984).

From the view point of the ordinary class teacher, most of these factors relating to pupils' personal and home characteristics and to school organisation are outside his control. The remainder of this paper concentrates on factors affecting disruption within the classroom itself. It is here that the classroom teacher could influence the situation directly, and it is here of course that disruption largely and importantly occurs. One major aspect of the Oxford study to be reported has been the development of techniques by which individual teachers may avoid or cope with disruption (Gray et al, 1985).

OXFORD STUDY — DEFINITION AND PREVALENCE OF DISRUPTION

The definition of 'disruption' used in any study will obviously affect the prevalence rates found. 'Suspension from school', used by Galloway et al (1982), gave a prevalence rate of only 0.001%, whereas Dawson (1982) found 1.5% of pupils to be causing an 'unusually high degree of concern for behavioural reasons' to their teachers.

In our studies a different definition of disruption was used, which seemed more meaningful than previous definitions for the following reason. Disruption occurs and is experienced in the classroom. As with all behaviour problems, identification of disruption arises out of a relationship between disrupter and disrupted. It depends not only on the observable disruptive behaviour, but also on the reaction of the disrupted individual(s). Therefore, the definition of disruption used in our study was simply to accept the identification of certain pupils as disruptive by teachers on the one hand by other pupils in the year group on the other.

We asked all the staff teaching the third year (ages 13–14 years) in two comprehensive schools in Oxfordshire to name pupils who disrupted their lessons. Altogether 18% (65 out of 364) were nominated by at least one teacher and 7.3% (26) were nominated by two or more teachers. Of these 26, it can be said that they were not nominated as a result of a 'personality clash' with a specific teacher (Gnagey, 1970).

All third year pupils were also asked to nominate disruptive pupils. Altogether 27% (97) received two or more nominations. The same prevalence rate of disrupters (about 7%) identified by two teachers was achieved by a cut off point of 10 or more pupil nominations. This produced 7.6% (27) pupils identified as disruptive.

All such cut off points (in this case two or more teachers, 10 or more pupils) are to some extent arbitrary, but the cut off points chosen gain validity when the coincidence of pupil and teacher nominations is investigated. This coincidence was high and significant (Table 10.1), suggesting that pupil and teacher nominations reflect more than idiosyncratic relationship problems.

Table 10.1 Pupil identification of disruptive pupils compared with staff identification

No. of nominations by peers	No. of nominations by staff		
	0	1	2 or more
< 2	249 (70.3)	8 (2.3)	1 (0.3)
2–9	37 (10.5)	26 (7.3)	7 (2.0)
> 10	3 (0.8)	5 (1.4)	18 (5.1)

Figures in brackets are percentages of 364, the total population surveyed

Taking the pupils nominated by both two or more teachers *and* 10 or more pupils, then the 5.1% jointly identified as disruptive may be taken as a possibly useful and relevant prevalence figure. This represents one or two pupils on average per surveyed class of about 30 pupils.

This figure is interestingly similar to the prevalence of school age behaviour problems (Rutter et al, 1970, 1975). However, our definition gains value only if it usefully discriminates children in terms of other characteristics. In other words, are the pupils nominated by two or more teachers and/or 10 or more pupils different in other ways too.

CHARACTERISTICS OF DISRUPTIVE PUPILS

Disruptive pupils were investigated in several ways, four of which will be reported here. These are:

1. self completion pupil questionnaire
2. staff questionnaire
3. sociometry
4. classroom direct observation

1. Self-completion pupil questionnaire

This questionnaire looked at several aspects of social relationships and attitudes in school (Gray, 1983). It was compiled from two main sources: (1) questions on social difficulty, from Lindsey and Lindsey (1982); (2) the National Foundation for Educational Research (NFER) questionnaire SF7 (Barker-Lunn, 1970; Ferri, 1971). In the same questionnaire pupils answered questions for a sociometric analysis and made nominations of disruptive pupils in their year group.

The original questionnaire data were initially analysed by means of a rotated factor analysis. This produced 10 factors with Eigen values above 1.0 and therefore of significance.

One factor that might have been thought to be particularly important for disruptive behaviour is 'attitude to school'. Most of the questions that loaded heavily on to it were derived from the NFER questionnaire and related to their construct 'attitude to school'. Low scores on this factor indicated that the child disliked or placed a low value on school. There is a considerable literature that is based on the concept of disruptive behaviour being derived from a child's underlying disaffection from school (e.g., Skinner et al, 1983; Bird et al, 1980). From this it would be expected that disruptive pupils would have significantly low scores on the factor described as 'attitude to school'. In practice, the relationship was not significant even at the 10% level. This suggests that the assumption that disruptive behaviour is importantly related to a disaffection from school needs to be re-examined.

A regression analysis was carried out on the original questionnaire data with the 'number of pupil nominations' as the dependent variable and the factor scores derived from the questionnaire as the independent variable. Two factors correlated highly significantly with the number of pupil nominations; these were 'adult social skills' and 'academic self image'.

Interesting differences in factor scores were found when seriousness of disruption, and sex differences were looked at. Two groups of disruptives, mild and serious, were distinguished on the basis of numbers of pupil nominations. (2–9, > 10). These results are shown in Table 10.2.

Table 10.2 Factor scores & disruption (peer nominations only)

No. of pupil nominations Sex	All disrupters 2+			Mild disrupters 2–9			Serious disrupters 10+		
	Both	Boys	Girls	Both	Boys	Girls	Both	Boys	Girls
Low social skills with adults	20	8	12	17	7	10	3	1	2
Low academic self esteem	20	20	0	17	17	0	3	3	0
Both low	32	24	8	17	10	7	15	14	1
Neither low	17	11	6	16	10	6	1	1	0
Total	89	63	26	67	44	23	22	19	3

Data incomplete – data could not be got from all pupils. Low = below average

It can be seen that two thirds of the serious disrupters had low scores on both factors, whereas this applied to only a quarter of mild disrupters. A further half of the mild disrupters had low scores on only one factor and a quarter on neither. There seems then to be an additive effect of both these two factors on the production of disruption.

An interesting sex difference also emerged. While boys and girls were equally likely to have low scores on both factors, when there was a low score on only one factor that factor was always 'low social skills with adults' in girls and tended to be 'low academic self image' in boys. This may reflect the generally greater concern of girls for direct social relationships and of boys for success in activities (activities which form media for social relationships).

2. Staff questionnaire

The finding that poor adult social skills and low academic self image are important characteristics of disruptive children gains validity when related to results of the teacher questionnaire. The constructs, used by teachers to construe the children, were first elicited from a sample of teachers using triads containing disruptive and non-disruptive pupils. Then the five most frequent constructs which distinguished disruptive and non-disruptive pupils were selected and all teachers asked to rate the disruptive children on them. The averages of each pupil's ratings were then correlated with pupils' scores on the two factors. The results are shown in Table 10.3.

Table 10.3 Relationships between pupil scores on factors and on teachers constructs

Teacher constructs	Scores on factor for social skills	Scores on factor for academic self image
Easily distracted/ not easily distracted	NS	$p = 0.002$*
Malicious/not malicious	$p = 0.001$*	NS
Rude/polite	$p = 0.02$*	NS
Hard working/lazy	NS	$p = 0.03$*
Short attention span/ long attention span	NS	$p = 0.02$*

* Fisher exact test

Data are incomplete, and scores of 41 disruptive pupils were examined. It can be seen that teachers' ratings of 'malicious' and 'rude' correlated with 'poor social skills with adults', whereas ratings of 'easily distracted', 'lazy' and 'short attention span' correlated with 'poor academic self image'.

Therefore, not only do pupils and teachers tend to identify the same pupils as disruptive (Table 10.2), but teachers and the disruptive pupils themselves make the same discriminations within the disruptive group. However, they make these discriminations in importantly different terms from their different perspectives (Marsh et al, 1978; Galloway et al, 1982; Frude, 1984).

3. Sociometry

A major aspect of children's lives in school is their relationship with other pupils. This is also of considerable interest to the staff, for instance Lawrence et al (1984) found that one significant group of teacher explanations for disruptive behaviour was 'friends lead him/her into trouble' (page 95). This makes it very important to learn how disruptive pupils fit into the peer friendship structures. To this end, our sample of pupils were asked on their questionnaire forms to name pupils who they did not like to be with in lessons. The answers to these questions were then analysed to determine whether disruptive pupils differed from controls in terms of their popularity and unpopularity in this situation.

These data showed that the disrupter's lot is not a happy one. Far from being a popular leader of an alternative culture in class, identified disrupters were unpopular. It is important, however, to distinguish between a pupil's score for popularity and his or her score for unpopularity.

Scores for popularity (nominations on the question 'a pupil I do like to be with') showed no clear relationship to disruptiveness. It seemed that disruptive pupils had neither a larger nor an abnormally small number of friends. No significant relationship was found. This lack of a significant relationship is probably due to the effects of cliques. Small groups within the class can nominate friends within the ranks of a group, so it is likely that many disrupters were effective members of small cliques.

This lack of relationship is not at all the case when nominations for being 'disliked' are considered. Here a very strong relationship ($p < 0.005$, gamma) was found. Disruptive pupils (two or more pupil nominations) were disliked, and seriously disruptive pupils (10 or more pupil nominations) are widely disliked by their peers. This is consistent with the findings of Galloway et al (1982), who found that over one third of the sample of suspended pupils had few if any friends.

If one of the explanations teachers use for disruptive behaviour is peer influences, then they ought at least to have some accurate conception of the social structure of their class. In our study staff were asked to name pupils who were popular, unpopular, isolated, members of groups 'positive to the working of the class' and members of groups 'negative to the working of the class'. The latter two categories were introduced to see if there was any relationship between them and pupils' popularity, since attitude to class work has been considered to be an important factor in the formation of groups in the classroom (Frude, 1984). The findings are summarised in Table 10.4.

It will be seen from Table 10.4 that, for girls, teachers' perceptions were accurate. Also, there was no significant relationship between popularity and teacher identification as being either a positive or a negative class member.

The picture for boys was very different. It was only the isolates that teachers identified accurately; their perceptions of popularity and unpopularity were, in fact, the exact reverse of their pupils' from the sociometric data. Boys identified as popular by the teacher were unpopular with the pupils and vice versa. There was also a relationship with being a positive or negative class member. Boys identified as being a member of a group 'positive to class working' tend to be unpopular and those in the 'negative' groups were popular with their peers.

In so far as disruptive boys are generally unpopular in class, teachers misperception of their popularity is likely to make classroom control rather difficult.

Table 10.4 Comparison with sociometry results — teachers 'right' or 'wrong'

Teachers classify pupils as:	Girls	Boys
(i) Popular	right	wrong
Unpopular	right	wrong
Isolated	right	right
	Relationship with popularity from sociometry	
(ii) Positive class member	none	unpopular
Negative class member	none	popular

(i)   Relationship between teachers' and pupils' identification of popularity
(ii)   Relationship of pupil identification of popularity with teacher identification
         of pupils positive or negative to classwork

The inaccuracy of teachers' perceptions of boys' social structures (social groupings are largely single sex at this age) — i.e., their perception of relationships *not involving themselves* but between two or more others — contrasts with their relative accuracy in perceiving good or poor social skills with adults — i.e., in perceiving relationships in which *they themselves are involved*. In this latter case, even though teachers and pupils are grouping together the same children, they are attaching very different labels to those groups. Teachers' descriptions of the disruptive children are generally perjorative ('rude', 'lazy'); they place blame on the pupil, and offer little that is constructive in the way of positive intervention.

This egocentricity militates against effective classroom control. Reconstruing the problem, in this case in terms of poor social skills with adults, offers a more constructive and actionable and less subjective alternative view of classroom management.

4. Direct observation in class

All the data so far presented have, strictly speaking, concerned the perceptions and attitudes of pupils and teachers of themselves and others. These data are incomplete if they are not related to publically observable behaviour and situations.

Forty lessons were observed by JRG. In each lesson a disruptive and a control pupil (matched for sex and verbal reasoning quotient) and the teacher were observed. Instantaneous scan sampling (Altman, 1974) on a 5 second interval was used to observe each of the three in turn. Eighteen child and 18 teacher items were recorded (Gray, 1985), but these were collapsed into four categories for analysis:

working
work related activity (e.g. collecting materials)
socialising
misbehaving.

(i) Work

Not surprisingly, disruptive pupils work less than controls, and on average 51% of observations were spent in a work or work related activity per lesson by disruptives versus 73% for controls. However, there was considerable overlap: the range for disruptives was 10–80% and, for controls, 40–90%.

(ii) Activity switching

The ratio of consecutive observations that were different ('switches') to those that were the same was calculated per lesson for each pupil. Disruptive pupils switched activity about twice as often as controls (mean ratios: 0.32 v 0.17).

(iii) Lesson type: whole class, group, individual

Lessons were divided into 3 minute periods, and each characterised by its predominant lesson type: whole class, group or individual. Comparisons were made between disruptives and controls on work versus non-work and on misbehaving versus not misbehaving.

(a) Work. Disruptive pupils worked less than controls for 129 of 405, 3 minute periods and more than controls for only 10 periods (Fisher exact test used on each 3 minute period). There was, however, no effect of lesson type.

(b) Misbehaving. As would be expected, significantly more misbehaviour was observed in disruptive pupils. In 37, 3 minute periods they misbehaved significantly more than controls, but significantly less than controls in only one. Lesson type was important here; misbehaviour was more frequent in periods characterised as 'individual' or 'group work' than in 'whole class' type periods.

Summary

To summarise the direct observation data, disruptive pupils work less and switch activity more, but the amount of work shows much overlap between disruptives and controls and it is not affected by lesson type. Amount of misbehaviour is, not surprisingly, more frequent in disruptives and is affected by lesson type, being more frequent when the class is meant to be doing individual or group work as opposed to whole class instruction.

DISCUSSION OF MAIN FINDINGS

Even from these preliminary analyses a clear picture of disruptive pupils emerges, in which data from all three main sources — pupils, teachers and observer — fit together coherently.

The disruptive pupil, we can hypothesise, is frustrated in the classroom and with his attempts at work, so he works less and switches activity more, has poor academic self image and is seen by the teacher as distractable, lazy and with poor attention span. He is frustrated in his interactions with adults so he misbehaves more often and is seen by the teacher as rude and malicious, but is also generally unpopular with his peers, in class at least, but teachers do not perceive this unpopularity accurately in boys, who form the bulk of disruptives.

This fits well with findings from the behaviour modification literature, which emphasises, as means of reducing disruptive behaviour, both structured remedial help and an increase in warm praise and encouragement from the teacher. Both would reduce frustration and increase academic and social self esteem (Yule et al, 1984).

These twin central characteristics, poor academic self image (related to poor academic performance) and poor social skills with adults, are also consistent with the background features of disruptive pupils. The first would be expected in a group with an excess of low IQ children, poor academic attainment and 'neurological' abnormalities. The second would be expected from a group from stressful home environments, with harsh inconsistent discipline and poor models for identification. Each factor refers to a major task in the classroom, namely, getting on with work and getting on with the teacher. Poor skills in either make for frustration, and disruptiveness therefore becomes more likely; poor skills in both make disruptive behaviour even more likely.

Let us emphasise again that disruption is a feature of a relationship between pupil and the teacher/school. Features in teacher behaviour and school ethos/organisation which heighten frustration in work or adult–child relations should increase disruption. Our first factor is related to poorly prepared, and therefore unstructured, lessons; inappropriate attention to academic standards (too much or too little) and, as we have found, too much inappropriately designed small group or individual work. These will increase work related frustration and so disruption. Decreasing frustration in adult–child inter-actions (our second factor) should decrease disruption, and do so by an emphasis on rewards rather than punishments, immediate action on discipline (to set limits and clarify relationships), ignoring some trivia and not encroaching on pupils out-of-school lives. Finally, frustration in relationships will be decreased if the pupil feels the teacher is approachable on personal matters, and, in turn, the teacher feels supported in that he or she is able to approach other members of staff, including the head, with his or her difficulties.

MANAGING DISRUPTION

If we accept that poor social skills with adults and poor academic performance/self image with their consequent frustration are important in promoting disruption, then improving these should decrease disruption. If disruption is to diminish it is necessary, although it may not be sufficient, to address it where it happens, in class. The teachers themselves need to develop class management techniques that enable them to avoid or to deal with disruption in the classroom. There is little reason to suppose that this task is any easier than trying to develop skills in the other half of the relationship, the pupil. Teachers are embedded in a social structure, the school, just as much as their pupils, and, like many of their pupils, espouse egocentric and perjorative views about their pupils, which stand in the way of the acquisition of successful class management techniques.

A recent manual of such techniques is currently being evaluated (Gray et al, 1985). A summary of its contents would be impossible here. It emphasises ways of observing and learning about pupils and of coping with the poor social skills and poor academic self image/performance of the more disruptive pupils, as well as more general class control techniques. By using these techniques the individual teacher can reduce disruption in class. They will do so even more efficiently if these measures are part of a wider 'package' where the school as a whole offers coherent support, a sentiment all teachers would agree with, but their intention is sometimes not translated into reality.

REFERENCES

Altmann 1974 Observational study of behaviour: sampling methods. Behaviour 49: 227–267
Barker-Lunn J 1970 Streaming in the primary school. National Foundation for Educational Research, Slough
Bird C, Cressum R, Furlong J, Johnson D (eds) 1980 Disaffected pupils. Brunel University Educational Studies Unit
Dawson R L 1982 Special provision for disturbed pupils: a survey. MacMillan Educational, London
Farrington D 1978 The family backgrounds of aggressive youths. In: Hersov L A, Berger M (eds) Aggression and antisocial behaviour in childhood and adolescence. Pergamon, Oxford
Ferri E 1971 Streaming 20 years later. National Foundation for Educational Research, Slough
Frude N 1984 Framework for analysis. In: Frude N, Gault H (eds) Disruptive behaviour in schools. Wiley, Chichester
Galloway D M 1980 Exclusions and suspension from school. Trends in Education 2: 33–8
Galloway D M, Bell T, Blomfield D, Seyd R 1982 Schools and disruptive pupils. Longman, London
Gannoway H 1976 Making sense of school. Stubbs M, Delamont S (eds) Exploration in classroom observations. Wiley, London
Gnagey W J 1970 The psychology of discipline in the classroom. Macmillan, London
Graham P, Rutter M 1968 Organic brain dysfunction and child psychiatric disorder. British Medical Journal iii: 695–700
Gray J R 1983 Classroom disruption and social skills. Dissertation for special diploma in educational studies. Oxford University Department of Educational Studies
Gray J R 1985 Classroom observation behaviour categories. Unpublished manuscript
Gray J R, Howarth R, Postlethwaite K, Richer J M 1985 A teacher's classroom control manual. Unpublished manuscript
Hargreaves D H, Hester S K, Mellor F J 1975 Deviance in classroom. Routledge and Kegan Paul, London
Lawrence J, Steed D, Young P 1984 Disruptive children – disruptive schools? Croom Helm, London
Lindsey W, Lindsey K 1982 A self report questionnaire about social difficulty for adolescents. British Journal of Adolescence 5: 62–69
Marsh P, Rosser E, Harre R 1978 The rules of disorder. Routledge and Kegan Paul, London
Power M J 1972 Neighbourhood school and juveniles before the courts. British Journal of Criminology 12: 111–132
Power M J, Alderson M R, Phillipson C M, Schoenberg E, Morris J N 1967 Delinquent schools. New Society, 19 October

Reynolds D 1975 When teachers and pupils refuse to truce: the secondary school and the creation of delinquency. In: Mungham G, Pearson S (eds) Working class youth culture. Routledge and Kegan Paul, London

Rutter M, Tizard J, Whitmore K 1970 Health education and behaviour. Longman, London

Rutter M, Cox A, Tupling C, Berger M, Yule W 1975 Attainment and adjustment in two geographical areas. 1. Prevalence of psychiatric disorder. British Journal of Psychiatry 126: 493–509

Rutter M, Maughan B, Mortimore P, Ouston J 1979 Fifteen thousand hours. Open Books, London

Shepherd M, Oppenhiem B, Mitchell S 1971 Childhood behaviour and mental health. University of London Press, London

Skinner A, Platts H, Hill B 1983 Disaffection from school. Leicester National Youth Bureau, Leicester

Sturge C 1982 Reading retardation and anti-social behaviour. Journal of Child Psychology and Psychiatry 23: 21–31

Yule W, Nerger M, Wigley V 1984 Behaviour modification and classroom management. In: Frude N, Gault H (eds) Disruptive behaviour in schools. Wiley, Chichester

Behavioural treatment of problems in children

The behavioural treatment of childhood problems had its origins in the 1920s and 30s, notably in the work on children's fears, phobias and enuresis carried out by Holmes (1936), M C Jones (1924) and Mowrer (1938), respectively. There followed two decades of relative uninterest in the approach. Then the 1960s witnessed a dramatic resurgence of activity — manifested by an outpouring of books and articles — which has continued unabated to the present time. The journal *Child Behaviour Therapy* was founded in 1979.

The terms 'behaviour therapy', and 'behaviour modification', at one time pedantically (and at times, disdainfully) differentiated, tend to be used synonymously today. They no longer refer to a monlithic, narrowly conceived theoretical system (see Kazdin, 1978). Social learning theory, which encompasses the social, cognitive and affective components of behaviour, informs the work of many practitioners who work with children in the behavioural modality. A major assumption of the behavioural approach is that, as a psychological therapy (or intervention), its proper subject is behaviour rather than hypothetical, underlying quasi-disease processes. Behaviour therapists generally acknowledge three main classes of behaviour: motor responses, psychological responses, and cognitive responses. Problem behaviours (be they aggressive actions, bedwetting or phobic avoidance patterns) are perceived as the central focus of therapeutic attention. Functional (prosocial, normal, appropriate) behaviours are construed as being, in large part, on a continuum with dysfunctional (antisocial, abnormal, inappropriate) behaviours, and are thought to be lawfully determined by the same principles. Frequently these are *learning* principles which underpin the acquisition, maintenance and elimination or reduction of behaviours.

Certain behaviours are defined as dysfunctional by social rather than objective, medical criteria; problematic activities are so-called because they are excessive or deficient, in quantitative terms (see Fig. 11.1); they are manifested in inappropriate situations (see Fig. 11.1); and the topography — the formal aspects — of behaviour is unacceptable and/or inefficient.

145

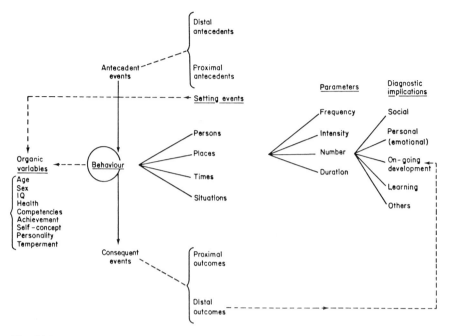

Fig. 11.1 Assessment framework. (Adapted, with permission, from Herbert, 1981)

Assessment

Behaviour therapists often refer to their assessment as a *functional* analysis (see the ABC terms, Fig. 11.1). In essence they make use of direct observation and interview methods (Herbert, 1981) in order to specify those *antecedent* (A) and *consequent* (C) conditions under which behaviour (B) is manifested. A specific description of the child's behaviour is offered on the basis of the functional relationship between the behaviour and the conditions under which it occurs.

As described by Ollendick and Cerny (1981), 'the description is generally data based (rather than theory based) and is obtained from a "sample' of the child's behaviour (rather than inferred from a test "sign')'. Thus, from a behavioural perspective, a child who indulges in frequent, intense temper tantrums would be observed in order to determine the specific circumstances and conditions in which the tantrums occur. Such conditions may involve antecedent organismic (O) and/or environmental stimulus events (A) which precipitate or set the scene for the temper outbursts and the consequent events (C) that maintain them. The functional relationship may be determined by.

1. Operant conditioning. Probably the best known learning principle in behaviour therapy is operant or instrumental conditioning. (This particular model is particularly (and sometimes exclusively) associated with fundamentalist versions of behaviour modification or applied behaviour analysis.) With operant conditioning the emphasis is on the response and consequent events (C). Behaviour is, to a large extent, a function of its consequences — 'favourable' or 'unfavourable' to the child. Thus, therapy involves the manipulation of reinforcement (rewards) and punishment (penalties).

2. *Classical conditioning.* In the classical conditioning model the emphasis is on the stimulus — antecedent events (A). The Pavlovian paradigm is well known. Counterconditioning treatments (e.g. desensitisation and flooding) and aversive procedures (embodying escape, avoidance and punishment para-digms) are rooted in classical conditioning.

3. *Observational learning (modelling and imitation).* Bandura (1969) states that one of the fundamental means by which human behaviour is acquired is through modelling (imitation) or vicarious processes. A distinction is made between *learning* an action and the subsequent *performance* of the learned behaviour. Although observational learning can occur in the absence of response consequences, the nature of the consequences (e.g. reinforcement) to both the model and the child determine whether the modelled behaviour is performed or not.

4. *Cognitive learning* Perceptions and cognitions influence learning and behaviour in a systematic manner (Mahoney, 1974). Cognitive based procedures aim to modify emotion and behaviour by influencing and changing the patient's pattern of thinking and 'self-talk'. An attempt is made to modify specific perceptions, images, thoughts and beliefs by the direct manipulation and restructuring of dysfunctional cognitions (Meichenbaum, 1977).

The point about these theories or principles of learning is that they explain *all* forms of learning; thus abnormal behaviour in children is no different from normal behaviour in the way it develops. Unfortunately — and it is the case with all forms of learning — the very processes which help the child adapt to life can, under certain circumstances, contribute to his or her maladaption. An immature child who learns by imitating an adult will not necessarily understand when it is undesirable (antisocial) rather than appropriate (prosocial) behaviour that is being modelled. The child who learns usefully on the basis of what are called 'conditioning' processes to avoid dangerous situations can also learn in the same way (maladaptively) to avoid social gatherings or school. A parent may unwittingly reinforce immature behaviour by attending solicitously to it.

Behavioural methods

The range of behavioural methods generated by the learning paradigms outlined above, is extensive as is the variety of problems to which they have been applied. Broadly speaking, childhood problems can be divided into three categories: (a) behaviour that is excessive (e.g. screaming, hitting, incessant pestering); (b) behaviour that is 'normal' or appropriate of itself, but occurs in restricted or inappropriate contexts (e.g. compliant actions to delinquent peer values but not to prosocial family norms); (c) behaviour that is absent from, or poorly represented in, the child's repertoire.

The categories of methods likewise fall broadly into three categories:

(a) Reducing or eliminating inappropriate behaviour. The methods include (inter alia) satiation, extinction, time-out from positive reinforcement, overcorrection, response-cost and promotion of alternative/incompatible actions.

(b) Providing the correct context for behaviours. The methods include discrimination training, prompting, cueing, modelling, skills training and problem-solving.

(c) Strengthening/developing patterns of behaviour. The methods include (inter alia) positive reinforcement, negative reinforcement, shaping, modelling and skills training.

Settings

There are three main settings in which behavioural work with children takes place. Therapy based on the dyadic (one-to-one) model tends to take place in the clinic; treatment on the triadic model (using significant care givers or teachers as mediators of change) takes place in the home or in the school.

The treatment of 'neurotic' and stress disorders is likely to occur in the clinic, although there is nothing absolute about such a demarcation. These problems tend to be of relatively short term duration (Herbert, 1974).

Short term problems

Although the distinction between treatment and training is, at times, indistinct, the treatment model is most appropriate to the 'emotional' disorders of childhood.

Fears and phobias

A commonly held behavioural view of anxiety and fear (and other powerful emotional reactions) is that they are acquired on the basis of classical conditioning (Watson & Rayner, 1920) and maintained by avoidance behaviour which is reinforced on an operant basis (Mowrer, 1960).

1. Desensitisation

The procedure called systematic desensitisation involves the presentation of the anxiety provoking stimulus while preventing the anxiety response from occurring. Counterconditioning is claimed to be one of the therapeutic mechanisms underlying the undoubted success of systematic desensitisation in the treatment of child fear states (Hatzenbuehler & Schroeder, 1978) including school attendance, physical injury, hospital, bathing, darkness, death, dogs and dentistry.

Emotionally, the child is trained to engage in an activity (e.g. relaxation) that is incompatible with the anxiety reaction. The anxiety stimulus may be *imagined* (conjured up by the child's fantasy in imagination) or presented in vivo (the child being exposed to the real life stimulus). Elements said to be important in the Wolpe (1969) version of systematic desensitisation — deep muscular relaxation, vivid evocation of images — can prove difficult for younger children (Ollendick, 1979). The necessary condition for change seems to be *exposure* to the feared object or situation. For children, participant modelling by the therapist seems to be a helpful ingredient.

2. Cognitive self-management skills

Stress-inoculation training has been used successfully (Meichenbaum, 1977) in the self-management of phobic anxiety, anger and pain. Children are provided with a set of skills and defences so as to deal with future crises. The training programme has three stages:

(a) Education. The child is provided with a conceptual framework for understanding the nature of his problem.

(b) Provision of coping strategies. A number of behavioural and cognitive coping skills, arising from the conceptual framework, are rehearsed by the child in the 'safety' of the home or consulting room.

(c) Practice. The opportunity is provided for the child to practise his coping skills while being exposed to a variety of real stress and/or practice by means of imagery and behavioural rehearsal.

3. Problem-solving

The treatment of various stress disorders may be based on a view of emotional disturbance as the consequence of ineffectual behaviour — instances of the child's inability to resolve certain life problems. Rather than thinking of the child as *being* a problem or *having* a problem, he is conceived of as trying to *solve* a problem, but in a self-defeating manner manifested in his difficult, unacceptable behaviour (see Herbert, 1985). This approach (Kendall, 1981) overlaps with the preceding one; children (and their parents) are taught rational thinking and problem solving strategies that can accommodate a variety of awkward situations. Where many of the cognitive problems associated with adult anxiety and depression can be conceptualised as *cognitive errors*, the focus of the therapies (for children) outlined above, are mainly to do with *cognitive absences*. The child fails to engage in the cognitive, information processing activities of an active problem solver and refrains from initiating the reflective thought processes that can control behaviour. Indeed, he may lack the cognitive skills needed to carry out crucial abstract, analytical mental activities. Thus he might be taught to analyse situations, shown how to negotiate and find compromises in conflict situations, to apply social skills to the peer group and so on.

Physical symptoms

Children with disorders involving bodily systems have been treated success-fully by behavioural methods, notably in the realms of enuresis and encopresis (Herbert & Iwaniec, 1981); ashthma (Creer, 1970); failure to thrive (Iwaniec et al 1985); stomach pains (Siegel & Richards, 1978) and obesity (Kingsley & Shapiro, 1977).

Most research has occurred in relation to the use of conditioning methods (implicit in the bell-and-pad) applied to enuresis and operant methods applied to encopresis; however, the work being carried out using biofeedback and other techniques for respiratory disorders and epilepsy has interesting ramifications for children's units in general hospitals and primary care teams (see Ollendick & Cerny, 1981, for an excellent overview).

LONG TERM PROBLEMS

There is insufficient space to do justice to the significant behavioural work (with long term objectives) carried out with mentally handicapped and autistic children and children with learning disabilities. Excellent reviews on these subjects are available by Weatherby and Baumeister (1981), Schreibman and Koegel (1981) and Lahey et al (1981), respectively. The training model of behaviour modification, involving the teaching of care givers and teachers (as well as children) in behavioural analysis and/or techniques, is particularly applicable in these areas and also in the potentially long term problem because of their grave prognosis — the so-called conduct disorders.

Conduct disorders

This is the generic (and somewhat loose) term applied to children whose behaviour can generally be described as 'out of control' as perceived by their parents, teachers and other long suffering peers and adults within their reach. Their problems are multitudinal and include aggressiveness, physical destructiveness, non-compliance, annoying and coercive actions (screaming, threatening, pestering) and other antisocial, sometimes delinquent, behaviours (e.g. stealing, fire raising). Some are also hyperactive, a feature which provides another 'turn of the screw' of misery for their hapless, often demoralised and depressed care givers (see Herbert, 1978).

Not surprisingly, parents figure significantly in the therapeutic programmes, not least because of their major contribution to the evolution of such problems. Parents of such deviant children display a significantly greater proportion of commands and criticisms and high rates of threats, anger, nagging and negative consequences than parents of non-referred children (Delfini et al, 1976; Lobitz & Johnson, 1975). There is frequently a lack of contingent consequences among the distressed family members. The probability of receiving a positive, neutral or aversive consequence for coercive behaviour seems to be independent of the behaviour — a gross inconsistency. Indeed, there may be positive consequences for deviant behaviour and punishment for those rare prosocial actions (Patterson, 1977; Snyder, 1977). Patterson and Fleischman (1979) hypothesise that the disturbed social interactions among the members of the family induce powerful feelings of frustration, anger and helplessness and low self-esteem.

Parent training programmes thus include methods designed to reduce confrontations and antagonistic interactions among the family members, to increase the effectiveness (and moderate the intensity) of parental punishment and establish consistent and genuinely rewarding patterns of reinforcement. Attention is paid to boosting parents' confidence and self-esteem and bolstering their expectations of success and sense of self-efficacy in their management of their offspring. Depending on the age of the child, he or she may be taught self-monitoring, the evaluation of their actions and self-control techniques. Problem solving and social skill training are components of many programmes designed for conduct disordered children (Herbert, 1981).

Parents are behaviour modifers

All parents are informal learning theorists and all are in the business of behaviour modification (i.e. changing behaviour). They use various techniques to train, influence and change the child in their care. Among those used are material and psychological rewards, praise and encouragement, giving or withholding love, reproof, corporal and psychological punishment, approval and disapproval, as well as direct instruction, setting an example and providing explanations of rules.

The basic principles of behaviour modification are clear and easily communicated to parents and other care givers and to professionals and paraprofessionals (Herbert, 1981). The characteristics of behaviour modification make it particularly amenable to employing individuals in a client's everyday surroundings as treatment intermediaries. Far from adopting an authoritative posture (as an esoteric cult) behaviour modification is willing and able to rally the support of people in the community to the task. This de-mystification process is important because many of the factors which contribute to the perception of and instigation of problem behaviour (and interactions) need to be influenced directly and immediately, and the social worker, psychologist or psychiatrist may not be in the best position to direct the needed change.

Parent training

Ayllon and Azrin (1968) propose a guideline: 'Teach only those behaviours which will continue to be reinforced after training'. The therapist's aim in using behaviour modification procedures is to introduce the child to behaviours which are either intrinsically reinforcing or which make reinforcements available to him which he was not previously experiencing. In a sense there are two therapeutic objectives in working with children.

(a) To enhance a child's responses to the controlling factors in his environment without deliberately altering the latter. Assuming a family environment to be essentially satisfactory, one might attempt to adjust a child to it.
(b) To change the controlling factors in an unsatisfactory learning environment as a means of modifying problem behaviour.

Where the latter strategy is predominant the therapeutic objective is to programme the environment so that it sustains the child's (and parents') 'improvement' after the formal programme has been terminated. The long term purpose of this phase of therapy is to help parents to become more systematic in their own behaviour so as to be more effective in managing their children.

There are several levels at which parent training might be pitched, four of which are listed by Gardner (1976) as follows:

1. The applicator is able to apply specific behavioural techniques under circumscribed conditions to solve particular problems.

2. The technician is able to apply a broader variety of techniques, but still under limited conditions, to solve specific problems.

3. The generalist has the 'know how' to apply theory and techniques to a wide spectrum of problems with a minimum of supervision.

4. The consultant is the person who trains others in behavioural theory and methods.

Of course, the rationale of the desire to train parents to the generalist level is the belief that the parents' ongoing contact with the child and possession of new skills might facilitate generalisation of treatment effects across time. Clients not only learn a new model of behaviour — a construct system which emphasises the significance of behavioural consequences and environmental causality — but assimilate new *methods* of understanding behaviour. They learn a new language for communicating about behaviour and a more precise way of specifying, defining, observing and thinking about behaviour — environment relationships. Various people are researching into the cost-effectiveness and cost-benefits of training parents in different ways. Sadly, the evidence in the area of temporal generalisation is mixed: positive with regard to long term persistence of favourable effects in some studies (see Griffin & Hudson, 1978), negative or minimal in others. A further hope is that thorough parent training will enhance the transfer of skills applied to one problem in the child's behavioural repertoire area to novel problems manifested by the same child. This expectation is difficult to translate into reality. The evidence is a little more positive when it comes to generalisation across children.

The time span for change is necessarily, in the case of conduct problems, a long one, given the slowly evolving, complex psychological attributes (e.g. internalisation of rules, resistance to temptation, empathy, self-control) we are dealing with. The goal of behavioural work (referred to as behavioural casework) in home settings, is to change not only the target child, but also parental and sometimes sibling behaviour (Herbert, 1985; Herbert & Iwaniec, 1981). Change is brought about by developmental counselling and by discussion, modelling and the use of more consistent sanctions for anti-social behaviour and effective and timely reinforcers for prosocial behaviour. Casework skills, such as clarifying problems, listening sympathetically, indicating empathic understanding and acceptance and so on, are an important part of the therapeutic armamentarium.

Initially, there were euphoric claims for the effectiveness of the behavioural approach; clinicians could be forgiven if they were seduced by the literature into believing that a panacea for all child problems had been discovered. The excessive optimism was founded on sometimes fragile data, derived mainly from single subject descriptive case studies. Research methodology since the late 1960s has become more sophisticated, critical and rigorous. Fortunately, much of the enthusiasm (properly tempered by caution) was not misplaced. Kazdin (1979), in a special issue of the *American Psychologist* entitled *Psychology and Children: Current Research and Practice*, concluded, on the basis of his review of the evidence, that 'for many problem areas, effective treatments have emerged that can be applied in naturalistic or treatment settings. For other problem areas, research has yet to make the necessary progress' (p.987).

REFERENCES

Ayllon T, Azrin N H 1968 The token economy: a motivational system for therapy and rehabilitation. Appleton-Century-Crofts, New York.
Bandura A 1969 Principles of behaviour modification. Holt, Rinehart & Winston, New York
Creer T L 1970 The use of time-out from positive reinforcement procedure with asthmatic children. Journal of Psychosomatic Research 14: 117–120
Delfini L F, Bernal M E, Rosen P M 1976 Comparison of deviant with normal elementary school children. In: Mash E J, Hammerlynck L A, Handy L G (eds) Behaviour modification and families. Brunner/Mazel, New York
Gardner J M 1976 Training parents as behaviour modifiers. In: Yen S, McIntire R (eds) Teaching behaviour modification. Behaviordelia, Kalamazoo, Michigan
Griffin M, Hudson A 1978 Parents as therapists: the behavioural approach. PIT Press, Victoria, Australia
Hatzenbuehler L C, Schroeder H E 1978 Desensitization procedures in the treatment of childhood disorders. Psychological Bulletin 85: 831–844
Herbert M 1974 Emotional problems of development in children. Academic Press, London
Herbert M 1978 Conduct disorders of childhood and adolescence: a behavioural approach to assessment and treatment. Wiley, Chichester
Herbert M 1981 Behavioural treatment of problem children: a practice manual. Academic Press, London
Herbert M 1985 Caring for your children: A practical guide. Blackwell, Oxford
Herbert M, Iwaniec D 1981 Behavioural psychotheraphy in natural home-settings: an empirical study applied to conduct disordered and incontinent children. Behavioural Psychotherapy 9: 55–76
Iwaniec D, Herbert M, McNeish S 1985 Social work with failure-to-thrive children and their families. Part 1.Psychological factors; Part 2.Behavioural social work intervention. British Journal of Social Work 15: 243–259; 375–389
Holmes F B 1936 An experimental investigation of a method of overcoming children's fears. Child Development 7: 6–30

Jones M C 1924 The elimination of children's fears. Journal of Experimental Psychology 7: 382–390

Kazdin A E 1978 History of behaviour modification. University Park Press, Baltimore

Kazdin A E 1979 Advances in child behaviour therapy: applications and implications. American Psychologist 34: 981–987

Kendall P C 1981 Cognitive-behavioural interventions with children. In: Lahey B, Kazdin A E (eds) Advances in child clinical psychology. Vol 4. Plenum Press, New York

Kingsley R G, Shapiro J A 1977 A comparison of three behavioural programmes for the control of obesity in children. Behaviour Therapy 8: 30–36

Lahey B B, Delamater A, Kupfer D 1981 Intervention strategies with hyperactive and learning-disabled children. In: Turner S M, Calhoun K S, Adams H E (eds) Handbook of clinical behaviour therapy. Wiley, New York

Lobitz G K, Johnson S M 1975 Normal versus deviant children: a multimethod comparison. Journal of Abnormal Child Psychology 3: 353–374

Mahoney M J 1974 Cognition and behaviour modification. Ballinger, Cambridge, Massachusetts

Meichenbaum D 1977 Cognitive-behaviour modification: an integrative approach. Plenum Press, New York

Mowrer O H 1938 Apparatus for the study and treatment of enuresis. American Journal of Psychology 51: 163–166

Mowrer O H 1960 Learning theory and behaviour. Wiley, New York

Ollendick T H 1979 Fear reduction techniques with children. In: Hersen M, Eisler R M, Miller P M (eds) Progress in behaviour modification. Vol 8. Academic Press, New York

Ollendick T H, Cerny J A 1981 Clinical behaviour therapy with children. Plenum, New York

Patterson G R 1977 Families: applications of social learning to family life. 2nd ed. Research Press; Champaign, Illinois

Patterson G R, Fleischman M J 1979 Maintenance of treatment effects: some considerations concerning family systems and follow-up data. Behaviour Therapy 10: 168–185

Schreibman L, Koegel R L 1981 A guideline for planning behaviour modification programmes for autistic children. In: Turner S M, Calhoun K S, Adams H E (eds) Handbook of clinical behaviour therapy. Wiley, New York

Siegel L J, Richards C S 1978 Behavioural intervention with somatic disorders in children. In: Marholin D (ed) Child behaviour therapy. Gardner Press, New York

Snyder J J 1977 Reinforcement analysis of interaction in problem and non- problem families. Journal of Abnormal Psychology 86: 528–535

Watson J B, Rayner R 1920 Conditioned emotional reactions. Journal of Experimental Psychology 3: 1–14

Weatherby B, Baumeister A A 1981 Mental retardation. In: Turner S M, Calhoun K S, Adams H E (eds) Handbook of clinical behaviour therapy. Wiley, New York

Wolpe J 1969 The practice of behaviour therapy. Pergamon Press, Oxford

The future of child guidance

INTRODUCTION

Unlike most other consultants in the National Health Service many child psychiatrists, for historical reasons, practise not in hospitals or clinics but in premises that are often owned by local education authorities. Furthermore, recent reorganisations of the social, education and health services and changes in the practice of child psychiatry have led to difficulties in the delivery of many child guidance services. The time therefore has come to question whether the present pattern of organisation is enabling modern child psychiatry to be practised at its best. This chapter outlines the history of the child guidance movement, describes briefly some of the growing points in child psychiatry, examines the problems that have arisen in the organisation of child guidance services and the reasons for them and concludes with suggestions for the future organisation of the specialty.

A SHORT HISTORY OF CHILD GUIDANCE

The first child guidance clinic was established in Boston in 1921, and the idea spread throughout the USA, coming to Britain in 1927 with the opening of the East London Child Guidance Clinic under the auspices of the Jewish Health Organization of Great Britain. From the beginning, the provision of a team of professionally qualified workers from different disciplines was considered essential. Thus, under the honorary directorship of a psychiatrist, Dr Emmanuel Miller, there came together a psychologist, psychiatric social worker and another psychiatrist. This team was later joined by voluntary social workers, research psychologists, remedial teachers and play therapists.

The large immigrant population of the East End of London, with its poverty and overcrowding, had posed many health problems for the Jewish Health Organization who 'viewed with apprehension the growth of nervous disorders among the children . . . Not only is there seen to be an increase of psychological maladjustment in home and school producing emotional disturbance and educational disorders, but an increase in disorders of behaviour from simple refractoriness to delinquency' (Renton, 1978). It is significant that even in the

20s a health organisation recognised that it had a responsibility to help children with emotional and behavioural disorders and that a multi-disciplinary team was needed for these disorders to be adequately treated. The idea caught on, though in a rather haphazard way, and child guidance clinics were established in many but not all parts of the country over the next 20 years. Normally they were funded by education authorities, but sometimes by health authorities and sometimes by charities. After the 1944 Education Act and the establishment of the NHS in 1946, the pace at which clinics were established, accelerated, but with little study of the needs of the target population or long term planning.

The model for practice that Britain imported from the USA was imaginative and very advanced for its time. From the first, the importance of the family and school in the genesis of disorders of learning, behaviour and emotions in children and the crucial need to involve them in treatment, were recognised. But the geographical isolation of the clinics from other health facilities had other, less desirable consequences. Child psychiatrists became alienated from their roots in biology, medicine and general psychiatry, educational psychologists from their roots in scientific method and from their clinical psychology colleagues, and clinic social workers from their colleagues in hospitals and local authorities, so that there was little cross-fertilisation of ideas between, say, paediatricians and child psychiatrists or between child guidance social workers and academic departments of sociology and social administration. Furthermore, the volume of clinical work which these small groups of staff faced left little time or energy for teaching, research or the development of the political expertise necessary to 'work the system' in order to enable effective expansion to take place. The lack of trainees, especially in child psychiatry (in 1960 there were seven senior registrar posts in child psychiatry in Greater London) to challenge established dogmatism led to the entrenchment of outdated and ineffective practices in some clinics. There was therefore little incentive to examine the best way of using scarce resources or to develop preventive services or to attend to professional development and the acquisition of new skills.

CHILD PSYCHIATRY DEPARTMENTS

When child guidance clinics started there were virtually no departments of child psychiatry in general hospitals. Disturbed children were normally referred, by general practitioners, to interested general psychiatrists or paediatricians; indeed, some valuable clinical observations were made by inspired practitioners in these specialties. One has only to think of Felix Brown's recognition of the frequency of childhood bereavement in adult depressives (Brown, 1961) or Donald Winnicott's observations on what constitutes 'good-enough' mothering, which was gleaned from his paediatric practice (Winnicott, 1965).

In the 1970s child psychiatry developed as a separate medical specialty, and a few academic departments were established in postgraduate and then undergraduate medical schools. This lent impetus to research and training and to the development of liaison work with paediatricians, obstetricians and other hospital departments.

Child psychiatrists began to have dual appointments to hospitals and child guidance clinics. This led to the development of services which although appearing to be very similar in the two settings, might be staffed by non-medical colleagues who might be notably different and have different employers (for example, clinical psychologists working in hospitals are employed by the NHS, educational psychologists working in child guidance or school psychological services are employed by the local education authority). Once more, child psychiatrists' medical roots became important and they began to contribute to improving the psychological environment for hospitalised children, cooperating in the treatment of children with psychosomatic disorders and becoming part of the treatment team which worked with children with life threatening disease. Some of this work occurred as children and their families had to adjust to painful, disfiguring and immobilising treatments, often involving 'high-tech' machinery (radiotherapy, haemodialysis, etc). Child and family psychiatrists and their teams had an important contribution to make to their adaptation and psychological well being.

THE CONTEMPORARY PRACTICE OF CHILD PSYCHIATRY

The epidemiological researches of Rutter and his colleagues (Rutter et al, 1970, 1975, 1976) established that between 6% and 10% of children and 20% of adolescents had handicapping psychiatric disorders. Of these, only a few were receiving specialised help (Kolvin, 1973). What kind of help were they receiving? For about 40 years the major treatment modality in child guidance clinics was individual psychotherapy for the child combined with social casework for the mother. This mode of treatment, a development of Freudian techniques by Sigmund Freud's daughter, Anna Freud, and by Melanie Klein, required a long time for its completion, and many professional man hours of highly trained staff. It was also difficult to evaluate and evaluation studies have been few. Eisenberg et al (1965) and Rosenthal and Levine (1971) both studied *brief* psychotherapeutic interventions and found them effective for neurotic disorders, but follow up studies of neurotic disorders in childhood indicate that most improve anyway. On the other hand, the conduct disorders have a bad prognosis and do not respond to psychodynamic psychotherapy (Robins, 1966). The subsequent development of behaviour therapies and family therapy produced changes in practice in some child guidance clinics while others continued to rely on one mode of treatment. These changes are well described by Graham (1976), whose account of current trends in practice is prefaced by the remark that it was 'merely a guide to the way in which quite a large number of presumably sensible child psychiatrists are working at the present time'. There was no way of knowing whether the wider spectrum of treatment and management techniques were 'one whit more effective than the approach used

20 years ago'. Current practice in child psychiatry now includes the use of many different therapies, singly or in combination. These include psychodynamic psychotherapies (individual, group, brief and long term, for child and/or parents(s)), behaviour therapies (desensitisation, operant conditioning, implosion and others including enuresis alarms) cognitive therapy, social skills training, family therapy and, in selected disorders, drug therapy. In addition, there is a wider use of consultation to institutions caring for children, and the establishment of residential treatment and educational facilities for children and adolescents.

Since Graham's paper, there have now been important evaluative studies of treatment in child psychiatric disorders. These indicated, for example, the effectiveness of behaviour therapy for sleep disorders (Richman et al, 1985), of family therapy in some asthmatics (Lask & Matthews 1979), of diet in behaviour disorders (Egger et al, 1985), of focused casework with abusive families (Nicol et al, 1984) and of court adjournment with truants (Berg et al, 1978). Other promising projects still await evaluation, for example the Tavistock Clinic project offering psychotherapy to severely deprived children (Boston & Szur, 1983).

Apart from the evaluation of treatment and management techniques, our basic understanding has also increased concerning the aetiologies of child psychiatric problems and as to how institutional change might lessen many disorders (see, for example, Rutter et al, 1979; Dowdney et al, 1985).

The application of this new body of knowledge now requires a much wider range of skills than was encompassed in the original child guidance team concept. Indeed, as with so many specialties, there is evidence that the fossilisation of the original establishments has hindered the application of new approaches (see Black, 1982). For example, few child guidance services employ community psychiatric nurses, family therapists, clinical psychologists or dieticians. Chance alone may therefore determine the type of therapy a child receives (e.g. family therapy or the more complex behavioural techniques, or a psychotic adolescent being nursed at home, etc.) This is in spite of the fact that the training of child psychiatrists and educational psychologists has broadened enormously in recent years and many social workers are training in family therapy. Even so, the staff of any one child guidance service may not encompass the wide variety of skills necessary to apply the new developments in knowledge.

ORGANISATIONAL PROBLEMS IN CHILD GUIDANCE

It is the organisational issues that appear to be the main stumbling block to change in child guidance. Traditionally clinics were headed by medical directors, but as other disciplines became better trained and developed a sense of their own identity, there was an understandable move to a more autonomous mode of working. This move arose because of changes in the organisation of education, health and social services and the need to employ scarce staff resources economically and effectively. It was given authority by the Department of Education and Science/Department of Health and Social Security circular on Child Guidance (DES/DHSS, 1974), which asked each health and local authority to submit plans for the future organisation of child guidance services in its area.

The concept put foward was of child guidance as a network of services (school psychological, school health, social work and child psychiatric) each with their own professional base but collaborating on those cases needing a combined approach. This collaboration would take the form of a permanent part-time team; but no thought was given to the knotty problem of its leadership. Teams need leaders if, for example, the most effective use of premises and resources is to be achieved, to take responsibility for the monitoring and development of the service, resolve differences etc (Brunel Institute of Organizational and Social Studies, 1976).

Since medical leadership was no longer mandatory, and often not acceptable to other team members, various solutions were sought. However, the Royal College of Psychiatrists (1978) identified the problems for the child psychiatrists and thought that patient care was best achieved if the consultant psychiatrist was the leader. This was because he or she cannot be subjected to managerial direction which was not the case with the other disciplines involved. Any other pattern of organisation would imply the need to set up a separate child guidance authority (i.e., not health, social services or education) with accompanying unacceptable financial and administrative implications.

In an attempt to resolve the apparent impasse which was threatening to disrupt patient care in some clinics, the Interdisciplinary Standing Committee of the four major child guidance professional associations (Association of Child Psychotherapists, British Association of Social Workers, The British Psychological Society and The Royal College of Psychiatrists) was reconvened. This identified some of the problems and proposed solutions, which included a clarification of the point at which each profession is qualified for autonomous practice and/or managerial responsibility and the devolution or rotation of some of the functions of leadership which could then be exercised by suitably senior and acceptable members of the team of any discipline. Although it made a helpful contribution to our understanding of how the problems arose, its recommendations were not accepted by all the professional bodies and an impasse remains (Interdisciplinary Standing Committee, 1981).

The Inner London Education Authority, which has the largest number of child guidance units of any local authority, also attempted to find a solution by having a 'coordinator' from among the staff of each unit appointed by County Hall. No study has been done of how successful this has been, and it appears to vary widely, some units virtually ceasing to function effectively and others finding they can do their work satisfactorily. It is, however, probable that the consultant child psychiatrists having been trained, like all consultants in the NHS, to head departments, find least satisfaction in a team coordinated by a non-medical professional. It is likely that this tendency will increase and that posts in which child guidance work accounts for a majority of sessions will therefore be less popular.

OTHER PROBLEMS

Financial stringencies make the development and expansion of child guidance services almost impossible, though this is occurring at a time when children are more at risk for psychiatric disorders because of social factors like increased unemployment, increase in family disruption and the pressures of urban life. One health authority's expenditure on child psychiatry is less than 2% of the budget for the adult mental health services and 0.2% of the total health expenditure (Black & Black, 1984).

Furthermore, child guidance is suffering from local political pressures. For example, there is the belief, among some politicians, that psychologists have consigned too many black children to schools for the educationally subnormal, and this has led them to try to deprofessionalise the school psychological service in some areas and the social services departments in others. In other places, child psychiatrists in the clinics are labelled as 'psychoanalytic cranks', and school teachers have been forbidden by their education authority to refer children to the child guidance service. In these cases, the need for change is seen only in political terms and so techniques for achieving intra-psychic or intra-familial change are suspect and to be discouraged.

THE FUTURE

The development of the medical specialty of child psychiatry with its relatively recent separation from paediatrics and general psychiatry, has taken place largely in child guidance clinics established by education authorities and where the consultant is all too often cut off from his or her medical colleagues. Consultants have therefore, until recently, had little influence on the psychosocial well being of children in hospital (Black, 1983) and in the development of psychiatric supports for staff and families facing life threatening illness in children.

The future of child psychiatry lies, however, in working closely with medical colleagues in the care of ill children as a team, in helping others with the care of disturbed children and in developing and applying treatments in association with other colleagues. These are all activities which should be adequately funded by health authorities, who should also recognise their responsibility for evaluating services and planning for the mental health needs of the community as a whole.

Many of the problems that have arisen in child guidance services as outlined above could be solved by the recognition that, because of financial expediency, a *health* service has been left to education and social services to develop. As the training of local authority social workers and educational psychologists is improved and widened, especially in family and behavioural therapies, they will obviously be able to deal with many of the milder learning and behaviour problems. Nevertheless, there remains a substantial number of children and adolescents with severe and persistent emotional disorders or behaviour problems stemming from psychiatric illness or complex familial problems who will continue to require the diagnostic and treatment skills of doctors as highly trained and experienced as other consultants in the health service. The present deployment of child psychiatrists and their dissatisfaction with their work conditions (Royal College of Psychiatrists, 1980) militates against achieving the excellence of service that these children need and deserve.

Disturbed children should be recognised as being extremely vulnerable and therefore in need of protection from the effects of the party political see-saw. This can only be done if the responsibility for their treatment is in the hands of a *national* health service. With the recent organisational changes in the NHS there will be a better opportunity to ascertain consumers' needs and wishes and to plan services accordingly. A recent study by Burck (1978) indicated that child guidance clinics were not fulfilling consumer needs. The pattern of child psychiatric services in the future must therefore change to take account of new knowledge, the changing pattern of practice and these needs of the community.

The problems which have arisen in child guidance are symptoms of a dysfunctional system. They reflect the fact that the concept of child guidance, pioneering though it was in its time, is no longer the appropriate one for our times and does not easily enable us to apply the knowledge we now have to the management and prevention of child psychiatric disorder. The first child guidance clinic in this country was established because of a concern by a health organisation about the mental health of children. It is appropriate that we return to the concept of mental health and place the responsibility for mental health services for children firmly back into the hands of the National Health Service. Consultant child psychiatrists and their multi-disciplinary teams should be based in health service premises both in hospitals and in the community. Only then might the integrated service envisaged by Court (1976) become a reality.

Meeting the needs of children with psychiatric disorder will also involve a greater flexibility in the use of resources, specialisation (for example services for victims of incest, children in care, children with long term illness, etc) and more mobility on the part of those providing the service, allowing children to be helped in school, hospital and family settings with a wide range of techniques and resources.

All this involves district planning and a willingness to cooperate and accept some changes. The need for a specialist multi-disciplinary team is greater than ever, but the members of the team must be headed by an employee of the owner of the premises (preferably the NHS), and, where possible, all the members of the team should have the same employer. The implications of such a policy are far reaching — for instance, the present social workers on the team, many of whom already have specialist knowledge and therapeutic skills of a high order, would be relabelled as child and family therapists and employed by the health service (as other therapists are); also, only clinical psychologists would be employed. Educational psychologists would continue to work in the school psychological service run by the education authority and social workers in the social services departments of local authorities. Although there would be cooperation, collaboration and cross referrals, the services would be separate. The National Health Service would be able to develop the child psychiatric services in accordance with new understanding and practice, backed by sound research evidence. This is no Utopia I have described, but a logical outcome of developments in our understanding of management and clinical practice.

REFERENCES

Berg I, Consterdine M, Hullin R, McGuire R, Tryers S 1978 The effect of two randomly allocated court procedures on truancy. British Journal of Criminology 18: 232–244
Black D 1982 Family therapy in child guidance clinics. In: Bentovim A, Gorrell-Barnes G, Cooklin A (eds) Family therapy: complementary frameworks of theory and practice. Academic Press, London
Black D 1983 Are child guidance clinics an anachronism? Archives of Disease in Childhood 58: 644–645
Black M, Black D 1984 Working arrangements of fifteen child psychiatrists in a child guidance setting. Bulletin of the Royal College of Psychiatrists, March, p. 49–51
Boston M, Szur R (eds) 1983 Psychotherapy with severely deprived children. RKP London
Brown F 1961 Depression and childhood bereavement. Journal of Mental Science 107: 754
Brunel Institute of Organizational and Social Studies 1976 Future organization in child guidance and allied work. Brunel University, Uxbridge, Middlesex
Burck C 1978 Study of families' expectations and experience of a child guidance clinic. British Journal of Social Work 8: 145–159
Court S 1976 Fit for the future. Report of the Committee on Child Health Services. HMSO, London
DES/DHSS 1974 Child guidance. A circular, DES 3/74. DHSS HSC(15)9
Dowdney L, Skuse D, Rutter M, Quinton D, Mrazek D 1985 The nature and qualities of parenting provided by women raised in institutions. Journal of Child Psychology and Psychiatry 26: 599–626
Egger J, Carter C, Graham P, Gumley B, Soothill J 1985 A controlled trial of oligo-antigenic treatment in the hyperkinetic syndrome. Lancet i: 865–869
Eisenberg L, Conners K, Sharpe L 1965 A controlled study of the differential application of outpatient psychiatric treatment for children. Japanese Journal of Child Psychiatry 6: 125–132
Graham P 1976 Management in child psychiatry: recent trends. British Journal of Psychiatry 129: 97–108
Interdisciplinary Standing Committee 1981 Multidisciplinary work in child guidance. Child Guidance Trust, London
Kolvin I 1973 Evaluation of psychiatric services for children in England & Wales. In: Wing J K, Häfner J (eds) Roots of evaluation. Oxford University Press, Oxford
Lask B, Matthews D 1979 A controlled trial of family psychotherapy in asthma. Archives of Diseases of Childhood 59: 116–119
Nicol R, Mearns C, Hall D, Kay B, Williams B, Akister J 1984 An evaluation of focused casework in improving interaction in abusive families. In: Stevenson J (ed) Recent research in developmental psychopathology. Pergamon, Oxford
Renton G 1978 The East London Child Guidance Clinic. Journal of Child Psychology & Psychiatry 19: 309–312
Richman N, Douglas J, Hunt H, Lansdown R, Levere R 1985 Behavioural methods in the treatment of sleep disorders — a pilot study. Journal of Child Psychology and Psychiatry 26: 581–590

Robins L 1966 Deviant children grown up. Williams & Wilkins, Baltimore

Rosenthal A, Levine S J 1971 Brief psychotherapy with children: process of therapy. American Journal of Psychiatry 128: 141–146

Royal College of Psychiatrists 1978 The role, responsibilities and work of the child and adolescent psychiatrist. Bulletin of Royal College of Psychiatrists: 127–131

Royal College of Psychiatrists 1980 Child psychiatrists and the organization of child guidance clinics. Bulletin of Royal College of Psychiatrists 4: 92–3

Rutter M, Tizard J, Whitmore K 1970 Education, health and behaviour. Longman, London

Rutter M, Cox C, Tupling C, Berger M, Yule W 1975 Attainment and adjustment in two geographical areas 1. British Journal of Psychiatry 126: 493–509

Rutter M, Graham P, Chadwick O, Yule W 1976 Adolescent turmoil: fact or fiction. Journal of Child Psychology & Psychiatry 17: 35–56

Rutter M, Maughan B, Mortimore P, Ouston J 1979 Fifteen thousand hours. Secondary schools and their effects on children. Open Books, London

Winnicott D 1965 The Family and Individual Development. Tavistock Publications, London

The conjoint family therapies

INTRODUCTION

This chapter is a short introduction in which I aim to explain to readers what conjoint family therapy is and what it hopes to achieve. In particular, I will attempt to discuss the status in child psychiatry and social work of this relatively new and fashionable set of techniques. Those who wish to practise family therapy will not be able to do so on the basis of reading this chapter, but some suggestions as to the ingredients of adequate training are included.

The title of the chapter is designed to emphasise two things. The first is that the essence of what is usually shortened to 'family therapy' is that interviews are conducted with all the family present. This is not always the case as some of a series of interviews may be conducted with parts of the family, e.g. the married couple, while at the other extreme a whole social network may be included, such as the extended family, neighbours or professional helpers. However, the nuclear family interview is the norm. The second implication is that there are many differences of emphasis among family therapists in their approach and techniques — hence 'therapies'. This in turn reflects the fact that family therapists come from many backgrounds both in their basic training and in their background of other psychotherapy experience. I should add that, in so far as I am a practising family therapist, I will inevitably bring some personal perspectives to this account. I will try to declare my own interest as I touch on the various issues.

Is there one central characteristic of family therapy which differentiates it from other forms of psychotherapy? The answer is yes, and I will now try to explain what this is. All child health workers are familiar with the need to view the developing child in the context of the family. Even so, to understand family therapy means crossing a big conceptual gulf. It can be likened to the positive and negative images of an X-ray plate. In ordinary practice one sees the child as a member of the family group while in family therapy one focuses on the family itself as the 'patient'. In ordinary practice the child remains the central focus whereas in family therapy the child as an individual becomes subordinate to the workings of the family as a whole. There are a number of implications of this contrast, and a description of them will help the reader to see the ways family therapy differs from other forms of therapy and casework in practice.

OBSERVATIONS

It is helpful to start by describing the types of observation that are important in family as compared with individual assessment and therapy. In modern child psychiatry, as in the rest of medicine, the main object of observation in both history and examination is the individual. The child mental state examination is designed to elicit the child's interests, attitudes and feelings and his account of events. Parents, who are seen separately, are also asked about these same areas and, in addition, about family and child development, health and relationships. Great attention is paid, with children and parents, to the way information is given: the hidden agenda of non-verbal attitudes and behaviours. What is *not* talked about is as important as what is talked about.

When information has been gathered, together with the results of special tests, the various perspectives are pooled in a diagnostic formulation. In this, a hypothesis of the causes, maintenance and prognosis of the problem is developed and treatment possibilities are advanced. The diagnostic formulation takes the place of diagnosis in conventional medicine in recognition of the fact that children's psychological problems characteristically have many different facets.

We can now highlight the ways in which conjoint family therapy differs from ordinary practice. Certainly the presenting problem is elicited and discussed as in individual assessment; however, family assessment focuses more centrally on how the family is responding to the problem. This is where the conjoint interview is essential. The therapist is looking for sets of interactions that relate to how the family has coped (often, in clinic families, in a self defeating way) with the presenting problem. The emphasis is on picking up and integrating non-verbal and verbal cues which help develop a picture of current family functioning. Often, for example, these verbal and non-verbal messages will seem to contradict one another — e.g., parents may attempt to control children by shouting at them, with the effect of making them more excited and disobedient, while at the same time complaining about how impossible they are to control. Issues such as who sits next to who and whether the family members talk to each other or just to the therapist are noted. Sometimes arguments and fights break out among family members, while at other times there is an atmosphere of frozen immobility. As the therapist spends time with the family he will come to recognise that many of these interactions, those which are relatively unremarkable as well as those which are more obvious and dramatic, have a repetitive and habitual quality. These are as characteristic of the particular family he is seeing as a finger print. They are called family transactions. The family therapist needs to acquire skills in observing and integrating these observations — so-called perceptual skills (see Epstein & Bishop, 1981; Goodyer et al, 1982).

As he sits down with the whole family group and starts asking them about their problems, the inexperienced family therapist will quickly find himself overwhelmed by the sheer quantity of information from the family. This will be both in terms of talk and discussion and in the non-verbal communication of looks and gestures, play, posture and so on. The struggling therapist will feel the need for a set of guiding principles to sift this mass of input. This brings us back to the central theme: the conceptual difference between individual and family work, which needs further elaboration.

Family therapy is characteristically based on some form of systems theory. This is simply the idea that the family as a totality is more than the sum of its parts, that what goes on in any part of the family influences all other parts, that individuals in the family cannot be understood in isolation from the whole and that the behaviour and development of individual members of the family is shaped by the structure and transactions within the family. Finally, the family is influenced by all that goes on around it.

A brief example from a therapy session will help to explain the implications of a systems approach. The F family, consisting of a couple with a 9 year old, mentally handicapped daughter and a 6 year old son, came to the clinic. The father, a Cypriot, was an unemployed mechanic and the family were obliged to live on unemployment benefit. The complaints were of the destructiveness of the little handicapped girl and her terrible, prolonged tantrums and wailing cries whenever attempts were made to impose limits on her behaviour. She was well known to the mental handicap service and was making good progress in a special school. Her behaviour showed a number of autistic features, such as pirouetting and hand flapping when excited or distressed, but on the whole she had quite good contact with her surroundings and had acquired some useful language.

The first session with the family was chaotic, with continual wailing and tantrums from the identified patient and marked disobedience and anxiety-based hyperactivity from the 6 year old boy, who continually tried to run from the room. As the session proceeded the therapist began to notice a marked difference in the ways the two parents controlled the children. The mother attempted discipline but was continually undermined by the father's comforting and indulgence of any sign of hurt or distress from either child. The second session was calmer, and the therapist was able to proceed with a systematic assessment of family function. It was during this exploration (to be described more fully later) that a fuller picture of the family system was developed. It turned out that, as well as being unemployed, the father's grasp of written English was poor and he was friendless in the local tight knit, traditional working class community. When there were marital difficulties, which, with their difficulties over the children, was often, the mother would take the children and go round to her mother, thus intensifying father's isolation. Further questioning revealed that the mother regarded the father as of little help in raising their children: 'He can't change, I have to be the father too'. The father's kindness and concern for the children knew no bounds. For example, he was often up half the night comforting the children and making them warm drinks and snacks. He is a delightfully warm and spontaneous man who said that he refused to let himself get depressed and constantly tried to humour his wife; despite this, his unacknowledged unhappiness was easy to see. Unfortunately his responses merely served to make the mother feel more alone with her responsibilities since she interpreted his smiling humour as further evidence of his essential childishness. She felt depressed, overate and, although still youthful, had intractible problems with her weight.

The many problems of this family system can be easily seen, as can the way in which they relate one to the other. No single 'cause' could be usefully isolated — not the handicap, the unemployment, the father's social isolation or personality or the mother's despair. Furthermore, there were many strengths in this small family: their warmth and humour, their underlying affection for each other and their expertise and care for the children once they could overcome their difficulties. Their motivation to do so was high. The identification of these strengths is a crucial task in the assessment and essential to successful intervention. There are some other lessons to note from this short illustration. It would have been easy to notice the obvious difficulties due to inconsistent handling between the parents and in doing so fail to understand the needs that were being served by this behaviour. With a fuller assessment it was possible to see the way the father was attempting to fulfil his need for love and the way the mother was coping with her anger and depression. The result in each case carried its own problems, but the attempt had to be respected and understood.

Different family therapist use frameworks which differ in emphasis when describing family systems. The most fundamental difference is between so-called behavioural approaches where the emphasis is on the detailed description of observable behaviour and psychodynamic approaches where the emphasis is more on understanding the feelings and motivations which, while unobservable, are generally acknowledged to be of great importance. I will briefly describe an example from each of these two traditions to illustrate the differences between them.

From among psychodynamic approaches my colleagues and I have adopted the McMaster model (Epstein & Bishop, 1981) in our clinical and research work (Goodyer et al, 1982). This consists of a systematic inquiry into family involvement, roles and behaviour control. This exploration enables the therapist to build up a picture of current family functioning and to identify areas of family malfunction and also — very important — of good function. The family therapist is much more interested in how the family is working in the present and less interested than the conventional practitioner in the history and development of the disorder. There are a large number of other frameworks of describing and attempting to understand the family among psychodynamic approaches. Some (e.g. Skynner, 1976) are much more clearly an extension and development of psychoanalytic concepts. In these formulations, symbolic communications by family members, often at an unconscious level, are given much attention. These may be detected from recurrent themes that come up in the therapy, from children's play or painting or from the therapist's detection of themes from his own emotional reactions to the family. Reactions by individual family members, such as denial of their feelings and projections on to other members of the family and the therapist, are carefully noted. This provides the therapist with an extremely complex picture of individual reactions and methods of coping with common family problems. The psychoanalytically oriented therapist is likely to be interested in the way that fundamental instinctual drives are coped with in the family. This would include both sexual and aggressive feelings, particularly oedipal and incestuous feelings.

A third influential school is that of the structural family therapists (e.g Minuchin, 1974). This approach focuses on problems in the boundaries within the family and the roles of family members. To take an example, in single parent families it is common for one child, usually the eldest, to assume a quasi-parental role with responsibilities for providing care for the others. These special duties may be rewarded by a special place in the parent's affection or other special privileges which in turn generate envy and rivalry in the other children. In other cases the so-called parental child may become overbearing in his or her disciplining role, instituting a subtle reign of terror among the children. Either of these situations is likely to lead to psychological disturbance in one or other of the children. This approach is particularly interesting to the paediatrician since it has been used in outcome research both with disadvantaged families and families of children with diabetes and anorexia nervosa (Minuchin et al, 1967; Minuchin et al, 1975). A final approach which merits attention within the dynamic tradition is the Palo Alto School (see Bodin, 1981). This group has made enormous contributions to the field over several decades and it is not possible to summarise them briefly. There has been an emphasis on understanding the families of very disturbed people (who came into the broad American definition of schizophrenia) in terms of the difficulties and abnormalities in family communication that are seen as being an integral part of their disturbance. In this approach the individual's disturbance is seen as merely a mirror of wider family disturbance.

The second type of framework, the behavioural, will not be discussed in detail here since the approach is somewhat different and relies minimally on the conjoint family interview. This does not mean that behavioural approaches are not extremely important; indeed, there is rather more positive evidence of their effectiveness than there is in the case of psychodynamic approaches (Gurman & Kniskern, 1978). Behavioural approaches do, however, come from a very distinct tradition of thought within psychology — one which is concerned with the very detailed dissection of behaviour and analysis of its relations with environmental stimuli. Since, particularly with children, the family is such a predominent source of such stimuli, family approaches have developed within behaviour therapy. These started from the idea that parents were in the best position to deliver rewards to children and so were the best 'therapists'. It was soon realised that parents may or may not be competent at giving consistent rewards, this depending on other family circumstances. Another approach arises from so-called social exchange theories (Thibauld & Kelley, 1959). Here each family member is seen as being involved in an exchange of 'rewards' with other family members while wanting to minimise personal 'costs' of the relationship. Problems arise when the reward system becomes disturbed and families begin to trade in mutual punishment instead of satisfying rewards. In a long series of studies Patterson and his colleagues (see Patterson, 1982) have investigated these mechanisms and their association with aggressive behaviour in children.

There have been some important studies, for example that by Alexander and Parsons (1973) on delinquents, which combine behavioural techniques with a more characteristically conjoint therapy approach.

PRACTICAL THERAPY TECHNIQUES

This is the section that the busy health worker is likely to turn to first. Any type of psychotherapy has some of the characteristics of an art form in that it is a blend of the inspiration and spontaneity of the therapist with a number of techniques he or she has learned through often prolonged training and experience. To start with, I have already mentioned that it is important that the therapist learns to observe interactions and the interplay of emotions in the family and that he learns to apply concepts and a framework in the practical situation. There are also a number of other skills to acquire and it is useful to ask: what does the therapist actually do when he or she sits down with the family? Again it is useful to draw contrasts with ordinary practice (for convenience only and at the risk of appearing sexist, I will refer to the therapist as 'he' from now on).

When I started learning psychotherapy I was helped to see that an important change of style was needed from that of the ordinary doctor. The psychotherapist listened and encouraged talk rather than talking and acting himself. When the talking stopped, the therapist did not ask questions but rather encouraged the patient to continue. The therapist follows passively wherever the patient takes him. We were taught that questions elicited answers but little else. This is an important change in emphasis, essential in the training of the psychiatrist, but a further modification of style is needed for the family therapist. The quiet passive approach does not work in family therapy because the family simply take over the session and the therapist becomes little more than a guest at the family meeting. It is not possible to do effective therapy under these conditions as the abnormal interactions and transactions in the family have a rigid quality which will change only with forceful interventions. Thus the family therapist must take a lead in the family session. He must have the capacity to listen but also be able to question and direct. He must be prepared to challenge long held assumptions by the family about how they should act towards one another. He must be sure that he both interacts with all family members (not just the spokespersons) and stimulates interactions among them.

We have found that our capacity to interact helpfully with families has been greatly enhanced by the use of a systematic routine, similar to that which one would use in history taking. Fuller details can be obtained from other publications (Epstein & Bishop, 1981; Goodyer et al, 1982), but briefly the sequence is as follows:

1. Orientation: the therapist explains and makes sure all family members understand the principles of the conjoint family approach.
2. Problem description: as seen from the point of view of all family members with the therapist encouraging debate and disagreement.
3. Systematic assessment: in which the therapist makes routine inquiries into problem solving, communication, roles, etc from all family members.
4. Clarification, feedback and agreement on the nature of the presenting problems and any other difficulties that have emerged. This stage is also an opportunity for the therapist to emphasise family strengths.
5. Outlining options: here the therapist makes recommendations to the family based on the assessment — Should they continue in treatment? Should they have individual therapy or some other treatment? Perhaps the assessment alone has clarified things enough so that the family can work on the problems themselves. In some extreme cases the therapist may be forced to conclude with the parents that the marriage should end.
6. Setting objectives: if the family wishes to continue in therapy it is necessary to decide what needs to change and to agree a treatment contract.
7. Setting tasks: one of the joys of working with families is that treatment can, indeed should, continue between sessions with the therapist. The designing of tasks which move the family towards change in a positive way while being at the same time concrete and specific enough for the family to carry out unambiguously is one of the high points of the therapist's art. The family should be involved in developing the tasks and these tasks should include all family members in the action.
8. Task evaluation: it is most important that the therapist checks and re-evaluates tasks at subsequent sessions. Attention to where the family has failed in task accomplishment will often give fresh insights into problems of the family system.
9. Treatment closure: includes a review of the changes that have been achieved and a discussion of what the family might do if faced with the same problem again.

This overall framework of stages usually takes up to eight sessions to follow, with long sessions of an hour or more in the early stages. It is, of course, a framework only and needs to be fleshed out with more detailed descriptions. Some of the important techniques include, as mentioned above, the ability to relate to all family members — not just the talkative ones — and to take a lead in the interview with the family.In addition, the therapist should be able to question aspects of family relationships in a way that the family finds non-threatening. He needs to be able to enter into the spirit of family life while not allowing it to carry him away and neutralise his therapeutic potential. He needs to develop the ability to focus on an issue or difficulty which is uncomfortable for the family even though they try to deflect him.

Conjoint family therapies have roots in many fields. Psychoanalysis and behaviour therapy have already been mentioned, but other influences have been equally important. One of these is psychodrama. In this series of techniques (see, for example, Moreno, 1971) the patient is helped with his problems through enactment in the therapy group. Enactment techniques are highly relevant to family therapy; indeed, the therapist is always swept up not in a discussion of the family but in the transactions and enactments of family life itself. It is therefore very important that he be able to work in the language of action, to know the power of physical closeness, to be able to detect non-verbal cues such as body posture and eye contact and intervene to alter non-verbal relationships. A more specifically non-verbal technique is called 'sculpting', where family members are invited to develop a non-verbal tableau of their relationship (see Walrond-Skinner, 1976, for a fuller description). Other important influences have been from hypnosis and existentialism. Concerning hypnosis, this is something of a renaissance of the older, more active psychotherapy techniques which preceded the dominance of psychoanalysis in the 20th century. The similarities to family therapy in terms of therapist activity are clear. It is from ideas derived from hypnosis and existentialism that so-called paradoxical techniques have developed (Haley, 1973; Frankl, 1973). It is impossible to do justice to these subtle and complex techniques in a brief account, and the interested reader is referred to these cited references (see also Palazzoli et al, 1978).

In order to illustrate some of the points we will return to the F family. The intervention consisted of a routine assessment as set out above and two treatment visits. The mayhem that constituted the first session has already been described. The fact was that this session, although difficult, was welcome (if somewhat exhausting) to the therapist since it allowed him to see the hellish circumstances that the family were living in. It also allowed him to enter into enactment techniques at an early stage. Wild behaviour prompted discussion of how one might control children and the separate parts that each of the parents might play in behaviour management. It was possible to promote control attempts within the session and then discuss the outcome. The therapist found it necessary to challenge the myth of the father's incompetence, choosing to reframe this as a misunderstanding of the children's needs that could be easily put right with the mother's help. The first treatment session consisted of a trial at child management by the two men (the therapist and father), with the mother watching through closed circuit television supported by a colleague who discussed with her what they observed. The therapist took a secondary supportive role while the father showed considerable competence with the children. The mother was, however, able to highlight some points where he had indulged both children and given in to their strident demands. This led to an agreement between the parents about the need for limits to the children's behaviour in a number of situations which both were able to honour. In turn, this led to the establishment of a viable behaviour modification regimen which had not been possible while the parents had interpersonal problems of their own.

This family illustrated well the importance of 'here and now' techniques in family therapy and the use of both enactment and discussion.

THE ROLE OF FAMILY THERAPY IN CHILD HEALTH SERVICES

For the most part, family therapy has been developed in the context of the private health care system in the United States. What relevance does it have to the development of services for children in a comprehensive health care system? Since it has never been tried, we have little direct data on this point, although some research is in progress at the present time (Nicol et al, 1984; Koziarski et al, 1986). There are a number of related questions and answers that can be given which might help us to see its role. These are discussed below.

1. What are the indications and contraindications for family therapy?

These have not been systematically worked out, but Walrond-Skinner (1976) gives some guidelines which can be augmented from experience. There is a case for family therapy in families which have several problems that seem to interrelate to one another, such as maternal depression and toddler behaviour problems (Nicol, 1984; Richman et al, 1982). There are many other cases where the identified patient's symptoms can be seen as an expression of pain at what is going on in the family, for example when rejected children steal from their parents. Family therapy is also the commonsense approach in families who are actually seeing their problems as a relationship difficulty rather than as the problem of one family member. It can be particularly useful when problems can be seen in the response of the family to illness such as uncontrolled diabetes or asthma. It has an important place where psychological incapacity, such as school phobia, can be seen as based on separation difficulties.

Family therapy is unlikely to be effective if any adult in the family is unwilling to take part or is persistently unable to take part. If children are unwilling to come the issue is somewhat different since it can be seen as the parents' responsibility to bring the children. If there is major violence or cruelty in the family I regard family therapy as contraindicated except under very special conditions. This is because family members who live in fear of each other are unlikely to speak openly and truthfully in an open family forum.

Psychotherapies in general are not usually very helpful in disorganised, multi-problem families, but several authors have claimed that some forms of highly structured family therapy can help (Minuchin et al, 1967; Jenkins 1984). This is an important claim that needs to be tested by controlled treatment trials.

There are three points worth making in connection with indications and contraindications. First, an introductory interview to explain the procedure and the reasons for which it can be helpful (Koziarski et al, 1986). This can prepare the family and give the therapist some idea of how to proceed. Second, a family assessment (as opposed to therapy) may be part of a broader psychological and psychiatric assessment and lead to other types of help rather than family therapy. Third, family therapy may be used in conjunction with other forms of help such as therapeutic fostering, individual or inpatient therapy or return of a child from care.

2. How much is needed in the way of resources?

Family therapies form part of a recent movement towards briefer and more problem focused therapies. Evaluation research has shown that, in contrast to traditional belief, short term therapies are as effective as long term therapies. The obvious conclusion is that from the point of view of professional resources and for most common disorders short term therapy is better (Bergin & Lambert, 1978).

3. How should a family therapy service be organised?

Some enthusiasts have seen family therapy as a revolutionary new development which is destined to surplant more traditional techniques of psychotherapy and behaviour change. There is no evidence that family therapy could or should be seen as a substitute for other techniques in this way. I believe that in a comprehensive service for children, family therapy should be one of a range of assessment and helping services which should be available. These would also include child care services of various types as well as a range of psychiatric and treatment services. There is no place for the arrogant statement, 'this family were unable to take advantage of our type of help' meaning 'our service is wonderful but these people are too deranged or stupid to see the light.'

4. How does one get training in family therapy?

Family therapists have not claimed that very prolonged or elaborate training is needed to be a family therapist. Having said this, the techniques are not easy and most of the leading family therapists and trail blazers of the movement have had extensive training in other forms of psychotherapy or casework. Training opportunities do now exist in colleges, child psychiatry clinics or psychotherapy institutes in the U.K. Self-knowledge, instruction and taking cases under supervision are particularly important, and the trainee should be prepared to devote considerable time and practice to developing into a competent therapist. It is important that, before attending a course, the trainee should satisfy himself that it is run by experienced, well qualified people.

5.   Is family therapy effective?

This must figuratively and actually be the bottom line. It is well known that psychotherapists have not been very eager in general to put their techniques to the rigorous test of a clinical trial. There are several reasons for this, not the least of which are the methodological problems of finding control groups, deciding on outcome measures, achieving 'blind' conditions (probably impossible), gaining cooperation, defining what the therapy is and so on. Despite these difficulties a review by Gurman and Kniskern in 1978 was able to identify some 19 studies of family therapy where a child or adolescent was the identified patient. Many of the research designs in these studies were unsatisfactory, although this situation was improving in the more recent studies. Overall, the authors concluded that there was evidence that family therapy was moderately effective: for example, of 13 reasonably controlled studies, eight showed some superiority over controls. More recently some good British studies have been carried out. Thus Dare and his colleagues (personal communication) at the Maudsley Hospital have been able to show good treatment effects with adolescents with anorexia nervosa. There is a great need for a positive attitude to evaluation and for more, better controlled studies.

REFERENCES

Alexander J, Parsons B 1973 Short Term behavioural intervention with delinquent families: impact on family process and recidivism. Journal of Abnormal Psychology 81: 219–225
Bergin A E, Lambert M J 1978 The evaluation of therapeutic outcomes. In: Garfield S L, Bergin A E (eds) Handbook of psychotherapy and behaviour change. 2nd ed. Wiley, New York, p 139–190
Bodin A M 1981 The interactional view: family therapy approaches of the Mental Research Institute. In: Gurman A S, Kniskern D P (eds) Handbook of family therapy. Wiley, New York, p 267–309
Epstein N B, Bishop D S 1981 Problem centered systems therapy for the family. In: Gurman A S, Kniskern D P (eds) Handbook of family therapy, Brunner Mazel, New York, p 444–482
Frankl VE 1973 Psychotherapy and existentialism. Selected papers on logotherapy. Penguin Books, Harmondsworth
Goodyer I, Nicol A R, Eavis D, Pollinger G 1982 The application and utility of a family assessment procedure in a child psychiatry clinic. Journal of Family Therapy 4: 373–396
Gurman A S, Kniskern D P 1978 Research on marital and family therapy: progress,

perspective and prospect. In: Garfield S L, Bergin A E (eds) Handbook of psychotherapy and behaviour change, 2nd ed. Wiley, New York, p 817–902

Haley J 1973 Uncommon therapy. The psychiatric techniques of Milton H Erickson, MD Norton, New York

Jenkins H 1984 A life cycle framework in the treatment of underorganised families. Journal of Family Therapy 5: 359–378

Koziarski M, Hodgson S and Nicol A R 1986 Family therapy in a community mother and toddler project. Journal of Family Therapy (in press)

Minuchin S, Montalvo B, Guerney B, Rosman B, Schumer F 1967 Families of the slums. Basic Books, New York

Minuchin S 1974 Families and family therapy. Tavistock, London

Minuchin S, Baker L, Rosman B, Liebman R, Milman L, Todd T A 1975 A conceptual model of psychosomatic illness in children. Archives of GeneralPsychiatry 32: 1031–1038

Moreno J L 1971 Psychodrama. In: Kaplan H I, Sadock B J (eds) Comprehensive group psychotherapy. Williams and Wilkins, Baltimore

Nicol A R 1984 Emotional problems of mother with young children who have behaviour problems. Maternal and Child Health 9: 161–163

Nicol A R, Stretch D D, Fundudis T, Davison I 1984 Controlled comparison of three interventions for mother and toddler problems: preliminary communication. Journal of the Royal Society of Medicine 77: 488–491

Palazzoli M S, Boscolo L, Leuchin G, Prata G 1978 Paradox and counterparadox. Aronson, New York

Patterson G R 1982 Coercive family process. Castalia Press, Eugene Oregon

Richman N, Stevenson J, Graham P J 1982 Preschool to school: a behavioural study. Academic Press, London

Skynner A C R 1976 One flesh separate persons. Constable, London

Thibauld J, Kelley H H W 1959 The social psychology of groups. Wiley, New York

Walrond-Skinner S 1976 Family therapy. The treatment of natural systems. Routledge and Kegan Paul, London.

Family Centres: prevention, partnership or community alternative?

INTRODUCTION

Family centres are increasingly popular as a new approach to providing services for families and young children. The coordination of services for the young child and his family, the recognition of the part that parents play in their children's development and the possibility of preventive work with families under stress are central themes in recent developments. 'Family centres', 'drop-in centres', 'combined centres, 'children's centres', are increasingly fashionable notions, but are they merely different labels for the same thing? What are family centres? What are their aims and activities? Who uses them, why and with what result? What assumptions underpin this approach?

There are two debates which lie behind the development of family centres. The first is the educational debate on the home/school partnership — the evidence on the one hand about the link between children's development and educational achievement, and what might be called the 'educational climate' of the home, and on the other about the feasibility of either centre-based or home-based intervention strategies with parents (Smith, 1984). We know that educational programmes with pre-school children and their parents can be effective in changing parents' expectations of their children and their own confidence and competence in adult–child interaction, and in boosting children's development, educational performance and self-confidence. Sociologists such as Douglas (1964; Douglas et al, 1968) and psychologists such as Clarke-Stewart (1973) illustrate the process through their clear picture of home influences and parent–child interaction. The recent longitudinal studies from the United States (Lazar & Darlington, 1982) confirm 'that preschool works' while leaving open the question of how the process operates through parents. In this context, family centres are an attempt to develop the partnership between parents, schools and teachers, focusing on the educational development of the child.

The second debate concerns formal and informal care — the relationship between statutory services and the informal networks of care and support

176

provided locally by family, neighbours and friends. Abrams (1978) points out the peculiar confusion over the term 'community care' and argues that the bases for such support by ordinary people in the community are links of kinship, religion and race rather than 'neighbourliness'. Much current research supports this view (e.g. Seyd et al, 1984), but it is also clear that networks can be created and supported (e.g. Challis & Davies, 1980). In this context, family centres represent an attempt at partnership between statutory services and the informal care system — a service that can respond sensitively to local needs and support, and if necessary help to create, local networks. The implications are for locally-based services, a preventive rather than crisis style, and a multi-disciplinary approach (Seebohm Report, 1968; Barclay Report, 1982; Leissner et al, 1971).

Oxfordshire, while by no means a pioneer in the development of family centres, provides us with an example of the range of approaches contained in four projects sponsored by different organisations — statutory and voluntary, education, social services and Manpower Services Commission — as well as in developments within the Social Services Department's own work, where the day nurseries have recently been renamed family centres (Note 1).

The Banbury Family Centre began in 1984 after several years of negotiation between the Children's Society and Oxfordshire's Social Services Department. Its aims are 'to coordinate and strengthen links among groups working with families; to foster community feeling by working alongside existing groups and supporting their continuing development; and to provide opportunities and enrich the lives of families and young children'. A 'community profile' of need in Banbury has led to considerable questioning of location and style. Currently operating from a rented room, with a leader, secretary, and an under-5s worker, the project has so far developed a mixture of styles of resourcing existing groups (the local under-5s network, summer play schemes, bulk buying scheme), developing new work (creche for an Asian women's language group, school/parent links), and supporting or initiating self-help groups (parents' groups, toy libraries, drop-in/welfare rights work). Debate continues on how best to reach those families and children most in need with an 'open access' service. After long debate, the decision is to combine a neighbourhood base in one area with outreach work in other areas.

The Bicester Family Centre (more properly the Bicester Under-Fives and Families Project) is based in a family room in one of the local primary schools. Funded by a five year Urban Aid grant to the local education authority, there is a project leader and a secretary, and a teacher seconded to work on links between the home, the school, and the community. Objectives are to increase parents' involvement in the education and development of their children. Local parents use the family room as a drop-in centre and for group activities and are beginning to plan and run the sessions themselves; play days and playschemes have been organised; and contacts made with other local groups for parents and young children. Discussion continues on how best to merge the work of the project with that of the school itself.

A third example comes from the Ambrosden Project, a small voluntary group employing a part time community worker to work with young army families. Objectives are to encourage families to make use of existing provision and set up their own self-help groups and to provide services which will enable people to develop self-confidence and a sense of control over their own circumstances. The worker operates from a family house used by the army's welfare workers, which serves as a base for a toy library, a drop-in for mothers with young children, a creche and as a 'front-line' for queries and problems. Groups are run mainly by local parents, with the worker's support, and there is close cooperation with other services — the local primary school, the health visitor and the doctors, the under 5s groups run by the army and in the village.

The fourth example is the Berinsfield Family Centre, funded by the Manpower Services Commission as part of a larger scheme, Employment Action Group (Berinsfield) Ltd. This is now a community programme agency employing about 40 local people on schemes including the family centre, a creche, an environmental improvement project and a needlecraft project producing toys for a reading scheme with such success that a private company has been formed to market the dolls and provide more secure employment. Berinsfield is a housing estate in the middle of the country — an area with health problems, high referral rates to the Social Services Department, children with special needs, isolation and poverty. The aim is to explore the blurring of employment and welfare functions. The Family Centre's objectives fit within the overall aims of the Employment Action Group (EAG) to promote employment opportunities in an area of stress and high unemployment; to promote the well being of local families and children; to develop and share skills already present in the community and to link with and support other groups.

The label of 'family centre', then, is used for a variety of activities and projects sponsored by widely different organisations. Some commentators stress the differences between centres — 'no two are the same' — others the similarities. So is the label a useful one? Jan Phelan, in her study of 12 of the Children's Society's family centres, argues that 'in reality they offer different things to different people in different situations' and takes a tough stand on the confusion: 'Let us try to use the same label for the same kind of centres. Let us ... call a centre for the preschool child and his family, which offers day care, a family day care centre; a centre which responds to the needs of a neighbourhood, a neighbourhood centre; a centre which promotes the general health of a family, a family health care centre' (Phelan, 1982, 1983).

Nevertheless, the label is important because, first, it describes a particular cluster of characteristics and, second, it implies a commitment to or aspiration towards a particular style or approach to services for families. There is no coherent and satisfactory definition of family centres that makes sense of the variety of work and little published evaluation (Note 2). In the absence of a satisfactory definition, three means suggest themselves to untangle the confusion: analysis of the history, objectives and types.

HISTORY AND STARTING POINTS

First, then, the starting points. If we look at the history, and the debates on home/school partnership, preventive work and community-based approaches, there have been seven major starting points from which family centre work has developed.

1. 'Nursery education plus' — nursery schools or classes which have shifted from a focus on 'education for the under 5s' to include work with parents.

2. 'Day nursery plus' — day nurseries which have shifted from a focus on 'day care for priority children' to work with families as a unit, ranging from generally supportive contact with parents to carefully planned therapeutic programmes with parent and child, usually on a 'referrals only' basis.

3. New joint schemes planned from the start with coordinated services — education, social services, health, voluntary groups.

4. 'From residential work to prevention' — the shift in both statutory services and the major voluntary child care organisations from 'residential care for the child' to varied patterns of day care, family support and community work.

5. Community development — small scale, locally initiated self-help groups and activities, often 'one thing growing out of another', dependent mainly on local people deciding on their own needs and getting together to meet them.

6. Family centres as patch-based or neighbourhood work — the focus for locally-based, decentralised social services, the 'open door'. This notion was developed in the 1960s with experiments in family bureaux and family advice services and is re-echoed in the Barclay Report.

7. Family centres as 'preventive community paediatrics' — the focus for multi-disciplinary preventive intervention in areas of high need, bringing together community health services such as health visitors and community nurses, education services for children and parents, and preventive social services.

Whatever their history, many centres develop a range of similar activities — toy libraries, parents' rooms, drop-in groups, mother and toddler groups, after school clubs, adult literacy work — but it is not clear what determines the particular mix of activities, of centre based or 'outreach' work, of 'open' groups and more intensive work with 'at risk' families.

OBJECTIVES

What are family centres trying to achieve? Broadly speaking, objectives fall under four headings, and these correspond roughly to the starting points already described. First, there is what Phelan (1983) has described as 'community-based preventive social work practice'. The major thrust for social services departments, health authorities, and national voluntary organisations reviewing their child care and family policies has been to promote family centres as part of 'preventive and rehabilitative services based in the community as an alternative to residential care'. In Birchall's (1982) overview of 30 centres, the main objective was to prevent family breakdown and reception of children into care, by improving the quality of parent–child relationships, supporting families to alleviate stress, and teaching practical skills. In Brill's (1976) account of the Langtry Young Family Centre in Camden, the objectives were to prevent 'the deprivation of parental care' and the 'fragmentation of families', and to provide 'supportive experience with the child'; but the improvement of parenting skills and family functioning, as some of the local authority planning documents recognise, depends on wider objectives of supporting a network of local services. Centres may act as resource bases for the local neighbourhood, and for social work area teams, and provide a mixture of day care, relief for families and after school and holiday activities. For example, in one local authority centre the aims are 'to assist good parenting ... and where inadequacies exist, to complement, compensate and develop [services] ... to a standard beneficial to the child' through 'a broad package of related complementary services' which match rather than substitute for parents' own efforts.

A rather different focus is illustrated by Nottinghamshire's review of the Crabtree Family Centre (Gilbertson). Here the objective is once again preventive work with families in an area of acute social need, but the overall intention is to decentralise a range of social work services with the ultimate aim of replacing the social services area offices with a network of local family centres. The context is thus the debate on neighbourhood work or patch based work.

Preventive work with young families is also the emphasis in centres with funding predominantly from the health authority (Polnay, 1984). Radford Family Centre in Nottingham, for example, brought together a multi-disciplinary team, including a health visitor, to work with 'multi-problem' families with a history of difficulties including child abuse and children failing to thrive. Aims included promoting practical parenting, home management skills, and better understanding of their children's development and needs. The effectiveness of the work was measured by 'hard data' such as a reduction in hospital admissions and receptions of children into care, as well as more 'subjective' information on parents' views, drawn from interviews with parents and workers in statutory agencies.

Second, there is what might be described as 'education outreach' — based on the assumption of parents as 'complementary educators', parents as the first teachers of the child. Here the objectives are to develop parents' understanding of the educational context of the home and the community, and their educational role in relation to their child.

Some family centres seem to have been particularly successful in moving away in their objectives from the dichotomy between 'education' and 'care' that runs throughout so much pre-school work. Pen Green Centre in Corby, for instance, aimed 'to establish a centre which combined the qualities of good nursery education with a flexible and responsive day care resource', serving the needs of the local community, providing 'a friendly and stimulating environment' for both parents and children and making no distinction between children's educational and welfare requirements. The Shiregreen Family Centre in Sheffield was designed as a 'flexible multi-purpose nursery unit', with a day nursery and educational input and parental involvement, and easy transition to the first school next door. These centres established from the start as joint ventures, or with staff from different backgrounds and with different training and experience, provide a clear illustration of joint objectives. However, joint objectives may have to be more explicitly stated if they are to be successfully implemented.

A third type of objective is found most clearly in the small self-help groups set up by local people to meet their own needs for friendship, support or child care (De'Ath, 1985).

A fourth type of objective is best described as employment initiatives to tackle the effects of poverty and unemployment at the local level. As with the Berinsfield Family Centre in Oxfordshire, or the EEC funded family projects studied by Willmot and Mayne (1983), these are usually self-help groups developing small scale schemes to employ local people. For the Downtown Family Centre in Rotherhithe, the aim was to recruit local mothers as staff for a centre in a declining dockland area, to help counteract the isolation of young mothers by setting up daytime activities at the centre for mothers with young children, run by 'new careerists' under the direction of the project leader.

KEY CHARACTERISTICS

Is there such a thing as a 'typical' family centre? Most writers agree on a list of 'core characteristics' to be found in most centres, although different 'core lists' may characterise different types of centre (e.g. Eisenstadt, 1983; De'Ath, 1985; Phelan, 1983; Willmot & Mayne, 1983; Birchall, 1982; Thamesdown's Voluntary Service Centre (TVSC)).

• A commitment to work with both parents and children. This does not necessarily limit work to parents and children together; it might equally well mean responding to families' needs and wishes by creating opportunities for adults and children separately. Nor does it necessarily imply a rigid definition of the nuclear family; family structure is diverse, and so are families' needs (Willmot & Willmot, 1981).

• A range of services for children and adults, and a commitment to integration and coordination.

• A range of flexible work styles, to suit families' and individuals' needs.

• A local neighbourhood base or catchment area, from which most users are drawn, although this varies with the activity and with the overall emphasis of the centre. A local base is thought to be essential if services are to be accessible to people and if workers are to be sensitive to local views of need and responsive to local issues. It is also essential if local people are to be involved in the work of the centre and the work is to be accountable to them and if centres are to build links with or support local networks and self-help groups (Phelan, 1983).

• An emphasis on consumer participation and local involvement, through 'open access' to the centre, consultation about identifying needs and planning services, and participation in management or running groups or training and employment as 'new careerists' (Willmot & Mayne, 1983; Brill, 1976). Few centres, however, have a users' committee or include local people in management.

• An emphasis on community work or a preventive approach — developing or supporting local groups, informal networks, self-help groups, mutual aid.

• An emphasis on 'reducing stigma and demystifying professionalism': 'the centres do not see themselves as a group of professionals providing services to clearly defined groups of clients, but ... to capitalise on the strengths and skills already there' (Phelan, 1983). The principle of reciprocity in self-help groups is that a 'client' in one situation may be a 'helper' in another (Knight et al. 1979).

• A set of common aims to do with increasing social people's self-confidence and self-respect, their sense of the potential of collective identification of problems or issues and collective action and their skills and understanding of their children.

• Work based in or from a centre (Birchall, 1982) — although small local self-help groups may operate from members' homes and borrow or rent different premises for different purposes (De'Ath, 1985).

TYPES AND MODELS

Now that we have reviewed some of the key features of family centres, their development and objectives, what can we say about different models?

A division along the lines of 'educational' or 'care' orientations is too simplistic: many centres combine both. Yet the extent of integration or separation between educational and care objectives, or concern for parents and their views and needs and work with children, remains one dimension. The first six months at Shiregreen Family Centre demonstrated that teaching staff and nursery nurses had very different priorities, and inaccurate views as to each other's roles and objectives, but had little opportunity to explore each other's objectives until they were faced with a crisis in the centre (Barnes, 1981).

Nor is a division according to type of premises entirely satisfactory. Local groups may: (i) operate activities from a 'scattered centre', using members' houses or rented church halls, or (ii) be premises-based, with different groups using the same building, perhaps with a coordinator and a users' committee, or (iii) offer a comprehensive service with a defined building, staff, funding and objectives; but there may be more interesting differences and similarities between them.

The most important question for family centres is who they serve, and how they provide that service. Do they operate a highly selective admissions policy for a priority client group or an open door policy to a local catchment area? This distinction separates centres into those which seek to provide a high quality, specialist service, often in the form of structured therapeutic programmes, for a selected group of recipients or clients on the basis of priority needs defined by professionals; and those which intend to provide a resource base for a wide variety of activities for parents and young children in the local area, with much emphasis on networks, self-help groups, participation and local definitions of need. The first type might be called a priority service model, the second a resource base model.

Eisenstadt (1983) characterises the different styles of work and philosophy thus:

> centres operating an open door community service for all v centres taking social services referrals only
>
> users as recipients of services v users as participants in services
>
> services as formally structured therapeutic programmes v informal drop-in services
>
> activities centre-based v based elsewhere in the community
>
> the extent to which policy decisions are shared between management, centre leader, staff and users

Hasler (1984) adds to these criteria the important question of how the community functions and how workers respond to the community's needs. In his argument, caring in or by the community requires both material resources and community norms and friendship networks, and communities vary considerably in their social make up. Centres may thus be divided into those which define problems as individual and devise individual solutions, and those which adopt a collective definition of the issues and the strategies to tackle them.

In practice many centres contain elements of both models. Coffee Hall Family Centre in Milton Keynes, for instance, runs therapeutic contract work with selected families alongside a range of drop-in 'open' mother and toddler groups, and for many families and children such a mix will be helpful. Nevertheless, it is important to be clear that the models are based on different styles of work and theories of learning. One suggests a didactic model with the 'expert'/worker teaching the 'learner'/client; the other suggests a sharing or catalyst model, when people share their experiences and insights with each other and the worker's skill is to act as catalyst when necessary.

ARE FAMILY CENTRES EFFECTIVE?

What criteria should be used to evaluate family centres?

Typically they are established in areas of acute disadvantage. Long lists of area and family indices of need — unemployment, poverty, inadequate services, and low take up of preventive services such as health care; large families, single parents, overcrowding, mental illness, children in care, non-accidental injury, juvenile crime — are often cited to justify location (Stone, 1981: (Note 3)).

Centres thus seek to meet needs of families who may be socially isolated and under enormous stress from poverty, poor housing and unemployment, and of children who may lack stimulation or adult encouragement or space to play in safety. Yet 'need' and 'disadvantage' are complex notions. Disadvantage may be defined as individual pathology, to do with an individual's own characteristics; or structural, more to do with the cumulative effects of social and economic circumstances in the area where people live (Brown, 1983), and strategies for intervention at this level will depend on the workers' analysis of disadvantage. Dawson's classification (Thamesdown's Voluntary Service Centre) of problem development usefully distinguishes between general background conditions (pre-conditions — e.g. poverty, unemployment, poor housing or health services), specific factors (causes — e.g. isolation from friends or family, lack of knowledge about welfare benefits, lack of understanding about child development), specific symptoms (effects — e.g. parental depression, anxiety over debts, housing conditions or sheer survival) and long term results (consequences — e.g. child abuse). These levels of analysis correspond to different levels of intervention — primary (campaigning for higher rates of benefit, better housing, better local pre-school facilities), secondary (developing or supporting family or friendship networks, or community groups) and tertiary (providing a casework service for families or priority day care for children). Family centres clearly operate at different levels of analysis and intervention.

At another level, there is considerable ambiguity over the concept of need itself. The debate over 'need' for pre-school provision provides an example. Social workers and health visitors operate with strict definitions of need for day care services based essentially on professionals' judgments about children 'at risk' in the home. The guidelines for day care priorities established by the then Ministry of Health in 1968, and the responses from social services departments up and down the country, ignore the needs of working mothers; yet working mothers by definition create a need for provision for their children. They also ignore the universal needs of children for educational challenge and stimulation. Education departments have tended to base their assessments of need for pre-school services partly on social priority, partly on the notion of shortfall or gap between the number of places for the under 5s compared with the number of children living in the area and partly on professional notions of parental demand. Depression among young mothers and the numbers of single parent families and working mothers are also cited as need factors.

This type of definition falls into the category of 'normative need' (Bradshaw, 1972). Yet user demand may be as valid a criterion of need as professional judgment. Any survey of pre-school services which has considered need, demand, and take up reveals large numbers of parents who would like pre-school places which they cannot get for their young children, and in particular for the under 2s. The transformation of day nurseries providing day care for children, into family centres emphasising parental involvement, as in Camden or Buckinghamshire, is a case in point. This may provide for the needs of isolated mothers or parents with child care problems, but at the expense of single parents or working mothers. Here the shift to more 'community-based preventive services' may not necessarily provide what families actually want.

How effective, then, are family centres in meeting needs?

Few centres would be likely to claim major success in structural change — poverty, poor housing, unemployment. Yet many centres provide advice on welfare benefits and, like the Walcot Centre in Swindon, initiate or support local campaigns or unemployed groups — the primary level of intervention. Willmot and Mayne's study provides examples of projects focused specifically at this level with the aim of providing employment and alleviating poverty, like the Downtown Family Centre. Their conclusion was that some projects undoubtedly provided services which alleviated or prevented poverty.

At another level, one might argue that provision should be judged by demand. If services are responsive to demand, then their effectiveness can be measured by whether there is increasing, and more discriminating, parental take up of those services (Note 4). We do not know whether family centres, as a new form of provision, are particularly effective in encouraging parents to demand more services for their young children.

What evidence is there that family centres are more accessible as a new form of provision for families with young children?

Studies of parents' views (Note 5) show that parents who use centres enjoy going, think their children benefit, view the centres as easily accessible places and find staff easy to talk to about problems. The informality of the service seems to be a keynote in consumer satisfaction.

How effective are family centres as a form of preventive work with 'at risk' children and families under stress?

This depends on how preventive work is defined and measured. Centres may hope that their work will result in fewer children being taken into care, less breakdown of family life, less juvenile delinquency. All this can be measured by 'hard data', but other aspects may be less easy to measure: whether a young mother feels less isolated and more able to cope with a young child, whether she has a network of friends to rely on. We have few studies so far of the impact of centres on their clientele, and the picture is far from clear. Two studies illustrate the problems.

A review of the Crabtree Family Centre in Nottingham (Gilbertson) suggested that fewer children were being taken into care, but there was no reduction in juvenile crime; more facilities for families and children had been brought to the area, and there was some evidence for increased 'community pride and stability'; but at the same time more families with acute problems were moving into the estate as a result of local housing policy, so no easy comparison could be made.

An evaluation of the Radford Family Centre, again in Nottingham, suggested some reduction in crises such as the hospital admission of a child as a result of attendance at the family centre. There was less evidence for changes in parents' health or behaviour, although the mothers themselves said they felt less depressed and had fewer child care problems. Again, however, it was difficult to get another group of parents for comparison (Leeming, 1985).

Some of the more intangible effects emerge in a study of a drop-in centre attached to the Moorlands Children's Centre in Milton Keynes (Eisenstadt, 1983). For the 'core users', the centre clearly provided a means to build new networks: this group had met nine out of every 10 friends and seven out of every 10 social contacts there. It is suggested that family centres manage to attract and keep families who would be less likely to make use of services for themselves or their young children, and that a locally based and more informal service lessens the stigma attached to provision for 'hard to reach' families, but we have little hard evidence as yet.

There is evidence of another kind that an integrated service which combines elements of 'care' and 'educational' approaches is effective at meeting children's needs for challenge and stimulation. The study by Ferri et al (1981) of 'combined centres' indicated that, in comparison with day nurseries, they were particularly successful at meeting the educational needs of the under 2s. This is supported by Holmes's study (1982) of the impact of introducing a teacher and an educational programme into day nurseries.

Creating an integrated service is, however, by no means an easy task. Ferri's study demonstrated that workers in combined centres spent more time talking to each other than to the children, and than workers in standard day nurseries and nursery classes — presumably because of the difficulties of working out new approaches. One study of staff in a new centre aiming to provide an integrated service (Barnes, 1981) showed that the teachers and the nursery nurses had very different objectives and misunderstood each other's roles. We need more information on the potential and difficulties of marrying family oriented and child oriented approaches.

Finally, what evidence is there that family centres reach people not touched by the more traditionally organised types of service? Studies of 'patch schemes', when social services teams have moved to local neighbourhoods, show that more people are likely to use their services, and more as a 'first call' than a 'last resort' (Hadley & McGrath, 1984; Cooper 1983). This is borne out by Willmot and Mayne's study of seven family projects funded by the EEC during the 1970s, which concluded that such schemes have the potential 'for reaching at least some of those whom the more traditional services fail to help'.

Willmot and Mayne's conclusions about family centres is that they represent a real attempt at affecting those most in need because of their flexibility and local base. 'The development of family centres, in all their variety, could play an important part in the movement towards the restructuring of social welfare services. ... The three "organising principles" of local authorities, it has been suggested, are uniformity (in the name of fair and equal treatment for all), administrative hierarchy, and functional division of services. Family centres work on quite different principles of flexibility, reciprocity, and participation ....'

THE WAY FORWARD

It remains to be seen whether family centres are more effective than other types of provision at meeting either the educational needs of families and young children or their needs for preventive services and locally based support networks. We have no longitudinal study of family centres, compared with either nursery classes or schools or day nurseries on the one hand, or more centralised support services, or residential provision, on the other. We know something of the different types of centre, their setting up and management, their activities, the views of their staff and users. Perhaps it is time to establish studies to compare family centre provision with good nursery classes, nursery schools and day nurseries on the one hand and alternative intervention such as good residential provision on the other. We shall then know more about who uses family centres, why and what they gain, and about the long term effects for both families and children.

NOTES

Note 1. I am indebted to the following people for material in this paper, and for discussion about family centres: Liz Yardley at Ambrosden; Nicola Breakell and Dave Wysling at Banbury; Barbara Bryant and Lin Pope at Berinsfield; Beryl Johnson and others at Bicester; staff in Oxfordshire Social Services and Education Departments; Dorothy Birchall; Jenny Dawson; Naomi Eisenstadt; Sonia Jackson; Anna Leeming; Sue Loveday; Peter Moss; Howard Williamson; and many others up and down the country.

Note 2. Most of the material written on family centres is of the case study description kind, attempts at a classification or small-scale reviews. Evaluation studies include Liffman's account (1978) of an Australian experiment, Willmot and Mayne's study of seven family projects funded by the EEC and a handful of short term studies of particular centres (for example, Barnes, Eisenstadt, Gilbertson, Leeming, Thamesdown's Voluntary Service Centre).

Note 3. I am grateful to Howard Williamson for his discussion of 'needs assessment' and 'community profiling' in relation to the Banbury Family Centre.

Note 4. I am grateful to Peter Moss for this point.

Note 5. The 'consumer viewpoint' is included in some of the short term evaluations — Loveday's study (1983) of the Walcot Centre in Swindon, Gilbertsons's study of the Crabtree Family Centre in Nottingham, Leeming's study of the Radford Family Centre and Jackson (personal communication) on the Gloucestershire centres.

REFERENCES

Abrams P 1978 Community care: some research problems and priorities. In: Barnes J. Connelly N (eds) Social care research. Policy Studies Institute, Bedford Square Press, London, p. 78–99

Barclay Report 1982 Social workers: their role and tasks. National Institute for Social Work, National Council for Voluntary Organisations and the Bedford Square Press, London

Barnes M 1981 Shiregreen Family Centre: the first six months. Clearing House for Local Authority Social Services Research, University of Birmingham, Report No. 7, 1–74

Birchall D 1982 Family centres. Concern 42: 16–20

Bradshaw J 1972 A taxonomy of social need. In: McLachlan G (ed) Problems and progress in medical care. 7th series. Nuffield Provincial Hospitals Trust, Oxford University Press, p.

Brill J 1976 Langtry Young Family Centre — a method of intervention. In: Olsen M R (ed) Differential approaches in social work with the mentally disordered. British Association of Social Work, University College of South Wales, Occasional Papers No. 2, 51–52

Brown M (ed) 1983 The structure of disadvantage. SSRC/DHSS Studies in Deprivation and Disadvantage, 12. Heinemann, London

Challis D J, Davies B P 1980 A new approach to community care for the elderly. British Journal of Social Work 10: 1–18

Clarke-Stewart K A 1973 Interactions between mothers and their young children. Monographs of the Society for Research in Child Development, No. 153. University of Chicago Press

Cooper M 1983 Community social work. In: Jordan B, Parton N (eds) The political dimensions of social work. Blackwell, Oxford, p. 146–163

Douglas J W B 1964 The home and the school. McGibbon and Kee, London

De'Ath E 1985 Self-help family centres: a current initiative in helping the community. National Children's Bureau, London

Douglas J W B, Ross J M, Simpson H R 1968 All our future. Peter Davies, London

Eisenstadt N 1983 Working with parents and the community: a study of two family centres. Unpublished MSc thesis, Cranfield Institute of Technology

Ferri E, Birchall D, Gingell V, Gipps C 1981 Combined nursery centres. Macmillan, London

Gilbertson G R Review of Crabtree Family Centre. Nottinghamshire County Council, County Management Services Division

Hadley R, McGrath M 1984 When social services are local: the Normanton experience. Allen and Unwin, London

Hasler J 1984 Family centres: different expressions, same principles. Family and Community Series, occasional paper No. 1. Children's Society, London

Holmes E 1982 The effectiveness of educational intervention for preschool children inday and residential care. New Growth 2(1): 17–30

Knight B, Gibson M, Grant S 1979 Family groups in the community. London Voluntary Service Council, London

Lazar I, Darlington R 1982 Lasting effects of early education: a report from the Consortium for Longitudinal Studies. Monographs of the Society for Research in Child Development, No. 195. University of Chicago Press

Leeming A 1985 Radford Family Centre — evaluation. Department of Child Health, University of Nottingham. Mimeo

Leissner A, Herdman K A M, Davies E V 1971 Advice, guidance and assistance: a study of seven Family Advice Centres. National Children's Bureau and Longman, London

Liffman M 1978 The family centre project: an experiment in self help. Allen and Unwin, Sidney and London

Loveday S 1983 A consumer evaluation of the Walcot Family Centre. In: Adams P, Dawson J, Loveday S (eds) The Walcot Centre, Swindon, Wiltshire: an evaluation 1980–1983. The Children's Society. Draft

Phelan J 1982 What's in a name? Social Work Today, 13: 20–21

Phelan J 1983 Family centres: a study. Family and Community Series. Children's Society, London

Polnay L 1984 The community paediatric team — an approach to child health services in a deprived inner city area. In: Macfarlane J A (ed) Progress in child health. Vol. 1. Churchill Livingstone, Edinburgh, p. 187–198

Seebohm Report 1968 Report of the Committee on Local Authority and Allied Personal Social Services. Cmnd 3703, HMSO, London

Seyd R, Simons K, Tennant A, Bayley M 1984 Community care in Dinnington: informal support prior to the project. Dinnington Neighbourhood Services Project. Paper No. 3. Department of Sociological Studies, University of Sheffield

Smith T 1984 Teachers and parents working together. In: Fontana D (ed) The education of the young child. 2nd ed. Blackwell, Oxford, p. 281–302

Stone W 1981 Identifying social need. Child Care Study Paper No. 1. Children's Society, London

Thamesdown's Voluntary Service Centre Local partnership in action: a look at family projects in Swindon. TVSC, Swindon

Willmot P, Mayne S 1983 Families at the centre. Occasional Papers in Social Administration No. 72. Bedford Square Press, London

Willmot P, Willmot P 1981 Children and family diversity. In: Rapoport R N, Fogarty M P, Rapoport R (eds) Families in Britain, Routledge and Kegan Paul, London. p. 338–354.

'Home-Start'

Home-Start is based upon an idea of remarkable and attractive simplicity: a bond of friendship between one mother and another, usually between a mother who has learned to cope and a younger mother who is finding it hard to do so. It is also a notably inexpensive scheme — with the volunteer mother unpaid and requiring only modest training.

Home-Start is a fresh and vigorous example of the partnership we need between the voluntary and public sectors; or, to put it another way, between the volunteer helper in the community and the professional in the statutory agencies.

Sir Patrick Nairne,
former Permanent Secretary at the DHSS,
now Master of St Catherine's College,
Oxford

Caring for a child from 0–5 years is a particularly crucial time, not only for the child, but for the parents too. In recent years sociologists, psychologists and educationalists have highlighted the impact of environment, relationships and stimulation on the infant during these special formative years. It would seem likely, that the developing child has a considerable effect on the parents too. They are not passive spectators watching their children growing up, but they are not necessarily able to provide endless resources and ideal circumstances.

In the past, young families relied for support on their extended family, or on close neighbourhood communities or, sometimes, on servants. In today's society, the traditional networks of family support have been eroded; yet society seems to have increased its expectations of parents. It is not surprising, therefore, that many professionals involved with families see depressed, dispirited mothers rather than young women delighting in their healthy energetic toddlers.

It was from perceptions such as these that the first Home-Start scheme began in Leicester in 1973, under the auspices of the Leicester Council for Voluntary Service. There are now over 50 Home-Starts around Great Britain, in both urban and rural areas, and two pilot schemes in Germany working with Service families. The Home-Start approach is simple: one mother visiting a family with at least one pre-school child, to offer support, friendship and practical help in their own home.

It was recognised from the beginning, however, that this attempt to recreate the extended family or good neighbour would have to operate within a formal administrative structure. This ensures that Home-Start is acceptable both to the families visited and to the statutory agencies and that effective standards of visiting are maintained.

The notion that formal organisation is needed to operate an informal befriending service could seem to be contradictory. Home-Start is an attempt to recreate what would normally be supplied by networks of support within a community. It is impossible to reproduce anything exactly in its original form. An analogy serves to illustrate this point: the kidneys under normal circumstances do their job cheaply, quietly, out of sight and without outside intervention. When kidney function ceases and is replaced by dialysis treatment, what was a hidden affair becomes public, takes up most of a room, is costly and requires a team of highly trained personnel.

All Home-Start schemes have a multi-disciplinary Management Committee with representatives from social services, health, education and probation departments, and from local voluntary agencies such as playgroups, marriage guidance and volunteer bureaux. The Management Committee raises funding and recruits a paid Organiser as well as an Administrative Assistant. The Organiser must be not only competent and committed but also acceptable to the families, the volunteers and to professional agencies making referrals to the scheme. The Organiser is responsible for the team of volunteers, who must be realistically recruited, carefully prepared for the visiting through an initial course, sensitively matched with families and then closely supported.

Just as each family is unique, so too are the difficulties which they experience. Although not all matchings are so successful, the following examples illustrate some of the families' needs and the approach of the Home-Start volunteers when the scheme is working at its best.

Anna

Anna was a 17 year old single parent, who had been brought up in care. Her first child, born when she was 16, had died a 'cot death', aged 11 weeks. The medical social worker requested a motherly Home-Start volunteer who could befriend Anna during her subsequent pregnancy, to help her to keep appointments and, above all, to give her intensive support after the baby was born. Anna had always found it impossible to make and keep friends and made several attempts to reject her volunteer — 'you're bossy like all the rest'. However, she allowed her to keep visiting and enjoyed being taken by car to keep her hospital appointments. Once the baby was born, Anna became close to her volunteer, who praised and encouraged her in all she did, supported her sensibly through potential crises and assured her that some of the problems of childhood are quite normal. Anna and her child have flourished, and, above all, Anna is experiencing family life such as she herself never had as a child. The volunteer is still a close friend.

Sue

Sue was depressed and suicidal over her uncontrollable 2 year old. She lived in a third floor flat, was socially isolated and felt she could not 'take the boy anywhere'. She was on anti-depressants and kept the radio on full blast to drown his noise. The volunteer gave ideas to the mother of how to amuse her son, went on outings with them, introduced the boy into a local playgroup so that Sue could have some time to herself. She was very soon off the anti-depressants and looked forward to the volunteer's visits.

Beth and Andy

Beth and Andy were both classified as educationally subnormal (ESN). When they had a son after 15 years of marriage they overprotected him. At $2\frac{1}{2}$ years he was still bottle fed at four hourly intervals and nursed like a baby. The parents were so proudly possessive that they would not let him out of their sight (to a day nursery) and were incapable of carrying out advice offered to them by professional experts. A local Home-Start volunteer, herself, 'just an ordinary mum' from the same estate, visited daily and gained their trust, so that gradually they began copying her methods of feeding and playing with their son. Eventually they accepted her suggestion that he would enjoy the local nursery. Now, seven years later, the boy attends the local school and is a normal, active child.

Sarah

Sarah was a doctor's wife whose experience of having young children did not match her expectations. Her 3 year old required little sleep and was actively demanding all day long. The baby caused sleepless nights, and the only response Sarah's exhaustion elicited from her overworked husband was, 'You should see what I've had to cope with down at the surgery all day'. When the health visitor called, Sarah put on a brave face but was reluctant to take up the suggestion to visit the local mother and toddler group. A Home-Start volunteer was introduced, who visited regularly on Tuesday and Thursday mornings. Sarah said, 'It breaks up the week nicely'. It meant that sometimes she could play the piano while the volunteer looked after the children; or they talked about topics other than parenthood; or they cooked a special meal with the 3 year old's assistance; or sometimes they all went out together. Regular visiting was needed only for six months, by which time this family had survived the bad patch.

Liz

Liz was reputed to be of a 'pestering and manipulative nature'. She showed no interest in her children, had no routine and was constantly in debt. Her two older children had been taken into care when her first marriage broke up, and there was proven sexual abuse by the co-habitee. Her third child had been hospitalised three times with symptoms of gastroenteritis by the age of 16 months. The fourth child, a baby girl, was born prematurely on the sofa without medical supervision when Liz heard of her own mother's unexpected death. Antenatal care had been almost non-existent. The baby was admitted to hospital until she was seven weeks old and she was not visited by the mother. She was re-admitted to hospital at 10 weeks, following bouts of vomiting. The social worker had a poor relationship with Liz, who feared that her two youngest children might also be taken from her. Therefore, the social worker had great difficulty gaining access to the family. The health visitor was unacceptable to Liz — 'She's never had kids, so what does she know about it'.

A local Home-Start volunteer was introduced to Liz — one who had herself been intensively visited for two years, had five children and knew exactly how Liz felt. She too was concerned that the baby was failing to thrive and spent hours each day with Liz 'doing everything together'. Through the Home-Start network, the volunteer was in contact with Liz's health visitor and social worker. Within a fortnight Liz was encouraged to go with the volunteer and the children down to the health clinic. The volunteer's husband also visited the home, helping to fix the fireguard and fence and encouraging the new co-habitee to get out of bed and attend the day centre. Six months later (not easy months) the mother was allowing the health visitor to visit her at home. Fifteen months after the Home-Start volunteer was introduced, the Social Services Department called a case conference to discuss removing the children from the At Risk Register. The case conference notes state,

> 'Since registration, it was agreed that there has been considerable improvement in the home situation and the children are developing satisfactorily. Liz attends clinic regularly with both children. The Home-Start volunteer will remain involved. The whole family attends the Home-Start playgroup and both Liz and George attend the parents' evenings and generally behave far more responsibly .... It was agreed that it was no longer appropriate for the children to remain on the Register and necessary procedure would be instigated to ensure their removal'.

Innumerable families who never use the health or social services are referred to Home-Start. Once a relationship has been established between the volunteer and the parent, the family can be encouraged to use all relevant community resources. Home-Start looks both inwards and outwards — inwards to the individual needs and qualities of each family member and outwards to the use of the whole network of community resources: the library, the family planning clinic, the schools, the health services and the park. A volunteer arrived late one morning to visit 'her family', where there were three children under 3, saying 'Sorry I'm late, but I've just been for my family planning appointment and look what they've given me!' The mother showed great interest and promptly made an apppointment for herself, knowing that the volunteer would be there to look after her three children while she went to the clinic.

Home-Start volunteers might visit for three months or three years. For some families the Home-Start approach is preventive, for others remedial. Individual family members can be respected as people rather than problems, and volunteers can respond with the help which the parents themselves seek, rather than to what outsiders might prescribe. A health visitor once said:

'The volunteers are down at the base level, and that is why it is important for them to visit young families. They have the time and can show they really care. All the problems that the professionals treat spring from a weak base and it is like a crooked tower — we might put some of it right at the top, but it will always go wrong again if we do nothing about the fundamental issues'.

The late Mia Kellmer-Pringle said that what every child needs emotionally is love and security, praise and recognition, new experience and responsibility. So often these needs have been unmet in the lives of the parents themselves. The Home-Start volunteer, in offering the parents care and nurturing, enables them in turn to provide emotionally for their children. Who, then, are the parents who become Home-Start volunteers?

Organisers, when they recruit a volunteer, are looking for someone with positive, hopeful, realistic attitudes, who also has a sense of *FUN*. Such people exist in all walks of life, with different social, cultural and educational backgrounds, at different ages and stages of their own lives, whether married or single, on supplementary benefit or financially secure. Christine Tracey a Home-Start Organiser, explains:

'When faced with the task of interviewing and selecting volunteers, it is interesting to remind ourselves what we are asking volunteers to do. We are asking them to form a caring relationship with another person or persons: to be reliable, flexible, non-judgmental; to offer friendship, support, encouragement and practical assistance where necessary. We ask them to be sensitive to the needs of the children; tactful with other members of the family, and to have the ability to give and receive. Surely we are looking for highly specialised paragons of virtue? However, let us now get this into perspective. I believe this forming of relationships,this sharing of the qualities mentioned is going on all the time in any community. It goes on in families, between friends, neighbours, work colleagues. It happens in Church fellowships, in clubs and societies of many kinds. It happens spontaneously without selection, training and matching. In Home-Start, we are organising a form of community support for those whose social network is depleted.

What am I looking for in a potential volunteer? I have discovered that age, background, social class, educational achievements, or lack of them, past careers, and so on, are not reliable guides. None of these factors alone indicates the right qualities or lack of them. We can recruit from the slum-dwellers and from the aristocracy. We can recruit the highly intellectual career woman and the simple homely mum who has never "worked". I have discovered that a person can make a good volunteer whether or not her particular personality appeals to me — whether I like her or not.'

Accepting a wide range of volunteers in Home-Start could be seen to be an irresponsible and even dangerous principle to follow. That would be true if acceptance relied solely on an interview. The close working relationship that an Organiser develops with each volunteer is an integral part of each Home-Start scheme, with the interview only the starting point. Once volunteers are accepted, they then join a Course of Preparation which normally lasts one day a week for 10 weeks. On the course the volunteers meet a wide range of professional workers involved with the under 5s. This provides an opportunity for volunteers to learn not only about statutory provisions and other community resources, but also about their role in relation to professional workers. In addition, each course also covers such topics as child development, budgeting on a low income, confidentially, listening skills and working in a multi-cultural society. The Courses of Preparation are non-academic and rely on discussion as well as speakers and visual aids to encourage the exchange of ideas. During a course, the Organiser comes to know well the individual volunteer, her strengths and her skills. That knowledge becomes the basis for careful matching of the Home-Start volunteer with the family she will visit. What then are the motivations and aspirations of the volunteers themselves?

Lila Yates, a Belfast volunteer who is typical of many others, describes her involvement in Home-Start:

'I thought about other mothers and how awful it must be to be alone with a baby. How easy it would be for a joyful time to become one of despair, depression and isolation.

I heard about Home-Start when my son was almost 18 months old, and at once felt that it was something I would like to be a part of. To me the idea of befriending someone seemed so simple, and yet it could be someone's lifeline, or for another an oasis for a short time to re-charge batteries with the encouragement that someone else would listen, care, try to understand and give what support they could for as long as was needed.

Before meeting my first family, I began to feel a little apprehensive. Do I really have anything to offer? Will I be able to make a big enough commitment? Will I be able to cope? I feared going out with the intention of helping someone, and of perhaps making the situation worse — would it be fair to expect them to cope with my incompetence? Will it infringe too much on my personal life?

Once the involvement with the family commenced, the fear of the unknown disappeared and the task of getting on with everyday life took over. I soon began to realise what Home-Start meant to me and the important place it was taking in my life. I enjoyed the company of the other volunteers, all coming as they did from different walks of life and all having their own individual personalities, and all working towards a common objective. It is a wonderful feeling, a feeling of belonging, a feeling of worth. It provides the opportunity to give back to the community in which we live — it is a privilege — it feeds the soul. I hope that the mothers we visit will feel the same sense of belonging as the volunteers, because we are all mothers and we are all part of the group. Perhaps in turn some of the mothers we visit will want to become volunteers when they are ready, after so much valuable experience. I think it is important to remember that no one ever knows what may lie around the next corner. A crisis could face anyone out of the blue, or a nagging anxiety could reach a peak. In this respect the volunteers are no different from the mothers we visit.

As a volunteer, the work is often difficult and demanding, and sometimes a feeling of uselessness can creep in. I have found that this has never been an on-going problem, because of the amount and quality of support that is given by the Organiser. Although the efforts of the volunteer can sometimes seem unrewarding and taken for granted, it is important to remember that one's expectations of the family visited must never be too high. Very often the rewards must be intrinsic. The work and effort that a volunteer puts in won't always be appreciated or even acknowledged by the family visited, but it is always recognised and appreciated by the Organiser and the group. In making a commitment to Home-Start, I feel that I am doing something worth while and the rewards that I get from being a volunteer more than compensate for the effort I put in.'

A basic principle in Home-Start is that everyone has a need to be needed, be they volunteer, Organiser or indeed, one of the families visited. With 12 years' hindsight, some of the most spectacular results have been with families for whom at first there appeared no hope. Yet, after years of sustained support, some have gradually evolved into volunteers themselves. 'It's been the best week of my life', said Jenny, the young single parent who had herself needed intensive visiting for over two years. 'The Council have just been in to do my front room, and now you've told me I can be a volunteer and come on the next course.' Suddenly there was hope, and Jenny has remained a loyal and valuable member of a Home-Start team ever since.

Maybe one of the reasons why Home-Start schemes are successful is that they each have a vital structure of support for everyone involved in the scheme:
• Families are offered regular support, friendship and practical help by their volunteer.
• Volunteers are offered regular support by their Organiser and by each other. Meetings are both formal and informal. They may consist of sharing ideas about the families visited, having a film or talk led by a professional person or it may be simply a coffee evening or summer party. There is always the opportunity for individual support for a volunteer by a health visitor, social worker or other professional who is also involved with the family.
• Organisers are offered support by their Management Committee members, by sympathetic local representatives from other statutory or voluntary

agencies, by meeting other Organisers in regional Home-Start groups bi-monthly and by Home-Start consultancy.

• Home-Start Consultancy was set up in 1981 in Leicester to offer consultation, liaison and assistance to all existing Home-Starts as well as in setting up new schemes. The Consultancy holds regular focus groups and study days for Organisers.

• Home-Start Consultancy also holds regular seminars to support Chairmen, Treasurers and secretaries of all Home-Start schemes, and to provide a forum for the exchange of ideas.

Each person involved in Home-Start thus has opportunities for support specific to their individual needs, allowing the breadth of support on offer to be unusually diverse.

What then are the general principles which guide Home-Start as a strategy for supporting young families and their children within the community? Willem van der Eyken, who undertook a descriptive study of Home-Start on behalf of the Social Sciences Research Council, sums it up most succinctly in his book *Home-Start: A Four-Year Evaluation*:

'1. Home-Start operates an "open door" policy of accepting referrals, many of which might be classified as "heavy" cases of severe environmental stress, and on the face of it would appear to effect "considerable change" within the majority of these families.

'2. It does so through a "reciprocity" model of community care, using volunteers whose sole qualification is that they are mothers, who benefit through their membership of a group, through a process of personal development and through the legitimisation of their child-rearing skills in a social context.

'3. An initial course of preparation, followed by discussion groups and lectures, offers status to the volunteers and this, coupled with a high degree of field support, the challenge of working "on the edge of experience" and of considerable autonomy of action, leads to an intense and lengthy involvement with the project for the volunteers.

'4. Because they are not paid, the volunteers wield a considerable, though unspoken, moral authority within the families they support, tacitly recognised by those families by the fact that few, if any, relationships break down.

'5. The volunteer and the family she visits develop a contractual relationship that might be described as "befriending" but is actually "befriending with commitment", in which the family can rely on empathy, constancy, non-possessive warmth and genuineness on the part of the volunteer, and open-ness, co-operation and honesty on the part of the family.

'6. This contract is very much family-focused, in that the object is neither simply the children, nor the mother herself. Rather, it is a "total" environment, in which every person can expect to benefit, while none need feel a "client" in need of some treatment, or a "case" demanding remedy.

'7. A more tentative point, and a more contentious one, relates to the characterisation of the families themselves. We stated in (1) that many of them were "heavy"cases. More generally they can be categorised as being under many forms of stress; not simply stress of the everyday form which we all experience, and which in many respects is beneficial, but stress which in its severity has in some cases caused the family either very temporarily or over a longer period, to *lose control*. This term, "loss of control" is a key point in the description of the families, who are so often inappropriately described as "at risk", "problem families", "deprived", or, even worse, "inadequate". What is useful about the term is that it strongly implies an environmental cause for the loss, in that it does not encompass, for example, severe personality disorders where, in a sense, "control" never existed. Further, it offers the possibility that, theoretically at least, "control" might be restored.

'8. Home-Start seeks to provide "support" for such families, while at the same time offering a positive educational stimulus and input for the children. It could thus be regarded, overall, as aiming to strengthen the parent–child bonds or relationships. More broadly, I believe that it actually aims to restore "control" to the family, to a point when it can again — or perhaps for the first time — function as a healthy, child-rearing environment.'

Most theories of child-development suggest that there are stages of dependency and growth through which a child must go before he matures. Only if each stage is satisfactorily completed does the child go on to the next stage. This has proved to be the pattern not only for the families visited and supported, but indeed for Home-Start itself.

FURTHER INFORMATION

For further information contact Home-Start Consultancy, 140 New Walk, Leicester, LE1 7JL. Telephone: 0533–554988.

Medical education in child health

INTRODUCTION

Teaching medical students has always been part and parcel of the work of doctors, and I am probably biased in thinking that paediatricians are more enthusiastic exponents of the art than are other specialists. Teaching is a central part of our work, but until quite recently it has not been thought proper for research to be done into educational techniques, for our long-established teaching habits to be assessed or, indeed for anyone apart from the head of department to play a significant part in organising the teaching. This deficiency is partly the result of the hospital career structure, in which a doctor's promotion depends more on clinical ability and on writing research papers than on interest and aptitude for teaching.

There are many students to be taught, both undergraduate and postgraduate. We take on this teaching sometimes with enjoyment and sometimes as a chore, but in general we spend little time analysing how we do it. Usually all grades of doctor join in the teaching, but the person doing it tends to be asked to take it on without knowing the stage the students have reached in their course, the extent of their previous teaching or the nature of their assessment. Little if any instruction is given on how to go about the teaching. Inexperienced teachers will most likely teach as they were taught — sometimes well, sometimes badly — but with little incentive to improve on their practice. Faults are sometimes laid at the feet of the students. One hears, 'You simply can't teach some students', when the problem is in truth that we teachers do not really know how to teach them (McIntyre 1979).

Fortunately, these attitudes are changing, and paediatricians have been at the forefront of change. In this chapter I will look at some new developments in undergraduate medical education — first, at what we are trying to achieve, second, at how we are to go about doing it and, third, at how we may assess the end results.

WHAT ARE WE TRYING TO ACHIEVE?

There are almost as many opinions concerning the aims of undergraduate child health teaching as there are teachers. In the course of discussions with teachers of the discipline around the country I have encountered three main themes on what are perceived as the objectives.

'Broad-based learning'

This rather vague phrase encompasses the feeling expressed by many teachers that we should teach 'the basics'. The undergraduate years are about education, not training, and the end product should be a person who has good scientific foundations and will be adaptable enough to take up any branch of medicine from general practice to neurosurgery or community medicine, with appropriate postgraduate training. According to this view, it would be wrong to attempt to teach specific skills which are better acquired later when the student is more mature and responsible. The paediatric course will therefore cover mainly the 'scientific' aspects of child health: growth and development, the differences in the main system disorders between children and adults, children's diseases as they are seen in hospital and the laboratory aspects of child medicine.

Students should have contact with children on the wards, but this contact does not need to be too close; it is not safe to expose children to 'procedures' undertaken by students, and there are also junior doctors who need to learn the same techniques.

I think there are few teachers who would profess this approach wholeheartedly in the 80s, but elements of the view are still propounded with emphasis. Teaching the 'basics' is indeed essential, but there is a wide agreement now that students learn theory and science better if these are placed in the context of patient problems and patient care. Few medical schools teach the 'scientific method' effectively, but instead fill the students with facts which are rapidly forgotten as soon as the requisite exam has been passed. If the facts are acquired at a time when students see their relevance, then they are more likely to be retained. This is an argument for a better integration of science-based with clinical learning.

'The flavour of child health'

This is shorthand for a widely held view that the undergraduate course should expose the students to contact with children so that they learn of their specific needs but not the details of their diseases. The approach described by Meadow (1979) perhaps expresses this philosophy best. Students should learn how to take a paediatric history and how to examine children competently and kindly; theoretical learning should take second place and can be acquired in the postgraduate period. 'These skills are more important than any amount of theoretical knowledge.' In a way, this approach is the converse of that described above. Some teachers supporting this view hold that specific skills beyond history taking and examination should not be taught or even described, but should be acquired by the student through close contact with good practitioners of the art. This idea of 'apprenticeship' has a long history in medical eduation and indeed, is the means by which our first doctors were taught, but for a number of reasons may be less apposite in present day medical schools.

The view that students will acquire the necessary skills simply by contact with paediatricians and other exponents of the art is a valid one if not yet validated. What the medical school often fails to ensure is that this contact is long enough to be effective and that inappropriate skills are not also picked up from practitioners whose art may be less perceptive. There is also the problem of excessive exposure to the hospital environment and to an unrepresentative spectrum of children's diseases in the conventional apprenticeship on a children's ward. If we profess to be training 'core-doctors' we should not concentrate the great mass of teaching within the hospital walls — otherwise it will be almost inevitable that an 'intramural' view of the world is adopted by most doctors and, in particular, that a negative view of general practice will emerge. This objection to the conventional undergraduate course is well developed by Tudor Hart (1985): 'The core curriculum for all doctors should be primary care . . . the doctor's sick shop, relying on episodic presentation of symptomatic illness, is inadequate for conservation of community health or the effective application of medical science'.

Howie (1984) presented the same view in comparing two approaches to medical practice: the 'cellular' and the 'behavioural'. The former describes much of today's high technology medicine espoused by the majority of medical academics, and hence influencing undergraduate teaching heavily. In the behavioural approach patients' problems are analysed in physical, psycho-logical and social terms: how patients present and cope with their symptoms, and how doctors respond. The cellular model fails to take account both of the less dramatic manifestations of ill health and of the behaviour of patients when confronted by chronic disease. Howie suggests that the behavioural model has more to offer to future medical practice.

A third approach to what we are trying to achieve in undergraduate child health teaching is based on the concept of 'competency'.

Competency-based teaching

Central to this approach is the concept that the end product of medical education is a 'competent doctor' (McGaghie et al, 1978). A practitioner may spend his or her life acquiring this status, but the process should start in the first year at medical school. Hence, in deciding what should be taught to the undergraduate, we must first decide what are the key attributes of the practising doctor in any given field, remembering that the majority of students will enter general practice. If it is decided, for example, that listening carefully to the mother's anxieties is an essential skill of the child health doctor, then this skill should be taught to medical students. The same would be true of making the diagnosis of meningitis in a neonate, or of explaining a diagnosis of Down's syndrome to a mother in the maternity ward. The process of acquisition of these skills (or 'competencies') is clearly a gradual one, which is represented schematically below:

1. awareness of existence of the ability
2. observing the ability in others
3. learning and practising the ability under supervision ⎤ increasing
                                                          ⎥ experience
4. practising the ability unsupervised
5. improving on the ability   ↓

The stage at which 'competency' is to be achieved, will vary in each case. We might expect competency at diagnosing tonsillitis from a medical student, but not competency at conveying the significance of handicap.

Clearly, the hardest task in this approach will be to define the requisite 'competencies' — remembering that students will not all be entering the same branch of medicine. Research techniques are available for defining competency (McGaghie et al, 1978), and one such method is the *'critical incident' technique* (Flanagan, 1954).

This technique has been used in the training of professionals requiring practical skills and has been shown by research to highly effective (McGaghie et al, 1978). It depends on analysing incidents of medicine care to select those which are especially significant — these then reflect the essential competencies. The 'critical' incidents are those which stick in the memory of observers, because they are examples of particularly good or poor medical practice. Greater objectivity is obtained by collecting a large number of such incidents. Indeed, the collection should continue until no *new* incidents are added to the list in 100 encounters. In the field of child health, the clinical practice analysed will be with children or their parents; the doctors practising the skills could be paediatricians, general practitioners, clinical medical officers or child psychiatrists. Incidents may be collected from anyone who has observed them including the above but also health visitors, social workers or parents.

The validity of the technique may be criticised on the following grounds:

• memory is fickle — the incidents may not be really important
• examples of poor practice may stick in the memory better than examples of good
• many important areas may not be illuminated in this technique — for example, the area of preventive medicine and epidemiology, which involves 'group medicine' rather than individual consultations with patients.

I personally share these reservations but would still consider the technique a valuable one. It does highlight key competencies which might otherwise be neglected in teaching, and orientates teachers towards those which are most important in practice.

Once the incidents have been collected they are grouped and the

---

Some incidents and competencies which they highlight

GP   I went to see a 10 week old baby and considered he had a cold. I was called to see the child again and found him to be blue and moribund. I took him to hospital in my car, and he was resuscitated. He had bronchopneumonia. I should have realised that his mother was 'slow' and that, as they lived in a slum, I must go back daily.
Competency: diagnosis and management of common ailments in a young baby at home, recognition of serious illness and assessment of parents' ability to cope

Pharmacist   A mother came in with a prescription for her 3 month old baby — it was for Conotrane. This is not recommended for children under 3 years. I telephoned the doctor and he altered the prescription.
Competency: correct prescription of drugs in baby and teamwork with pharmacist

GP   A mother of an 8 year old boy telephoned me to say her son had a 'chill on the bladder', and would I just leave a prescription for him and advise her how to treat him. I insisted that she bring the boy to see me first, and when she did I found him to have diabetes.
Competency: recognition of serious complaints over telephone, management of urinary complaints, early recognition of diabetes mellitus

GP   At 11 p.m. a paediatrician sat down next to the mother of a Down's Syndrome baby with congenital heart disease, who was dying in hospital at 9 months of age. He discussed what was happening and what should be done and the mother was very comforted.
Competency: counselling in bereavement

'competencies' extracted. Examples of 'good' or 'poor' practice may still highlight the same competency. It is essential that details of the encounter are recorded, but without naming the individuals concerned or otherwise allowing them to be identifiable. An example of four incidents with their relevant competency, are given in the box. A lengthy list will be generated, but this can be categorised into smaller groups, as shown in Table 16.1. Some of the detailed competencies from one of these groups are listed in Table 16.2 (Waterston, 1984a).

Table 16.1   Major groups of competencies

Inter-personal skills with parents and children (including counselling)

The diagnostic process (problem recognition; data collection; data processing)

Clinical management

Teamwork

Health maintenance skills

Inter-professional communication

Data recording

Administration

Personal qualities

Table 16.2   Some key diagnostic skills (arising from critical incident study)

Listen to the mother in a child with persistent abdominal pain, deafness, squint or limp — there may be an organic cause

Consider epiglottitis in child with croup

Consider asthma in a wheezy toddler

Suspect pyloric stenosis, intussusception and inguinal hernia in a baby with persistent vomiting

Consider otitis media in a child with persistent crying

Exclude diabetes before treating for urinary infection

Ability to recognise serious illness in a baby at home, especially in deprived circumstances

It will be seen that, since the incidents relate to clinical practice, each may include several 'parameters' of content and these must be detailed if they are to be taught to medical students. The conventional grouping of teaching divides content into knowledge, practical skills and attitudes. The disadvantage of such a grouping is that in practice we use these components together and not independently. Thus to make a diagnosis of meningitis we require a *knowledge* of the disease, a *skill* in history taking and examination and in problem solving, and a *sympathetic* attitude to a mother who will be anxious. Knowledge alone is not enough. In the 'incidents', and the 'competencies' derived from them, knowledge, skills and attitudes are integrated. In most cases, teaching of the different parameters should be integrated too.

Another means of establishing the 'competencies' is by the *'Delphi'* *technique.* (Dunn et al, 1985). In this method a group of doctors experienced in various fields of child health are interviewed individually. Each is asked to define the competencies required in their particular field. A list is collated and the experts are asked to rank each competency on a five point scale, according to how necessary it is for the doctor to acquire it. A consensus picture is then built up of the priority to be given to the different skills. Table 16.3 lists the competencies rated most highly in a Delphi study carried out by the author.

Table 16.3   Competencies ranked most highly by experts in Delphi study

Talking and relating to parents and children

Recognition of serious features of common conditions in children, and problem-solving at primary care level

Practice of prompt emergency care

Recognition of stage or condition of illness requiring referral to a higher level of care

Correct transmission of information to pharmacist concerning drug dosage and formulation

Maintenance of high ethical standards

Maintenance of confidentiality with patients

Some teachers object to a system of undergraduate teaching based on 'competencies' because they consider that it will be too structured, and that the necessary skills are better learned later. Proponents of the system would hold that later is too late.

ARE WE ACHIEVING OUR AIMS?

It may well be said that, even if we adopt a competency-based curriculum, our teaching need not change, as we are already successful in producing competent doctors. Is this in fact the case?

It is hard to measure quality, particularly in general practice where most graduates are still heading. Tudor Hart asserted (1985) that 'general practice is a disaster area', that what these doctors learn is inappropriate to the work they do, that those who succeed in general practice do so despite their undergraduate training, not because of it. Meadow (1978), in a study of undergraduate teaching, found that doctors questioned about their paediatric course 10 years after graduation still rated the different components in the same way. They were not, however, asked to relate the content of their teaching to their clinical work.

When junior doctors in hospital and in general practice were asked (Waterston, 1984b) to rank different items in their practice according to their current importance and their degree of deficiency in their undergraduate teaching, the majority indicated that teaching of the diagnosis and management of 'minor ailments' had been highly deficient yet was now seen as being extremely important. Table 16.4 summarises the areas of practice which were felt to be both important yet deficient in the undergraduate course. These findings do not indicate that all is well with our undergraduate teaching.

Further evidence of deficiencies in the undergraduate teaching of primary care paediatrics comes from the Knowelden report (Knowelden et al, 1985) on post-perinatal mortality. This study of 988 child deaths between the ages of 1 week and 2 years suggested that two thirds of 131 infants seen by general

Table 16.4 Areas of clinical practice felt by doctors to be particularly important, yet deficient in their undergraduate teaching

Handling of babies

Examination of ears

Diagnosis and management of minor ailments

Feeding problems in babies and their management

Techniques of health education

Use of home remedies in children

practitioners and a quarter of the 69 admitted to hospital had received inadequate management.

HOW TO ACHIEVE THE AIMS OF THE UNDERGRADUATE COURSE

It is essential to relate the content of an undergraduate course in child health to what we are trying to achieve. This will be easier if we adopt educational objectives. The writing of objectives is too often an exercise similar to the writing of a constitution of a learned society. It is seen as a lengthy and tedious chore which is pursued with interest only by a minority of the members of a department, and the end result is confined with relief to a dusty backwater, to be extracted for perusal only on an exceptional and rare occasion. Certainly, the adoption of educational objectives is essential if a curriculum is to be realistically and relevantly orientated. These objectives must, however, be brief, practical (Wyn Pugh et al, 1975; Carswell F, 1983) and should be used regularly — both students and staff need to be quite familiar with them and ideally should review them together at the beginning and at the end of the course. Some examples of practical objectives are:

1. Elicit an appropriate history from the parent of a child admitted with asthma.
2. Keep a 4 year old child amused for two hours and gain her confidence.
3. Feed a young baby and change her nappy.
4. Competently examine and recognise abnormality in the ears and throat of a young child.
5. Assess developmentally a 9 month old baby.
6 Diagnose a urinary tract infection in the side room.
7. Work out (a) an oral feeding regimen for a newborn infant and for a 5 month old baby
    (b) an intravenous fluid regimen for a 3 month old infant with hypotonic dehydration.
8. Prescribe the drug therapy for
    (a) a 2 year old with acute asthma
    (b) a 5 year old with chronic asthma
   and explain the management to the parents, in each case.
9. Prescribe the immunisation programme for a newborn baby who has an uncle with epilepsy.
10. Give a talk on the effects of smoking on children to an audience of teachers.

An important way of ensuring that objectives are adopted by all teachers within a department is to review them yearly as a group. Objectives of this kind are an aid as much to teachers as to students.

Agreement on objectives may well lead to a reassessment of priorities within the child health course, and I would now like to look at the balance of the different components within the whole.

THE CONTENT OF A CHILD HEALTH COURSE

In a competency-based curriculum teaching is organised around the various competencies which have been collated by methods such as the ones described above. Whatever method is chosen, the following major areas will probably be included within the course:

1. history taking and communication with children and parents
2. examination of children, and assessment of their growth and development
3. clinical skills — investigation, practical procedures and problem-solving
4. diagnosis and management of common problems in babies and young children, including their effect on the family
5. health supervision, screening and preventive aspects of child health (including the effect of the environment on child health) and the health services for children, including the handicapped
6. ethical aspects of the care of children.

Some would place a separate category of *Newborn care* within the above.

There is not space here to discuss all aspects of course content, but I would like to develop further the questions of the *priority* to be accorded to different components of the course, the *place* of teaching and make some comments on *teaching methods*.

Priorities

Unless clear objectives have been accepted by all members of a teaching department (and sometimes even in spite of this), there will be disagreement over the priority to be accorded to different components. Traditionalists will wish to emphasise teaching on the diseases they are interested in; others will wish most of the students' time to be spent on the ward seeing sick children; others will not wish to specify the topics, but simply attach students to a paediatrician or 'firm' for the period. Clearly the priorities will depend on the total time allocated to child health and on the years in which it is taught. In the end, however, the adoption of objectives should help to promote a more rational allocation of priorities. The critical incident study alluded to above highlighted communication with parents as being of especial importance in child health practice. It may well be that some departments should give greater priority to communication techniques as part of history taking, and there are now well established methods for achieving this (see below).

The place where teaching occurs

At present, most teaching is done within the teaching hospital or its outlying centres for the very simple reasons that this avoids the complications of travel and of finding additional teachers outside hospital, but, inevitably, this emphasis on the hospital reinforces the view that the 'central aim of medical education remains the production of specialist excellence' (Tudor Hart, 1985). If we are concerned for students to learn the primary care aspects of child health, and indeed for them to understand the root causes of ill health in children, then they must be exposed to reality outside hospital. As Harden et al (1984) pointed out, some aspects of medicine can *only* be taught adequately in the community setting (for example, the need for continuity of care, the effect of illness on a family, the early signs of disease and the importance of teamwork), while much of the medicine presently taught in hospital *could* be taught in the community if the resources were available. An additional reason for teaching more in the community is that many hospitals have insufficient inpatients for teaching large numbers of students.

Some teachers will feel that such teaching outside hospital should be the responsibility of general practitioners rather than paediatricians, and this is true given the present structure of the service. However, to entrust all teaching about children in the community to GPs would be an abrogation of responsibility by child health teachers. Ideally, a child health department should coordinate its community teaching with the department of general practice to ensure that the objectives of each are met. In general practice, the students should learn about the recognition and management of commonly occurring problems in children, and their impact on the family. They should visit children in their homes and begin to understand the relationship of the different services for children in the community. It may not be so easy to convey the environmental and preventive aspects of child health within general practice given its present curative orientation. The community child health service may perform this task better, since students will make contact with ordinary children in their natural environment in situations such as day nurseries, primary and secondary schools. However, our experience in Dundee indicates (Waterston, 1985) that there are constraints in using this service for teaching medical students, which may be grouped as follows:

Who will teach in the community? Hospital staff lack knowledge; community doctors lack teaching experience.

How will the learning be assessed? The skills and attitudes learned in the community are hard to assess in a conventional examination.

How can the students obtain experience of integrated child health care? In practice, there may be a lack of integration between hospital and community services and between preventive and curative services.

There are also practical difficulties with transport, with teaching space and with the provision of a sufficient number of suitable settings.

All these constraints can be overcome, but they must first be recognised. It is too easy, as Coles (1985) suggested, to 'graft on' community expriences to an otherwise traditional curriculum which itself remains essentially unchanged. When this was done in Southampton, the students felt that the experience was 'relevant to being a doctor, but totally irrelevant to being a medical student'.

Teaching methods

I wish to indicate here some ways of teaching certain of the important aspects of child health, for which traditional methods are not suitable. I am referring particularly to methods for teaching about communication skills, about the place of teamwork in child care, and about the problems of the social environment. These areas depend on the acquisition more of skills and attitudes than of knowledge.

Communication skills These skills are vital to child health clinical practice but are poorly taught at present, and inadequately assessed. Even the process of history taking is not usually assessed as such in our clinical examinations, though the facts elicited from it may be. Many medical schools are introducing a course on communication skills in the early years, but this does not absolve child health teachers from developing the paediatric aspects. *Role play* is a particularly appropriate technique for teaching these skills and helping the student to become more aware of his or her own strengths and weaknesses. Video-taping such a session helps the participants to analyse their own performance, but it may be sufficient for those students watching to discuss the interchange afterwards. The use of role play is discussed by Meadow (1979) and, in more detail, by Cox and Ewen (1982). Teachers may be reluctant to try out this technique because of their own unfamiliarity with the method. Certainly, more experience of its use and research into its effectiveness would be very helpful. Maguire in Manchester has extensive experience of teaching interviewing skills to medical students. He has shown both that the apprenticeship method of training often fails to equip students with these skills (Maguire & Rutter, 1976) and that methods such as feedback by audiotape (Maguire et al, 1978) are effective in improving interview technique.

Teamwork Doctors are well known for their authoritarian attitudes and individualistic approach to patients, and it is difficult to provide more cooperative examples unless students have the opportunity to learn outside hospital. A deficiency of successful role models of teamwork in action make this process even harder. Two approaches to teaching teamwork to medical students are described below.

The most radical is to promote *joint training* of doctors and other workers such as nurses or health visitors. This has been frequently suggested (Dowling, 1983) but rarely attempted. A method accessible to all paediatric teachers would be to organise a project jointly between medical students and students from another discipline. This would get round the criticism that sitting in a lecture theatre with nursing students will not help medical students to work with them more effectively (though it might promote the marriage rate). Again, more published examples of this kind of work would be helpful.

A second method of teaching teamwork is through a *case study*, as practised in Newcastle (Steiner, 1984) and Dundee. In Newcastle, third year students are allocated a child as a community case. Their task is to present the child to a multi-disciplinary group and also to write up the case as an essay. In studying the child, the student is expected to visit as many of the people working with the child as possible — as well as the family themselves. The case study proved popular with students and seems effective as a teaching method, though it has not yet been formally evaluated. Its main aim is to teach the students what the roles of different team members are rather than to help them function in a team themselves.

The social environment The social environment and its effect on child upbringing is a difficult but important area of teaching. Students should learn something of the problems that parents from deprived backgrounds face in bringing up children, and of the cultural differences which exist in child rearing. We approach this in Dundee through a case study where students are allocated a child with a social or behavioural problem in a day nursery. The student acts as a nursery nurse to the child, looking after him or her throughout the day and performing the usual chores, pleasant or unpleasant, of the child's parent.

This exposure to the realities of child care is particularly important for male students. The case is reported to a multi-disciplinary group, and cultural aspects are exposed whenever possible. It is not easy to give students insights on cross-cultural differences in such a brief period. Poulton & Rylance (1985) from Birmingham have produced useful teaching material which highlights deficiencies in the health care of ethnic minorities.

Meadow's (1979) suggestion of letting students take on the role of nurse for a day is another way of giving students practical experience as a child minder. The Newcastle scheme of attaching a student to a family with young children early in the course, and allowing him or her to follow them over the next two years, is valuable and well tried in the United States, but careful supervision is necessary.

These descriptions of what to some will sound like difficult and experimental methods, may be offputting to teachers better versed in the traditional techniques of lecture, ward round and seminar. However, these latter methods are unlikely to make the students better communicators, teamworkers or observers of children. As Harden (1984) points out, techniques such as role play should not necessarily be used in place of a lecture. It is a question of deciding what our educational objectives are and then selecting out of the extensive 'toolkit' of available methods, those which are most suitable to help the students achieve these objectives. It is therefore essential that teachers are familiar with as wide a range of methods as possible. Another objection to this type of teaching (which relates to attitudes and skills rather than to knowledge) is that it is better done as part of postgraduate education, when the doctor can see its value more clearly. The counter to this objection is that students' views are formed during their undergraduate years, but neglect of certain important areas of practice even at the postgraduate stage may lead to deficiencies being perpetuated throughout life.

Cooperation with other departments

A final point to raise in the discussion on how we achieve our aims in child health teaching, concerns cooperation with other departments in the medical school. As yet, few schools have abolished individual departments. Students need to learn about people and their health problems rather than about bits of people — hence an inter-disciplinary approach is to be preferred. This rarely takes place because of the constraints of time and motivation. Traditionally, child health has considered itself more closely aligned to adult medicine than to any other specialty. However, if the course is to be orientated more towards the requirements of primary medical care, child health will become more closely aligned with the departments of general practice, community medicine and obstetrics and gynaecology than with medicine. Indeed, the teaching of geriatric medicine with its emphasis on family care in the community may have more in common with present day paediatrics than does acute adult medicine. Yet at present these departments tend to remain distant relatives rather than partners. Can a greater degree of cooperation be achieved?

ASSESSMENT

The way we assess our medical students is not only critical in providing information on whether the aims of the course are being achieved but also concentrates student attention on certain aspects of the content. It may, in addition, assist in reforming the curriculum. Problems with present assessments are that:

1. They concentrate on factual knowledge.
2. They tend to emphasise the esoteric.
3. They omit areas such as history taking, problem solving and community skills such as the ability to work in a team.
4. Effective feedback is rarely provided to the students on their performance, especially in clinical examinations.

If we accept that students learn best what they expect to be examined on then we should alter our assessments to take into account our revised priorities. As with teaching methods, a 'toolkit' of assessment techniques is also available from which we may select the one most appropriate for assessing a particular area of knowledge or skill.

Assessment of competence

If a curriculum is intended to educate/train doctors in competence, then we should attempt to assess performance towards this end in our examinations. This implies setting in advance a level that we expect most students to achieve. In the conventional system, teachers are surprised if most students obtain over 80 percent and say that the test was 'too easy', but a patient would probably prefer *all* students to perform well, as he or she will then have more confidence in the ability of the end product. It is still possible to pick out 'high-fliers' using a test which assesses competence (the so-called 'criterion-referenced' assessment (Cox & Ewan, 1982) as opposed to a norm-referenced system which relates each student's performance to that of his or her peers).

Most teachers will be familiar with techniques such as multiple choice questions (MCQs), modified essay questions and continuous assessment in testing achievement as these methods now have their own extensive literature. However, the assessment of clinical performance is less comprehensive, and students tend to obtain little feedback. The conventional clinical exam is formal, lacks objectivity and neglects important aspects such as history taking, attitude to the patient and problem solving ability. A more appropriate method is the objective structured clinical examination (OSCE) (Waterston, et al, 1980) now in use in a number of medical schools in Britain and overseas. The method may be adapted by the users to give more feedback to the student (Black et al, 1985) and any clinical area may be selected for special emphasis. The OSCE is particularly good at indicating students' strengths or weaknesses on particular topics and in directing teachers' attention to areas of deficiency within the course.

A further point about the OSCE is that it may rapidly alert teachers to the need to alter the content of a course — should deficiencies be shown on topics (such as urine microscopy or history taking) which had not previously been amenable to testing.

REFORMING CHILD HEALTH TEACHING

I would like to look finally at some of the constraints to change that occur in a conventional child health course, and some ways of circumventing them.

Lack of primary care orientation by teachers

Primary care concepts are poorly understood by clinicians working in hospital in the UK. Walton (1983) noted that even in departments of general practice, only half of 32 heads of department surveyed in the UK were familiar with the components of the WHO declaration of Alma-Ata on primary health care. It might be said that this concept is intended more for developing than for developed countries, but those familiar with the elements of primary health care would not agree. Illingworth (1979) has amusingly described the heavy emphasis on rare disorders in most student paediatric textbooks — more detail being given, for instance, about double penis, which might be seen in general practice once in 137 500 years, then about temper tantrums and nappy rash. 'Common' problems are thought not worthy of great consideration by some paediatric teachers, and yet their epidemiology, natural course, effects on the family and value as indicators of disease elsewhere are little studied; nor is much known about effective management in many cases, yet the Knowelden report (1985) on sudden infant deaths has shown how much this information is needed. These deficiencies are being remedied and perhaps the influence of increasing numbers of community paediatricians will do much to improve the status of primary child health care.

Lack of time, lack of interest

Constraints of time in altering a teaching programme are commonly heard, but may in fact be due more to lack of interest. However, the system whereby advancement in the profession depends on clinical or basic science research rather than on teaching skills is a big factor in deflecting this interest. It is also true that any innovative teaching method *is* likely to require more time and preparation, at least in the early stages. This is particularly so for methods which depend on teaching in small groups. However, it must be recognised that paediatricians will be unable to rely in the future on ward rounds and case demonstrations in hospital as extensively as before, given the smaller number of children who are admitted to hospital. This welcome change will force us to take different approaches to teaching, with greater use of outpatient departments and community facilities. Such an opportunity for innovation should be grasped positively rather than greeted with dismay.

Child health within the curriculum

A further constraint is the very brief time actually allocated to child health within the curriculum. Almost all paediatricians will assert that their teaching time is too short, especially if the community and preventive aspects of the course are to be fully covered. They may, however, have difficulty convincing their colleagues, who usually also feel that their own time allocation is inadequate. A better case may be made if all community orientated departments such as child health, general practice, community medicine, obstetrics and gynaecology and geriatrics reach some agreement over their arguments for more community 'time' and then consider using integrated or coordinated teaching.

It is also valuable if certain aspects of child health such as growth and development, child psychology and sociology are taught in the early years with input from paediatricians, as is done in Dundee and in some other medical schools. Meadow (1979) pointed out the advantage to child health teachers of making contact with students before their attitudes are set, but that it helps if students have practised the use of a stethoscope on an adult before using it on a child. It would therefore seem appropriate that paediatricians should have several points of contact over the whole course.

The way forward

I would like to finish by suggesting some ways by which interested teachers can try to introduce change in their own departments, with the agreement rather than over the dead bodies of their colleagues. They are also ways of stimulating interest in medical education in general. McGaghie et al (1978) have presented useful discussion on strategies for curriculum change.

1. Introduce an OSCE

This type of examination can be introduced without affecting any other aspects of the course. One person will need to spend a fair amount of time initially in setting it up and preparing and 'banking' material, but the work becomes less as a routine is developed. The OSCE is also a stimulus to reforming the context of the course and in particular to reviewing its objectives. Those interested should refer to Harden and Gleeson (1979).

2. Introduce a community attachment or community project

Many departments of paediatrics are in future, likely to try to expose their students to more community child health. This may be better done within general practice than by the community child health services, for reasons already alluded to above. However, it is essential for defined objectives to be adopted if a new venue and new teachers are introduced. A project which involves the students in collecting information for themselves, or which allows them to follow up a child at home after admission to hospital, is likely to be more fruitful than a simple clinic attachment where the students quickly become bored.

A community study of the kind initiated by Steiner (1984) in Newcastle may fulfil the same function. As more and more teachers look to the community as a resource, the supply of suitable children and facilities may become overstretched, but this has been a problem in hospital for many years and should not prove insuperable.

3. A course for teachers

My own interest in teaching methods stemmed from attending a medical education course, and I have observed this phenomenon in other teachers. Yet it is still the exception rather than the rule for medical lecturers to attend a course on teaching methods. Perhaps there is a lack of good courses. It is up to heads of departments however, to ensure that their lecturers are exposed to a review of their own teaching styles as well as to some analysis of how students learn. These teachers will then have to be given more time to organise their tasks; a clear statement of recognition will then be required from the medical profession that such a use of time is appropriate.

After all this, will it make any difference to change the way we teach? The Lancet (1984) stated that 'some believe that irrespective of the medical school of origin, much the same sort of young doctor emerges on the wards at the start of the pre-registration year'. This is a statement that the students themselves, and the general public, will be in a better position to answer than the teachers.

Acknowledgements

I am grateful to Ross Mitchell for having the foresight to see that time could usefully be spent in medical education, and to Ronald Harden for providing most of the ideas.

REFERENCES

Black N M L, Urquhart A, Harden R M 1985 The OSCE: an aid to learning. Medical Education 19: 85–86
Carswell F 1983 Instructional objectives in child health. Medical Teacher 5: 114–115
Coles C R 1985 The effects of Southampton's community experiences on student learning. Medical Education 19: 196–198
Cox K R, Ewan C E 1982 The medical teacher. Churchill Livingstone, London
Dowling S 1983 Health for a change. Child Poverty Action Group, London
Dunn W R, Hamilton D D, Harden R M 1985 Techniques of identifying competencies needed of doctors. Medical Teacher 7: 15–25
Flannagan J C 1954 The critical incident technique. Psychological Bulletin 51: 327–358
Harden R M 1984 Medical teaching. Workbook of a course at Centre for Medical Education, Dundee
Harden R M, Gleeson F 1979 Assessment of clinical competence using an objective structured clinical examination (OSCE). ASME medical education booklet No. 8. Association for the Study of Medical Education, Dundee
Harden R M, Sowden S, Dunn W R, 1984 Some educational strategies in curriculum development: the SPICES Model. ASME medical education booklet No. 18. Association for the Study of Medical Education, Dundee
Howie J G R 1984 Research in general practice: pursuit of knowledge or defence of wisdom? British Medical Journal 289: 1770–1772
Illingsworth R S 1979 Does it matter? World Medicine 7 April: 31–36
Knowelden J, Keeling J, Nicholl J P 1985 A multi-centre study of post neonatal mortality. DHSS, London
Lancet (Editorial) 1984 Medical student selection in the UK. Lancet ii: 1190–1191
McGaghie WC, Miller GE, Sajid A W, Telder TV 1978 Competency-based curriculum development in medical education. Public health papers No. 68, WHO, Geneva
McIntyre N 1979 In defence of students. World Medicine, 10 March: 19–22
Maguire G P, Rutter D R 1976 History taking for medical students. I: Deficiencies in performance. Lancet ii: 556–558
Maguire G P, Roe P, Goldberg D, Jones S, Hyde C, O'Dowd T 1978 The value of feedback in teaching interviewing skills to medical students. Psychological Medicine 8:695–704
Meadow R 1978 Students' assessments of paediatric teaching and their opinions 7 years later. Archives of Disease in Childhood 53: 653–655
Meadow R 1979 The way we teach paediatrics. Medical Teacher 1: 237–243
Poulton J, Rylance G 1985 Cross cultural medicine: a teaching aid, Medical Teacher 7: 157–163
Steiner H 1984 Personal communication
Tudor Hart J 1985 The world turned upside down: proposals for community-based undergraduate medical education. Journal of the Royal College of General Practitioners 35: 63–68
Walton H J 1983 The place of primary health care in medical education in the UK: a survey. Medical Education 17: 141–147

Waterston T, Cater J I, Mitchell R G 1980 An objective undergraduate clinical examination in child health. Archives of Disease in Childhood 55: 917–923

Waterston T 1984a Teaching child health — use of the critical incident technique. Paper read at Scottish Paediatric Society, Glasgow, 23rd November

Waterston T 1984b Relation between undergraduate child health teaching and graduate clinical practice. Paper read at Paediatric Research Society, Bristol 21 September

Waterston T 1985 Constraints in the introduction of community-based teaching in child health. Paper read at Association for the study of Medical Education, Newcastle, 20 September

Wyn Pugh E, LloydG J, McIntyre N 1975 Relevance of educational objectives for medical education. British Medical Journal iii: 688–691

The paediatric nurse practitioner

The paediatric nurse practitioner (PNP) is a registered nurse who has integrated non-traditional skills into nursing practice, enabling her to provide more effective health care to infants, children and adolescents in a variety of community and institutional settings. A formal programme of study and clinical supervision is required. Generically, nurse practitioner skills are understood to encompass:

1. The ability to elicit, organise and record a health history which includes, but is *not* limited to, the traditional, detailed medical and developmental history;

2. The ability to use the basic instruments required for physical examination;

3. The ability to conduct a classical physical examination and identify physical findings abnormal for age;

4. Working knowledge of the indications and interpretations of commonly used diagnostic tests;

5. The ability to diagnose acute minor illness frequently seen in a specific area of practice, recognising clusters of symptoms and ruling out indications of more serious disease requiring consultation and/or referral; initiating and monitoring treatment based on protocol and on an understanding of pathophysiology and pharmacology;

6. The ability to implement immunisation programmes;

7. Refined skills in health, illness, behavioural/developmental counselling and anticipatory guidance;

8. The ability to collaborate, consult and coordinate the management of the child and family dealing with chronic illness — the extent of PNP contribution in this area is determined by skill and experience level;

9. Referral to inter-dependent members of the health care team and to a broad range of community resources;

10. Coordination of multi-disciplinary input and services;

11. Willingness to negotiate a collaborative practice;

12. Commitment to continuing education to meet individual learning needs as well as licensure and certification requirements.

ROLE TRANSITION

'Practitioner' training promotes an appreciation of and introduction to the clinical language and the process of medical diagnosis, enhancing communication between the two disciplines. It builds on generic nursing education, which in the United States prepares nurse generalists with entry level skills in care of the acute and chronically ill child and adult as well as maternity and psychiatric patients. Role transition requires an initial period of intense skill development, the focus of which is the deliberate, systematic process of physical assessment and its validation. The time frame is variable and dependent on duration and intensity of the training programme, intensity of the clinical exposure, availability and quality of the clinical supervision, individual learning styles and abilities. Optimally, assimilation and integration occur over time, in practice permitting the emergence of a flexible clinical style maximising traditional nursing competencies along with new skills. A mentor and/or formal group process providing a forum for issues and support during the transition are desirable.

Paediatric nurse practitioners are not a homogeneous group. Their credentials and PNP training vary from short term certificate progammes to formal graduate programmes. Moreover, skill level, experience and talent contribute further to the diversity, as in other fields. Although this has created confusion for patients, physicians and nurse colleagues, it reflects philosophical differences in development of the role. This is probably unavoidable at this point in nursing history in the United States as the profession evolves in the context of a rapidly changing health care delivery system. Legal sanction for this type of practice varies from state to state — amendments enabling nurse practice to encompass non-traditional skills have required considerable legislative activity across the country. As a group, nurses in the vanguard demonstrated clinical competence, autonomy and an ability to tolerate the uncertainties associated with shifting role boundaries and re-definition. Conflict within the profession and with the medical community, the necessity of educating the public and political, regulatory battles continue to be taxing realities. The distinction, for instance, that has been made between physician practice and nurse practice as curing versus caring is a most unfortunate one. To imply that a physician sincerely committed to his or her practice is an uncaring clinician or uncaring person is unfair and disparaging and justifiably provokes resentment and creates a barrier to collaboration and cooperation.

PRACTICE SETTINGS

A 1983 National Association of Paediatric Nurse Associates and Practitioners membership survey (Butler, 1984) with a 51% response rate reported the following practice setting distribution:

Community health clinic or centre	22.8%
Hospital-based outpatient clinic	17.2%
Private medical practice	16.4%
Schools — grade K-12	8.3%
In-hospital patient unit	7.0%
Military clinic	5.6%
Prepaid group practice	4.9%
School of nursing	4.8%
Self employed — independent	1.3%
Hospital emergency room	0.6%
Rehabilitation Centre	0.3%
Other	11.2%

In addition, paediatric nurse practitioners are employed by, or consult to, day care centres, summer camps, community based early intervention programmes for physically handicapped children and those at risk for developmental delay, residential and institutional settings for the severely retarded or multi-handicapped and paediatric nursing homes.

As in any other field, a mature clinician may have developed a specific area of expertise either in a clinical sub-speciality, or as a nurse-educator, nurse-researcher, nurse-manager. A wide range of actual and potential practice settings exist.

ROLE DEVELOPMENT

In ambulatory primary health care settings, the PNP role varies somewhat depending on the primary care model adopted. A collaborative model team practice identifying a primary care physician and PNP for each child/family has the advantage of making available, in an ongoing way, a broader range of clinical skills, talents and perspectives.

Establishing any collaborative practice is a process. The impetus for collaboration, whether personal choice versus organisational decision or mandate, impacts that process. The dynamics are determined by both the personal and professional needs, goals and motivations of the collaborators. Some of these characteristics are revealed during the 'breaking-in' or negotiation phase. Respective practice styles and philosophy must be explored. What does each find most rewarding and fulfilling in practice? What are individual areas of expertise and special interest? How does each approach specific problems? What are individual biases relative to child rearing and the management of behaviour problems? The team must recognise similarities and differences, confront problems and negotiate a compatible approach to practice. The challenge of 'sharing' patients requires cooperation and a willingness to address inevitable issues of competition and territorialism. Guidelines delineating who does what, consultation and referral mechanisms, provision for case review and coordination must be established. Commitment to the negotiated plan must be followed by orientation of colleagues and ancillary personnel and patient education. Periodic re-evaluation and re-negotiation are important in response to increased awareness of relevant individual and practice variables, change and growth. Effective teams are characterised by mutual respect, trust and a willingness to learn from and teach each other. In addition, it is important to accept and respect a family's choice of clinician, recognising that it is their individual needs and dynamics, and not exclusively the clinician's skills or credentials, that mediate this choice.

In a parallel practice model, a physician or PNP is identified as the primary caretaker, with consultation and referral between the team members based on negotiated guidelines.

In, yet other, primary care settings, the PNP serves primarily a consultative role and accepts referral for direct care of children and families with specific problems — e.g., feeding problems, developmental delay, a wide range of behaviour problems, child abuse/neglect, chronic disease management and preparation for hospitalisation

In long term institutional settings the PNP tends to focus on maximising day to day functional level of residents, monitoring chronic conditions such as a seizure disorder and its associated drug treatment, coordinating medical treatment and serving as a resource for the family.

In contrast, camp settings require a focus on safety and accident prevention, promotion of adjustment to the setting, emergency treatment of acute illness and trauma and monitoring chronic health problems.

The current trend in the United States limiting hospitalisation to the most acutely ill and fragile patients presents a challenge to the health care delivery system to provide careful patient monitoring, equipment and coordinated support services in the home. Hospitalisation is a potent social signal designating patient status and freeing the individual from many social responsibilities. Increasingly, the burden of providing a nurturing environment that motivates towards wellness falls to the family. Guidance and support in creating an environment conducive to rest, repair, recovery, adjustment and adaptation, whenever possible, and comfort and palliation in the case of terminal illness will be assumed more and more by nurse practitioners. Advanced physical assessment and decision making skills integrated with traditional nursing competencies should prove to be a valuable clinical resource in home care.

A NURSING IDENTITY

The PNP role described represents an overlap of functional responsibility with physicians, for example, in implementing immunisation programmes and screening for signs and symptoms of disease, malfunction and deviations in growth and development. The PNP function in illness is complementary to that of the physician in that its *central* focus is the realistic integration of the acute or chronic condition and its treatment into the lives of the child and family.

Exploring, for example, How the treatment regime *fits* into the family routine? What significance does the disease have for the child and parents? Does compliance with any part of the treatment and follow up plan conflict with family priorities? The patient education and counselling under which this activity is subsumed involves more than the conveying of facts about the disease and its treatment. It is a facilitative relationship — a process — aimed at a healthy integration permitting physical and psychosocial growth of all family members while deriving maximum benefits from available treatment and prevention or early detection of complications.

I would propose that a measure of the influence of the PNP in the health care system is the measure of the PNP's efficacy, or ability to mobilise individual and family resources, appropriate health and medical care services and community resources, in order to preserve or restore health, maintain safety and promote growth and development.

REFERENCE

Butler C 1984 The 1983 National Association of Paediatric Nurse Associates and Practitioners membership survey. Paediatric Nursing 10: 187–190

Child health in general practice

In 1892 Budin, a physician in Paris, started a clinic for infant consultation. Mothers returned to the hospital where they had been delivered for advice on breast feeding. His work was widely publicised, and a few pioneers in the United Kingdom followed his example and set up similar infant consultation clinics, often involving layworkers to help them. Their success led to the realisation that there was a nationwide need for centres where parents and their children could obtain advice on all the aspects of infant care, feeding, health, clothing and hygiene. As they evolved, some centres in addition offered advice to the mother on her health and care, and in many parts of the UK layworkers made house to house visits to seek out problems or follow up treatment and to visit routinely all the mothers and children known to them (and until 1950 these original layworkers were working still, alongside the trained health visitors).

The benefits were quickly noted, and by the beginning of the First World War many local authorities had set up such centres and appointed doctors and health visitors to staff them.

In 1918 the Maternity and Child Welfare Act required all local authorities to prepare and implement schemes for the establishment of child health clinic centres. Supervision was the responsibility of the Board of Education, unconsciously echoing the oft quoted remark of the doctors and lay staff in the early days that the centres should be, 'Schools for parents rather than clinics for babies'.

Not until 1920, with the Local Government Act, did the Ministry of Health become responsible for the central supervision of local authorities operating such centres. Then, as now, at the insistence of general practitioners, clinic doctors were unable to prescribe treatment for illness and were forced to refer the sick children to the patient's own general practitioner (if he or she had one and could afford his fees), or to the local authority run hospitals. This had the effect of forcing many hospitals, and particularly children's hospitals, to organise and staff a dispensary service which often swamped the existing outpatient consulting services.

General practitioners viewed the infant welfare centres with scorn and distrust. The work did not seem to them to have much to do with illness care as

222

taught in medical school. In addition, it reduced the consulting workload and therefore their income. The more astute privately admitted that, in all but the wealthier areas of the country, the fees that could be earned, charged and collected for such work were not adequate recompense for the outlay of time and energy. In some parts of the cuntry, however, general practitioners ran their own infant consulting clinics successfully, often virtually free to their own patients despite the unofficial sanctions on such 'free' services.

By 1930 health visitors had proved themselves invaluable as their training, for the first time, matched the requirements of the task in hand. They usually became the key workers as the success of the individual infant welfare centre depended on their skills in persuading mothers of newborn babies and new arrivals to the district to attend. Much house to house visiting was carried out, and the health visitor became a familiar figure to mothers with chilen. In the 1930s and 40s maternal health and, in particular, antenatal care were accepted as further responsibilities, and, at the beginning of the National Health Service in 1948, the Child Health Movement could claim, with justification, that much had been achieved. Maternal and infant morbidity and mortality were falling fast. Deaths from diphtheria, whooping cough and tetanus were fast becoming fewer each year, and the Movement appeared in full flower.

However, voices were insistently claiming that the work done should properly be done by adequately trained, motivated and recompensed general practitioners. Sir Leonard Parsons (1947) stated that, 'the present Child Welfare Service would probably never have arisen if in years gone by general practitioners as a class had taken a real interest in the care of young children'. He went on to qualify the statement by remarking 'the teaching in medical schools contained little, if any, instruction in the subject, as a result that the keen general practitioner had to equip himself for the care of children after he had started practice'.

In 1949 the White Paper (Cmnd 6502) on the future National Health Service Report commented, 'There is no doubt that in much of the general care of the young child and handling of many of its day to day problems, the clinics and the family doctor who have the general medical care of the child must be enabled to work in better contact for their common purpose.'

Despite this confident and, to some, self-evident statement the final National Health Service Act left untouched the existing structure of local authority funded clinic services and ensured their separate continuation. Research continued, however, into the effectiveness of child health centres and their staff. The results of the Newcastle 1000 families study, published in 1954 (Spence et al, 1954) and 1960 (Miller et al, 1960) showed that the number of mothers attending clinics with their children fell from 67% in the first years to less than 10% during the fifth. Doubt was cast on the perceived role of the child health clinic as currently organised at the time.

A special inquiry undertaken by the Ministry of Health into the staffing of child health centres in 1961 showed the amazing variety of staffing arrangements. In the City of Gloucester, in Oxfordshire and in Cambridgeshire, for instance, general practitioners undertook nearly all the child health clinic work. In some counties fewer than 2% did so.

In 1964 (Cartright, 1967) a survey carried out by the Institute of Community Studies in 12 parliamentary constituencies revealed that the fall off in attendance as children grew older, so apparent for local authority clinics, did not in fact occur in clinics organised by general practitioners covered by the survey.

Change, however, was occurring. In 1964 health visitor attachment to child health centres was still virtually the rule (94%). In a few areas, enlightened medical officers of health began to experiment with health visitor attachment to general practices. The success of the experiments was such that, by 1974, official government policy was to encourage the complete detachment of health visitors from their traditional child welfare centres and geographical base to individual general practices, and, by 1976, the transition was virtually complete.

Meanwhile, the Sheldon Committee had reported to the Ministry of Health on child welfare centres (Sheldon, 1967) and stated that, in its opinion, 'in the long term it will be part of a family health service provided by family doctors' and went on to outline the functions, covering routine examinations, advice, nutrition and hygiene, health education, immunisation, etc. It also made recommendations on the training of medical staff, noting, once more, the current deficiences.

This report's findings failed to stimulate either the leaders or the rank and file of general practitioners, who saw that a lot of extra work and responsibility would receive little or no financial recompense, and the perceived worth of the work was of doubtful value to many general practitioners, untrained as they largely were. For instance, only a small minority (5%) possessed the DCH, a rough indication of how much more postgraduate training was needed if general practitioners were to take over the task.

The report was not, however, wholly disregarded; its publication acted as a catalyst, and the numbers of general practitioners running developmental care programmes in their practices steadily rose. The previously mentioned wide scale attachment of health visitors to general practice, who brought with them badly needed organisational ability, injected a new enthusiasm for preventative care, and the health visitor acted as the eyes and ears of each programme: on their ability to persuade mothers to attend clinics rested the success of the individual practice programme.

By the time the Court report was published in 1976 (Department of Health and Social Security, 1976) about 15% of all general practitioners, in cooperation with health visitors, were running child health clinics in their practices. Again, a call was made in this report for general practitioners to take over total responsibility for child health. Again, the general practitioners' leaders dismissed the report as unrealistic, poured scorn on its recommendations that general practitioner paediatricians should be appointed and paid for carrying out the work, both of the pre-school services and also the school health services. In fact, the detailed recommendations were flawed. Unfortunately, the medical profession used the flaws to deny the good sense in the rest of the report, which again attempted to place the health care of children back into the general practitioners' hands. However, many general practitioners saw now, for the first time, that there was good sense in taking over the responsibility for child health in total for those children registered with them in their practices.

Since the beginning of the National Health Service in 1948, individual general practitioners had made a valuable contribution to child health. Pioneers like Cook, working outside Bristol, who ran an exclusively paediatric general practice for many years until the problems of pension funding forced him to accept parents as well as children, demonstrated what commitment and skill could bring. One hundred per cent immunisation rates; low levels of behavioural problems; early, speedy diagnosis of developmental disorders, coupled in Cook's case with regular psychological assessments through the school years and careers guidance, forming just a part of his complete package of care.

Pollak (1972), working in Brixton, had demonstrated that in the most unpromising and deprived surroundings, enthusiasm and commitment could result in near 100% uptake of immunisation, and she reported a commendably high level of attendance for routine surveillance examinations. It was obvious too that the parents greatly welcomed the opportunity that such a service provided to obtain child health care and advice.

In Livingstone in Scotland the radical reorganisation of health services in the new town showed how the traditional demarcation between hospital, community and general practitioner services could be eliminated. The general practitioners with special paediatric interest worked a third of their time in general practice, a third in the community child health service and a third on the hospital paediatric services (Stark et al, 1975).

SURVEILLANCE

The routine surveillance examination had already become a sine qua non of all 'quality' child health programmes as a result of the 1966 United Nations declaration. Many general practitioners took on this task. Starte (1974, 1975, 1976) and others addressed themselves to the problem of the content and recording of examinations in the face of the lack of any such guidance from the community paediatric care planners and providers. His lead put in train the work of the Ashford Developmental Paediatric Research Group, which set itself the task of producing an accurate, reproducible surveillance examination system and an effective recording system to go with it. I and others, have reported on its use (Curtis Jenkins et al, 1978), and the Group will shortly be reporting its findings on a national 3500 child sample.

That such a tool was urgently required was demonstrated by Bain (1977), who showed how appalling the standard of examination and recording was in general practitioner child health clinics. It is probable, however, given the similar lack of tools and guidance, that a similar situation existed in many community run clinics.

By 1970, however, the first doubts were being cast on the value of routine surveillance examination. Already, many local authorities were running large scale progammes, but a combination of low attendance rates for the over 1 year olds, poor follow up of disorders found, occasional lack of commitment and sometimes non-existent training of the community paediatric medical staff, together with the basic organisational problems, had allowed few of the ambitious programmes to fulfil their planners' hopes (Roberts & Khosla, 1972.

Researchers in general practice too were quick to find fault with the concept. Few, if any, validation studies had been attempted of the tools to be used, their uses and their outcomes.

Despite this drawback, general practitioners continued to set up similar programmes in their practices. The results were sometimes very successful but, on occasion, disastrous, as unskilled and untrained general practitioners reported examining hundreds of children yet failed to detect the expected deviations from normality because of their lack of expertise.

Harvard Davis (1975) went so far as to say that there was no good evidence that any condition other than hearing and vision defects justified screening, and his views were echoed by many in the profession who used such arguments to justify their decisions not to organise child health clinics in their practices. In addition, many argued that as every child was seen so often for illness care, opportunistic assessment could be carried out at this time. (The argument still grumbles on (Houston & Harvard Davis 1985), but I feel that the arguments voiced against such a stance (Williams, 1985; Piper, 1985) are now winning the day.)

However, many skilled and highly motivated general practitioners continued the task. The volume of research increased as those doctors felt that organising child health surveillance programmes that incorporated regular examinations in their practices was a logical extension of good general practice. (Barber, 1982; Bassett, 1981; Willmot et al, 1984).

The formal attachment of health visitors to general practice had already demonstrated the benefit to the children in the care of those general practitioners who understood the health visitors' role and were able to work with them. Health visitors stood squarely at the centre of practice based child health programmes. In many cases they acted as the spur to the setting up of child health clincs, where they sometimes carried out screening procedures alongside the general practitioners who performed regular medical paediatric surveillance examinations. In addition, they shared traditional consulting and immunisation activities. Age–sex registers enabling accurate identification of all children in the practice care enhanced their effectiveness.

After 16 years, there are *still* many problems to be resolved about who does what, the levels of cooperation and the professional problems caused by, for instance, nurse managers regurgitating half understood concepts of independent professionalism. Health visitors have been ordered sometimes actively to withdraw from paediatric consulting sessions run by general practitioners in their practices. Clinic nurses have been encouraged to take upon themselves the ultimate decision about who and who not to immunise without discussion with the doctor and even where to put the injection! — not the best way to demonstrate to parents how well the professionals cooperate in the care of their children!

Developmental guidance and advice benefits from policies of concensus. If each member of the team involved in child care — doctor, midwife, health visitor, clinic nurse — can agree on management strategies and policies, the parents' trust in the programme is greatly enhanced, ensuring that they will use the resources both effectively and routinely when required, seeing their worth and trusting in the advice and help given (Robinson, 1983) and trust is vitally important if reassurance is to be effective (Williams, 1983).

Despite these difficulties, successful practice based child health clinics have proved their worth in achieving: (1) high uptake of immunisation; (2) parent satisfaction manifested by high uptake of appointments provided for surveillance examinations; (3) similar 'find' rates of disorders found when compared with research studies (Drillien & Drummond, 1983). All these advantages must point to a greater cost effectiveness in terms of services provided when compared with the overall low rates of immunisations nationally and the low rates of appointment uptake at surveillance clinics in the community.

TRAINING

Individual general practitioners have in the past had to learn their skills the hard way. Few, if any, training programmes were available, and, if available, few were relevant to the needs of the individual general practitioner who wished to start a child health clinic in his or her practice. I confess to neither having held a hospital post in paediatrics nor possessing the diploma in child health (despite being an examiner); such has been the case for many — but not for much longer.

The quality initiative of the Royal College of General Practitioners stated clearly the needs and objectives of training for child health. *Healthier Children* — Thinking Prevention, the report of the working party appointed by the Council of the Royal College of General Practitioners, has proposed a number of far reaching changes in the way child health is organised. The Northern Regional Study of Standards and Performance in General Practice, which is hoped will be completed by 1989, involves 65 training practices and 90,000 children on their lists and 'a before and after' study of the effects of setting performance standards for a number of symptomatic conditions of childhood. This is where the underpinning of the research into effectiveness and cost benefit has to begin. It is as true today as it was in 1976 that 'the recommended programme of surveillance has only limited research support and a great deal remains to be done in evaluating the effectiveness of surveillance procedures and in measuring their cost and effectiveness' (Court, 1976).

Apart from the work of Drillien and Drummond (1983), there is a shortage of research data which to base a scientific argument that there 'should be' surveillance. This is not to damn the concept but could allow more time and thought to the protagonists and antagonists to prove their cases. However, it is vital to take parents' needs into account and their perceived notions about what is on offer (Sefi & Macfarlane, 1984; Hart et al, 1981) and to be sure that scientific validity or surveillance per se *is not* the sole criterion on which to base an opinion either way.

ORGANISATION

Local initiatives are many. In the Isle of Man child health surveillance has been 'sold' to the general practitioners of the island for an annual fee per child with, in return, proof of a basic service provided, including immunisation, health checks and an agreement from the general practitioners taking part to receive further training and regular updating.

In some other parts of the UK, the exact reverse holds true, with high quality, whole population services being carried out by general practitioners, in the Isle of Wight for instance being totally ignored and unrewarded by the community services (Hooper P D, 1985, Personal communication).

In many parts of our inner cities the organisation of child health clinics in general practices poses special problems (as they do when community based (Zimkin &Cox, 1976)). The low morale and low self esteem of parents conspire to cause low attendance rates for all preventive services from antenatal care to cervical cytology, despite great efforts on the part of the individual practices and community health services to produce change and increase the uptake of such services. In addition, the fact that between one in four and one in seven children under 10 years of age are not registered with general practitioners poses additional problems. To solve these problems will take more than individual initiative. Linking maternity and child benefits to attendance at child health clinics is one way (as is the case in France), coupled to powers to prevent unimmunised children attending nurseries and play groups. In the USA no child is allowed to enter schooling without proof of immunisation. The recent successful virtual elimination of measles in the USA rested on such methods, and there are many people in the UK coming to the same conclusion. I am one of them.

In France, the change in legislation which coupled the paying of maternity and child benefit to attendance at child health clinics resulted in the biggest fall in infant mortality in any 5 year period since recording began. This was not due to the fact that the doctors and other professional staff became cleverer or more attentive; instead, it merely proved the point that contact between mother, child and health professional is the key factor.

Whether in the UK this contact should be with a clinic staffed by health visitors or doctors is at the moment under discussion. A recent, provocative document produced by the Health Visitors' Association suggested that properly trained health visitors could carry the bulk of the clinic work of surveillance examinations, allowing the clinic doctor to examine children of 6 weeks old and immediately pre-school and 'any other children that they or the health visitor were concerned about'. Where the extra health visiting staff were to come from and where they were going to find time to carry out all their other tasks inside and outside the clinics without a massive backup of secretarial and clerical services were not clear. In addition, the suggestion that doctors should give all the immunisations seemed an expensive way of using valuable 'doctor time'.

Unfortunately, the research data that should underpin such proposals are not available. Indeed, what information is available points to the difficulties that lie ahead in training if such a programme was instituted (Health Visitors' Association, 1983).

In addition, little account has been taken of the expectations of the health visitors, their ability to offer the continuity of care over years not months and the suitability of prior nursing training as a basis for this work. The evidence from the USA demonstrates the very clear difference in work styles, performance and effectiveness in the clinical role between paediatric nurses and paediatric 'aids', who have no nurse training but a degree in medical sciences. The latter out perform the former on all parameters, and in my view this demonstrates that prior nursing training is perhaps a positive hinderance for this particular extended role.

We must also wait to see if parents would accept the judgment of a health visitor that their child is medically and clinically normal as the result of a surveillance examination carried out by one.

Finally, it is apparent to me that my skills at developmental paediatric surveillance rely on my ability to identify the normal. This I do by constant practice with the normal. By knowing the normal I learn what the developmental variation from the normal is. I also learn when the sum of variations in an individual child alert in me a suspicion that all is not well. Further close observation spread over days, weeks or months confirms or denies my suspicion. How I can maintain my skills in the face of such a change in organisation I do not know — and I suspect a lot of other doctors are in the same position. It is important that any changes to be made in organisation can be allowed to grow organically, as is the tradition in the UK and particularly in the first 80 years of 'public' child health.

The future of the movement seems uncertain; lack of money and low morale in the health services are acting as hefty constraints to change. More and more general practitioners are expressing a willingness to organise child health clinics in their practices. In many areas clinical medical officers are finding their work more cost effective when they share the work with general practitioners. Having worked in this way for 20 years we can vouch for the good effects of cross fertilisation of ideas, shared research, a mutual understanding of each other's roles and an ever more effective service. Maybe, after 60 years, the wheel will turn full circle and child health will return to its home in general practice.

REFERENCES

Bain D J G 1977 Methods employed by general practitioners in developmental screening of preschool children. British Medical Journal ii: 363–365
Barber J H 1982 Preschool developmental screening. The results of a four year period. Health Bulletin 4: 170–178
Bassett W J 1981 Child and family health in a Scottish new town. Health Bulletin 1: 7–20
Cartright A 1967 Patients and their doctors. A study of general practice. Routledge Keegan and Paul, London, p 88
Court 1976 Fit for the future: report of the Committee on Child Health Services. HMSO, London [Cmnd 66.84]
Curtis Jenkins G H, Collins C, Andrea S 1978 Surveillance in general practice. British Medical Journal i: 1537–1540
Davis R H 1975 The school child. In: Screening in general practice. Churchill Livingstone, London, p. 101
Department of Health and Social Security 1976 Fit for the future. A report of the Committee on child health service. HMSO, London
Drillien C, Drummond M 1983 Developmental screening and the child with special needs: a population study of 5000 children. Heinenann Medical, London, p. 84–86
Hart H, Bax M, Jenkins S 1981 Use of the child health clinic Archives of Disease in Childhood, 56: 440–445
Health Visitors' Association 1983 Hearing screening survey No. 2, Health Visitor 56: 191
Houston H L A, Davis R H 1985 Opportunistic surveillance of child and development in primary care: is it feasible? Journal of Royal College of General Practitioners 271:77–79
Miller F J W, Court S D, Knox E G 1960 Growing up in Newcastle upon Tyne. A continuing study of health and illness in young children within their families. Oxford University Press, London.
Parsons L 1947 Child health education. In: Moncrief A, Thomson W A R (eds) Practitioners handbook. Eyre and Spottiswoode, London p. 14
Piper A R 1985 Opportunistic Surveillance of Children. Journal of Royal College of General Practitioners 35: 250
Pollak M 1972 Today's three year olds in London. William Heinemann, London.
Roberts C J, Khosla T 1972 An evaluation of developmental examination as a method of detecting neurological, visual and auditory handicaps in infancy. British Journal of Preventive and Social Medicine 26: 94–100
Robinson P J 1983 Uptake of preschool immunisation in a rural practice. Journal of Royal College of General Practitioners 33: 500–504
Sefi S, Macfarlane J A 1984 A survey of 103 child health clinics, Oxfordshire 1980–81. Oxford Regional Health Authority
Sheldon W (Chairman) 1967 Child welfare centres. A report of the sub-committee of the Standing Medical Advisory Committee. HMSO, London
Spence J C, Walton W S, Miller F J W, Court S D 1954 A thousand families in Newcastle upon Tyne. An approach to the study of health and illness in children. Oxford University Press, London
Stark G S, Bassett J J, Bain D J G, Stewart F I 1975 Paediatrics in Livingstone New Town. British Medical Journal iv: 387–390
Starte G D 1974 The development assessment of the young child in general practice. Practitioner 213: 823–828
Starte G D 1975 The poor communicating 2 year old and his family. Journal of the Royal College of General Practitioners 25: 880–884
Starte G D 1976 Results from development screening clinic in general practice. Practitioner 216: 311
Williams P R 1983 Does your child health clinic meet the needs of mothers as well as children? Journal of Royal College of General Practitioners 33: 505

Williams P R 1985 Opportunistic surveillance of children Journal of Royal College of General Practitioners 35: 248–250

Willmot J F, Hancock S, Bush T, Ullyett P 1984 Paediatric surveillance performance review and the primary health care team. Journal of Royal College of General Practitioners 34: 152–157

Zimkin P M, Cox C A 1976 Child health clinics and inverse care laws evidence from a longitudinal study British Medical Journal ii: 411–413

Index